HANS KÜNG is president of the Global
Ethic Foundation, Germany/Switzerland, having
retired in 1996 as professor of ecumenical theology and director of the Institute for Ecumenical
Research at the University of Tübingen. He is the
author of more than fifty books, including *The
Catholic Church* and *On Being a Christian*.

The Beginning of All Things

The Beginning of All Things

SCIENCE AND RELIGION

—⟨◎⟩—

Hans Küng

Translated by

John Bowden

William B. Eerdmans Publishing Company

Grand Rapids, Michigan / Cambridge, U.K.

Originally published 2005 in German as
Der Anfang aller Dinge: Naturwissenschaft und Religion
© 2005 Piper Verlag GmbH, Munich

English translation © 2007 John Bowden

Published 2007 by
Wm. B. Eerdmans Publishing Co.
2140 Oak Industrial Drive N.E., Grand Rapids, Michigan 49505 /
P.O. Box 163, Cambridge CB3 9PU U.K.
www.eerdmans.com

Printed in the United States of America

12 11 10 09 08 07   7 6 5 4 3 2 1

Library of Congress Cataloging-in-Publication Data

Küng, Hans, 1928-
[Anfang aller Dinge. English]
The beginning of all things: science and religion / Hans Küng;
translated by John Bowden.
p.   cm.
ISBN 978-0-8028-0763-2 (cloth: alk. paper)
1. Creation.   2. Religion and science.   I. Title.

BT695.K8613   2007
261.5′5 — dc22

2007005206

The author and publisher gratefully acknowledge permission to reprint excerpts
from Ingeborg Bachmann's "To the Sun," translated by Peter Filkins, from *Darkness
Spoken: The Collected Poems of Ingeborg Bachmann*. Copyright © 1978 by Piper Verlag
GmbH, München. English translation copyright © 2006 by Peter Filkins. Reprinted
with the permission of Zephyr Press, www.zephyrpress.org.

Contents

—◦◦◦—

Let There Be Light!   xi

I. A Unified Theory of Everything?   1

  1. The Riddle of Reality   1

    A Twofold Riddle   2

    The New Model of the World: Copernicus, Kepler, Galileo   3

    Church against Science   5

    The Victory of Science   6

  2. A Physical Description of the Beginning   8

    The New Physics: Einstein's Relativistic Space-Time   8

    An Expanding Universe   9

    The Big Bang and Its Consequences   10

  3. What Holds the World Together in Its Innermost Being?   12

    Heisenberg and Quantum Theory   13

    The World Formula — a Great Hope   14

    GUT instead of GOD? Hawking   15

    The World Formula — a Great Disappointment   17

  4. The Dispute about the Foundations of Mathematics   19

    Mathematics without Contradiction? Gödel   19

No Ultimate Theory of Everything   21

Occasion for Self-Critical Reflection   22

5. The Inadequacies of Positivism   24

Rejection of the Meta-empirical? Popper   25

Only Meaningless Pseudoproblems?   26

The Impossibility of Proving All Statements True,
    Even in Science   27

The Autonomy and Limits of Scientific Knowledge   29

6. The Questionability of Reality   31

Universe — Human Being — Self   32

Multidimensional and Multilayered Reality   33

Reason, but Not Reason Alone   35

7. Science and Theology: Different Perspectives   36

Science: The Foundation but Not the Totality   36

Theology Too Needs Self-Criticism   37

Physical Knowledge Cannot Transcend the World
    of Experience   40

A Model of Complementarity instead of a Model
    of Confrontation or Integration   41

II. God as Beginning?   43

1. The Question of the Beginning of Beginnings   44

The Singularity of the Beginning   44

The "Copernican Shift" in Philosophy: Descartes   46

Proofs of God — Doomed to Failure: Kant   46

Counterproofs Also Fail   47

2. Science Blocked by the Critique of Religion?   48

The Rights and Wrongs of the Critique of Religion:
    Feuerbach, Marx, Freud   49

The Death of God? Nietzsche   50

Contents

Science Must Leave God Out of Account   51

Atheism Is Understandable but Not Necessary   52

3. Where Do the Constants in Nature Come From?   54

A Universe Finite in Space and Time   54

Intellectual Helplessness in the Face of the Question
of Origins   56

Where Do the Principles of Cosmic Order Come From?   58

Instinctive Opposition   60

4. Reactions to the Cosmic Fine-Tuning   62

Cosmological Speculation: Alternative Universes   62

Is Our Universe One among Many?   64

A Cosmological Demonstration: A Designer Universe   68

Can God Be Proved by Physics?   69

A Questionable Basic Motivation   70

5. Why Isn't There Nothing?   72

A Solution to the Riddle of the World   73

Ignorance Also Grows with Knowledge   75

Approaching the Primal Mystery   78

God as Hypothesis   80

God as Reality   81

An Archimedean Point   82

III. Creation of the World or Evolution?   85

1. The Beginning as the Beginning of a Becoming   85

Evolution of the Biological Species: Darwin   86

The Descent of Human Beings from the Animal Kingdom   88

2. Theological Defense   90

Anglican Perplexity   90

A Second Galileo Case for the Catholic Church   91

Protestant Creationism   93

3. Evolution with or without God? — 95

    Progress without God: Comte — 95

    Evolution to God: Teilhard De Chardin — 97

    God in Process: Whitehead — 100

4. How Are We to Think of God? — 103

    An Alternative to the Word "God"? — 103

    God — a Being above the Earth? — 105

    Space-Time, Embraced by Eternity and Unfathomability — 106

    Is God a Person? — 107

5. Bible and Creation — 110

    Creation Myths of the World Religions — 110

    A Need for Information? — 112

    The Magna Carta of the Jewish-Christian Worldview — 114

    A Metaphorical Language — 117

    No Harmonization or Mixing — 118

6. The Testimony of Faith to the Ultimate Origin — 120

    Creation of Space and Time from Nothing — 120

    What Is the Meaning of Belief in Creation Today? — 122

    "In Light Inaccessible" — 125

IV. Life in the Cosmos? — 129

1. How Long Has There Been Life? — 129

    What Is "Life"? — 130

    Are We Alone in the Universe? — 131

    A Vain Quest — 133

2. How Did Life Arise? — 136

    The Vehicles of Life — 136

    Matter Organizes Itself — 137

3. Chance or Necessity? — 139

    The Primacy of Chance? — 140

Contents

Natural Laws Guide Chance   141

Is God Superfluous?   143

An Existential Alternative   144

4. Why a Universe That Is Friendly to Life?   145

Evolution toward Human Beings   146

An Anthropic Principle?   147

No Ultimate Foundation   148

5. Miracle   151

Breaking the Laws of Nature?   151

Results of Biblical Criticism   152

Pointers for Faith   153

6. How Are We to Think of God's Activity?   154

A Spiritualized Understanding of God   155

The Infinite Has an Influence on the Finite   156

No Competition between God and the World   157

V. The Beginning of Humankind   161

1. The Physical Development of Human Beings   161

Phylogenesis   162

Human Beings Come from Africa   163

Earliest Traces of Religion   165

2. The Psychological Development of Human Beings   168

The Body-Soul Problem   168

Psyche instead of Soul   169

Conditioned Freedom   171

Environmentally Conditioned and Preprogrammed   172

3. Brain and Mind   174

Determined by Physical-Chemical Brain Processes?   174

Is Free Will an Illusion?   175

*The Trivialization of Responsibility and Guilt
   by the Neurosciences*   177

4. The Limits of Brain Research   179
   Ignorance about the Decisive Levels of the Brain   180
   The Big Questions of the Neurosciences   181
   Chemistry and Physics Do Not Explain the Self   184
   Experience of Freedom   187
   The Spiritual Cosmos   189

5. The Beginnings of the Human Ethic   191
   Evolutionary Biological and Sociocultural Factors   192
   The Primal Ethic as the Basis for a Global Ethic   193
   Even the Biblical Ethic Has a History   194
   The One Light and the Many Lights   195

Epilogue: The End of All Things   199
   Hypotheses of the End in Physics   199
   Apocalyptic Visions of the End   201
   The Significance of the Biblical Visions   203
   Dying into the Light   205

A Word of Thanks   207

Index   209

Let There Be Light!

—⟨⟨∘⟩⟩—

"Let there be light!" That is what the Hebrew Bible says in its first sentences about the "beginning" of "heaven and earth." The earth was "without form and void": "darkness was upon the face of the deep; and the spirit of God was moving over the face of the waters" (Gen. 1:1-3). Light was created before all other things, even before sun, moon, and stars. Joseph Haydn in his oratorio *The Creation* expressed this more vividly than any words could, better even than Michelangelo could depict it in the Sistine Chapel: with the surprising fortissimo change in the whole orchestra from dark E minor into radiant triumphal C major, the biblical saying about light is, as it were, re-created in music.

But, scientists will ask me, do you seriously believe, as many fundamentalists — and not just in America — believe, that the Bible gives us an answer to the prime question of cosmology: Where does everything come from? Are you arguing for naive and unenlightened biblical belief in an anthropomorphic God who even created the world in six "days"? Certainly not! I want to take the Bible seriously, but that doesn't mean I want to take it literally.

"Let there be light!" That was rightly also the slogan of the Enlightenment, which started in England and in France *("les Lumières")* and sought to help bring about "man's release from his self-incurred tutelage" (as Kant put it)[1] with the aid of reason. All those pious so-called

---

1. Cf. I. Kant, *Foundations of the Metaphysics of Morals, and What Is Enlightenment* (Indianapolis, 1959), 85.

"friends of light" who at a very early stage argued even in the church for free research and preaching in accordance with reason and the times, with no compulsion and spiritual restriction, were men of the Enlightenment. And they all had on their side that post-Copernican natural science that had ultimately proved victorious in the process of the Roman Catholic Church against Galileo. So there can be no going back behind Copernicus and Galileo, behind Newton and Darwin.

But I must now ask scientists in return: Hasn't enlightened reason sometimes also led us astray? With all its progress, so rich in blessing, hasn't it increasingly created murderous machines of war? Hasn't it often destroyed the natural foundations of life, so that today many people fear for the future of our earth? There is indeed a dialectic of enlightenment, of the kind acutely analyzed by Max Horkheimer and Theodor W. Adorno,[2] a transformation of scientific and technical reason into unreason. So don't we perhaps need another view of things than just that of the natural sciences?

"Let there be light!" Albert Einstein could also have said that when he established the speed of light as the great constant, and on this basis went on to "relativize" gravity, space, and time. With reference to "heretics" such as Democritus, Francis of Assisi, and especially Spinoza, Einstein argued for a "cosmic religious feeling" free of dogmas, which "knows no God devised in the image of human beings."[3] In his view this cosmic religious feeling is "the strongest and noblest motive for scientific research."[4] "What a deep conviction of the rationality of the universe and what a yearning to understand, were it but a feeble reflection of the mind revealed in this world, Kepler and Newton must have had to enable them to spend years of solitary labour in disentangling the principles of celestial mechanics! . . . Only one who has devoted his life to similar ends can have a vivid realization of what has inspired these men and given them the strength to remain true to their purpose in spite of countless failures. It is cosmic religious feeling that gives a man such

2. Cf. M. Horkheimer and T. W. Adorno, *Dialectic of Enlightenment: Philosophical Fragments* (London, 1979).

3. Cf. A. Einstein, "Religion and Science," *New York Times Magazine,* 9 Nov. 1930, reprinted in *Ideas and Opinions* (New York, 1954), 36-40, here 37.

4. Einstein, "Religion and Science," 38.

strength."[5] I know that not every scientist cultivates a cosmic religious feeling, and in this book I certainly will not force upon my readers either this or any other form of religion. But if scientists want to see more than their own limited field, they, too, could at least feel challenged by the *question* of religion.

"Let there be light!" This book too attempts in a modest way to shed light: to pass on the light that the great findings above all of physics and biology shed on the beginning of the world, life, and human beings. This light still shines out in a completely different way from the testimony of the Bible understood in contemporary terms; and it is still shed by the humble self-confidence of an enlightened philosophy and theology. Here intellectual integrity is more important than dogmatic conformity, than ecclesiastical or secular correctness.

However, this is a difficult enterprise. For over recent decades research in cosmology, biology, and anthropology has progressed so far and become so extensive that it is almost impossible for those outside these disciplines to comprehend. That is often true even for scientists. One of the great figures of physics formulated the dilemma of a universal approach at a very early stage and saw "only one way out": "that some of us venture to look at facts and theories together, even if their knowledge is in part only second hand and incomplete — and they run the risk of making themselves look ridiculous." Erwin Schrödinger, the founder of wave mechanics and a Nobel Prize winner, the man who began to look at the living cell with the eyes of a physicist, wrote this in 1933 in his book *What Is Life?* I hope the reader will graciously accept his excuse as mine.

If one is to think in broad spans and not lose sight of the whole among all the necessary specialisms, one needs a basic knowledge of philosophy and theology. My book is meant to provide help toward this in a concentrated form. It goes without saying that here I shall be referring back to everything that I have studied, lectured on, and published over five decades. That makes it possible to write a book that I have deliberately kept short. I want not only to gather further information about scientific topics that have become fashionable but also, I hope, to give a

5. Einstein, "Religion and Science," 38f.

coherent and convincing answer to some basic scientific questions. The book culminates in a section on the beginnings of the human ethic, which shows that it, too, has its place in the global ethic project.

I wrote this introduction to the first draft of the manuscript at Montserrat, during the Fourth Parliament of the World's Religions in Barcelona, in some free time during the preparations for the Parliament. To my right were the powerful and steep natural massif with its ridges and pinnacles, and to my left a view of the Benedictine basilica, with the broad landscape of Catalonia in between. That makes me wonder. Would it really be just a dream at the point of transition from modernity to postmodernity to envisage the overcoming of conflicts between science and religion — which often have ideological coloring — by a new sharing, even though there are so many different perspectives on the evolution of the cosmos and human beings?

I have thanked all those who helped me with this survey of the "beginning of all things" in the postscript to this book.

Tübingen, July 2005   *Hans Küng*

CHAPTER I

A Unified Theory of Everything?

—⟨ʘ⁄ʘ⟩—

Physicists can be proud of all the results of their research that have been discovered, reflected on, and confirmed by experiments. In fact, all scientists have to keep returning to this basic science, which investigates and analyzes the elementary particles and basic forces of material reality. So we can understand that on the basis of the indisputable triumphant successes that have been achieved, some physicists expect that one day it will be possible to decipher our universe. How? By finding a theory for "all things," for all the natural forces, for everything that is: a formula for the world that could solve the deepest riddles of our cosmos, our universe, and explain the whole of reality by physics.

1. The Riddle of Reality

The Greek word *cosmos* has a long history. Originally it meant "order"; the earliest mention in Homer in the eighth century B.C.E. refers to the army drawn up in order. Then it meant "decoration"; this meaning is attested for the first time by Pythagoras in the sixth century B.C.E. Finally, at the beginning of our era, it meant "harmony," related to the universe, and later was used in the same way as we use "world order" and "universe" today. So "cosmos" denotes the world as an ordered whole, cosmos as opposed to chaos.

The word "universe" means "turned into one," from the Latin *unus*

1

+ *vertere, versum,* summed up as a unity. So, strictly speaking, "universe" means the "whole as the embodiment of all its parts." In this book I shall use "cosmos" and "universe" interchangeably and attempt to fathom the origin and meaning of the universe.

A Twofold Riddle

A twofold question underlies the simple title *The Beginning of All Things:*

- The *key question* about the *beginning generally:* Why does the universe exist? Why doesn't it not exist?
- The question about the *conditions surrounding the beginning:* Why is the universe as it is? Why does it have these particular properties that are decisive for our human life and survival?

So the issue is no less than *the origin and being of the universe as a whole,* indeed, *of reality as a whole.*

But what is the *whole* of reality? Is it only "nature," or is it also the "spirit"? Can the sciences also embrace the spirit? And must we in some circumstances reckon with more than one universe, with several universes, each perhaps of a rather different kind, a "multiverse," though this would be hardly more than a mere hypothesis, not supported by any direct observation? What is *reality?* I shall begin from an elementary and completely open description that includes "all things": reality is *all that is.*

In the Middle Ages people framed their questions above all in terms of purpose: What is a thing for? In modern times the question is put above all in causal terms: Why is a thing as it is? How is it made, what does it consist of and what laws does it obey? If we want to know what everything is, we must know how everything came into being. If we want to know what the cosmos is, we must know how it came into being. What often solitary thinkers conceived of theoretically even in the early modern period, discovered by experiments, championed against all resistance, and so struggled toward a new picture of the world, is impressive.

Today "world history" must be understood no longer just as human history (lasting a couple of hundred thousand years) but as the real history of the world, extending over 13.7 billion years since the Big Bang. However, it took around four centuries for the new astronomical and physical model of the world, the scientific foundation of the modern view of the world, to become established.

The New Model of the World: Copernicus, Kepler, Galileo

It was not a secularized scientist but a Catholic canon (from Poland or Germany) named Nicolaus Copernicus (1473-1543) who took up an idea of Aristarchus of Samos (third century b.c.e.) and, on the basis of his own observations, calculations, and geometric-kinetic reflections, presented the brilliant sketch of a new, truly revolutionary model of the world. He had studied above all in Italy and, as is well-known, in his work *De revolutionibus orbium coelestium libri VI* (Six Books on the Revolutions of Heavenly Spheres)[1] replaced the traditional, closed, geocentric model of the world constructed by Ptolemy, which had proved increasingly unsuitable for calculating the positions of the planets over longer periods, with an open heliocentric model.

This was a paradigm change par excellence, first in physics, which then had an effect on the whole picture of the world and human "metaphysics." The "Copernican shift" became the slogan for a variety of fundamental revolutionary "shifts" that constitute modernity. It is also a prime example of what is meant by a "paradigm shift": it is more than just a change in a "pattern of thinking" that shapes the worldview of a time; rather, it is the shift in what Thomas S. Kuhn has called "the entire constellation of beliefs, values, techniques and so on shared by the members of a given community."[2]

The model of the world presented by Copernicus in purely theoretical terms was confirmed and corrected by Johannes Kepler (1571-1630), who had studied Protestant theology in Tübingen but soon turned to mathematics and astronomy: the courses of the planets are not circular

1. Cf. N. Copernicus, *De revolutionibus orbium coelestium libri VI* (1543), new critical edition (Hildesheim, 1984); ET, *On the Revolutions of Heavenly Spheres* (Jackson, Tenn., 2004).
2. T. S. Kuhn, *The Structure of Scientific Revolutions*, 2nd ed., with a postscript (Chicago, 1970), 175.

but elliptical. Kepler's three laws of planetary motion became the foundation of an *Astronomia nova* (1609).[3] Knowledge that could be experienced empirically and measured now became the only way to explain nature. However, for Kepler, an astronomer whose philosophical thought was holistic and ecumenical, this did not exclude belief in a creator God or, indeed, in a divine harmony of the world in all things and all relations that had a mathematical foundation.[4]

The new model of the world appeared extremely threatening to the traditional picture of the world when the Italian mathematician, physicist, and philosopher Galileo Galilei (1564-1642)[5] discovered with a telescope (developed on a Dutch model) the phases of Venus, four moons of Jupiter, and the rings of Saturn, and found out that the cloudy luster of the Milky Way consisted of individual stars. By this irrefutable confirmation of the Copernican model, according to which the earth revolves around the sun, and the introduction of quantitative experiments (the laws of the pendulum and of gravity), Galileo became the founder of modern science.

The foundations had now been laid for the demonstration of the laws of nature and unlimited research into it. Of course, Galileo himself recognized how threatening his researches were to the biblical view of the world. In principle he wanted to take the "book of nature" written in the language of mathematics as seriously as the "book of the Bible." In a letter to the Benedictine B. Castelli in 1613 he presented his views on the relationship between the Bible and the knowledge of nature: if scientific knowledge is certain and contradicts what the Bible says, a new interpretation of the Bible is due.[6]

But how did the church react to this new picture of the world? How did it stand on this Copernican "shift of overall constellation," this "paradigm shift"?

---

3. Cf. J. Kepler, *Astronomia nova* (Prague, 1609), in *Gesammelte Werke* (Munich, 1937ff.), vol. 3; ET, *The New Astronomy* (Cambridge, 1992).

4. V. Bialas, *Johannes Kepler* (Munich, 2004), especially chap. 3, "The Harmony of the World," paints a new overall picture of Kepler.

5. Cf. G. Galilei, *Dialogo* (1632); ET, *Dialogues concerning Two New Sciences* (New York, 1954).

6. Cf. Galilei, letter to B. Castelli, 21 Dec. 1613, in *Opere*, vol. 5 (Florence, 1965), 281-88.

Church against Science

It is well-known and significant that Canon Copernicus himself delayed the publication of his lifework until shortly before his death — out of fear of the Roman Catholic Index of Prohibited Books and the stake. Was this perhaps a typically Roman Catholic fear of the new, above all of the new natural philosophy and natural science? No, the Reformers Luther and especially Melanchthon also rejected his work. As it had been given only a theoretical foundation and allegedly had been presented only as a hypothesis, they thought they could disregard it. Moreover, Copernicus was put on the Index only in 1616 — when the case of Galileo was becoming acute. Thus religion became largely an opposing force and the Catholic Church an institution that, instead of being concerned for intellectual understanding, effort, and acceptance, called for censorship, Index, and Inquisition.

In 1632 Galileo was called before the Inquisition and condemned for transgressing a ban on his heliocentric theory that had already been pronounced in 1616. He probably did not make the much-quoted remark about the earth that is attributed to him, "And yet it moves." Nor was he subjected to torture, as is often claimed. But the pressure was so great that on 22 June 1633 the scholar recanted his "error" as a loyal Catholic. Nevertheless, he was condemned to indefinite house arrest at his villa in Arcetri; there Galileo, who went blind four years later, lived a further eight years with a group of his pupils and wrote his work on mechanics and the laws of gravity that was so important for the further development of physics.

"According to the present state of 'Galileo research' it cannot be disputed that in 1633 the Holy Office passed a false judgment and that Galileo was only partly responsible for what he was charged with." With these words the Catholic church historian Georg Denzler, in a book entitled *No End to the Galileo Case,*[7] opposes the Roman Catholic apologists who are still active today.

Was Galileo's conflict with the church an unfortunate isolated oc-

---

7. G. Denzler, "Der Fall Galilei und kein Ende," *Zeitschrift für Kirchengeschichte* 95, no. 2 (1984): 223-33, here 228.

currence? No, it was a symptomatic precedent that poisoned at the roots the relationship between the new and rising science and the church and religion, especially as in the subsequent period too Rome's attitude did not change but even hardened further in the face of the progress of science (and later especially Charles Darwin's biological research). After the disastrous excommunication of Luther and the Protestants by Rome, the Galileo case was followed by an almost silent emigration of scientists from the Catholic Church and a permanent conflict between science and the dominant theology. So Italy and Spain, under the lash of the Inquisition, had no scientists worth mentioning until the twentieth century. Still, ecclesiastical repression could not prevail against the evidence of the natural sciences.

The Victory of Science

Even Rome could not stop the collapse of the medieval structure of the world with its firmament between heaven above and hell beneath; it could not stop the demystification of nature and the overcoming of medieval belief in the devil, demons, witches, and magic. Granted, fifty years after Galileo's condemnation, when the Catholic Church was at the height of the Counter-Reformation and baroque triumphalism, the old medieval view was depicted in the Jesuit church of San Ignazio in Rome: the whole nave was still programmatically decorated with a gigantic fresco of heaven, adorned with the Trinity and all the saints and angels, as though the telescope had never been invented and no paradigm shift in astronomy and physics was taking place. But in the long run the artistic illusion did not prevail against the scientific revolution. The traditional authorities became increasingly unconvincing.

The case of Galileo has provided the material for many plays — by the Marxist Bertolt Brecht, the Jew Max Brod, the Catholic Gertrud von Le Fort, and others; in our day Pope John Paul II, whose judgments on birth control and the ordination of women were as infallibly wrong as were those of his predecessors on astronomy and heliocentricity, caused amazement among some scientists and historians by his ambiguous remarks on it. In 1979 he solemnly announced that 350 years after Galileo's death, he wanted to have his case investigated by a commission. But when this investigation was concluded, in his speech on 31 October 1982 he avoided clearly conceding the guilt of his predecessors and the Sancta Congregatio Inquisitionis (today the Congregation for the Doctrine of Faith) and instead foisted it on a "majority of theologians" of the time, which was not more closely specified. This was "a rehabilitation which did not take place."[8]

However, Galileo had long been rehabilitated by competent figures. In fact, his findings had been confirmed two generations later by the no-less-brilliant English mathematician, physicist, and astronomer Sir Isaac Newton (1634-1727), a professor in Cambridge. In his magnum opus, *Philosophiae naturalis principia mathematica,*[9] published in 1687, Newton had formulated three axioms of mechanics and his law of gravity, discovered two decades earlier — all also applied to the movement of heavenly bodies. So a "heavenly mechanics" was also possible. One and the same force of gravity makes the apple fall to the ground and ties the moon to the earth. Moreover, Newton discovered the nature of light and electricity and simultaneously with Leibniz invented calculus.

Whereas Kepler and Galileo had provided fragmentary elements of a comprehensive theory, from their discoveries and those of others Newton formulated a convincing new system for the world, rationally demonstrated in quantitative and mathematically precise laws. Thus Newton became the second founder (after Galileo) of exact science, the founder of classical theoretical physics.

Only at the beginning of the twentieth century was the immediate realism, determinism, and reductionism of Newton's picture of the world put in question by Einstein's theory of relativity and quantum

---

8. Cf. the investigations by the historian of science M. Segre, "Light on the Galileo Case," *Isis* (History of Science Society) 88 (1997): 484-504. This documents how in a second speech at the end of the 1992 proceedings Pope John Paul II in practice took back what he had announced in 1979. Cf. Segre, "Galileo: A 'Rehabilitation' That Has Never Taken Place," *Endeavor* 23, no. 1 (1999): 20-23; Segre, "Hielt Johannes Paul II. sein Versprechen?" in *Der ungebändigte Galilei. Beiträge zu einem Symposion,* ed. M. Segre and E. Knobloch (Stuttgart, 2001), 107-11.

9. Cf. I. Newton, *Philosophiae naturalis principia mathematica* (London, 1687; 3rd ed. 1726; new edition in 2 vols., Cambridge, Mass., 1972).

theory. Here it became clear that physics by no means simply describes the world in itself, independently of the standpoint of the observer, as Newton presupposed. Its theories and models are not literal descriptions of reality at the atomic level (naive realism), but are symbolic and selective attempts that depict the structures of the world and are responsible for special observable phenomena: a critical realism, which recognizes physical reality — not, however, simply through observation but in creative conjunction with interpretation and experimentation.[10]

2. A Physical Description of the Beginning

Many precise calculations and further discoveries were made subsequently within the framework of this paradigm developed by Newton, until physics was ripe for a further paradigm change: to the new physics, which unexpectedly showed that space and time are extremely flexible entities that can no longer be thought of separately.

The New Physics: Einstein's Relativistic Space-Time

At the beginning of the twentieth century Albert Einstein (1879-1955) developed this new model of the world that deviated completely from the infinite world of Newton's classical physics.[11] It could be derived from the basic equations of the general theory of relativity he put forward in 1914-16. He elevated the speed of light (ca. 300,000 kilometers per second) to be the absolute and unchangeable constant of nature: no report can be communicated faster than the speed of light, which is identical for all observers, however quickly they may be moving relative to one another. In this way Einstein relativized gravity and with it also space and time, the constants in Newton's system; these now fused into

10. I. G. Barbour, *Religion and Science* (San Francisco, 1998), chap. 7. The American physicist and theologian, who has distinguished himself in the dialogue between science and religion, offers a precise scientific and philosophical analysis of the epistemological differences between classical physics and modern physics.

11. Cf. A. Einstein, *Relativity: The Special and the General Theory* (1917; New York, 1961), especially §§30-32: "Considerations about the World as a Whole."

a new physical entity, space-time. Mass warps space and time. Accordingly the force of gravity is none other than the "warping" of space-time by the masses contained in it.

The result is an amazing four-dimensional space-time that cannot be envisaged: in it calculations must be made with a non-Euclidean geometry of space and time coordinates. Einstein's prediction that the light of remote heavenly bodies is measurably warped by a massive star such as the sun (around twice as strongly as might be expected according to Newtonian mechanics) was confirmed by measurements during a total eclipse of the sun in May 1919. "Space warped" was the sensational news. A universe warped in space means that the universe must be thought of as unlimited, but can have a finite volume. We can understand that better in analogy to a three-dimensional (not four-dimensional) space, for example, the surface of a sphere: a beetle that crawls around it and does not find an end possibly regards it as infinitely large. It has a finite surface but knows no limits.

An Expanding Universe

Einstein's space-time model also has defects: like almost all the nineteenth-century scientific establishment, he initially thought of the universe in static terms as eternal and unchangeable. Aristotle had already assumed that the cosmos was limited in space, but had no beginning and end in time.

By contrast, despite much resistance, a dynamic view of the universe soon became established. Interestingly it was a theologian (for that reason also suspected!) who is often passed over, an astrophysicist at the University of Louvain, Abbé Georges Lemaître (1894-1966), a pupil and colleague of Eddington and Einstein, who within the framework of the general theory of relativity in 1927 developed the model of an expanding universe and was the first to put forward the hypothesis of the "primeval atom" or the "Big Bang" (which was initially a nickname).

As early as 1923-24 in Pasadena, the American physicist Edwin P. Hubble (1889-1953), after whom the famous Hubble Space Telescope was named many decades later, had determined the distance of the

Andromeda Nebula from the earth by means of classifiable stars in the fringe area and so for the first time demonstrated the existence of heavenly bodies outside the Milky Way; he thus laid the foundations for modern extragalactic astronomy. In 1929 he concluded from the red shifts in the spectrum lines of Milky Way galaxies (the Hubble effect) that our universe was continuing to expand.[12] That means that the vast systems of galaxies no longer simply occupy space but are extending exponentially in all directions at tremendous speed (like a balloon on a flask of helium).

Thus in the utterly dark universe the stars are not equally distributed as far as the apparently infinite depths of space. Rather they constantly change and develop. Outside our own Milky Way the galaxies are moving away from us with a speed that is proportional to their distance from us. How long has this been happening? It cannot have been for an infinite length of time. There must have been a beginning, the Big Bang; now that seemed to be proved by physics and mathematics. After Einstein had visited his colleague Hubble on Mount Wilson, he too abandoned his static cosmology and accepted the expanding model of the universe. But he did not accept the quantum theory that had been developed in the meantime, though it had been confirmed by experiments more and more frequently. Therefore, despite his world fame, he increasingly became a solitary and almost isolated researcher.

The Big Bang and Its Consequences

On the basis of these fundamental discoveries and calculations that I have described briefly, astrophysicists today can give a precise description from the perspective of science of the *beginning of the cosmos,* how it came into being, how, so to speak, creation took place. The consensus of scientists achieved here is so great that we can speak of a standard model, against which rival models have not been able to prevail. Here is a brief sketch of it.

In the beginning all energy and matter was compressed into an unimaginably tiny and hot primal fireball of the smallest dimensions and

---

12. Cf. F. Hubble, *The Realm of the Nebulae* (New Haven, 1936).

the greatest density and temperature. This was a mixture of radiation and matter so dense and hot that neither galaxies nor stars could exist in it.

Since the explosion of comparatively "tiny" atom bombs, we can more easily understand how 13.7 billion years ago (this is the most recent calculation of astrophysicists) our universe began with a gigantic cosmic explosion, a Big Bang. It rapidly expanded and became cooler, but after 100th of a second it still had a temperature of 100 billion (100^{11}) degrees and a density about 4 billion times (4×10^9) that of water. It kept expanding in the same way in all directions (isotropically).

In the first seconds elementary particles must have formed from photons that were extremely rich in energy, especially protons and neutrons and their antiparticles, along with light elementary particles, especially electrons and positrons. After a couple of minutes nuclei of helium were formed from protons and neutrons by a fusion process, and some hundreds of thousands of years later neutral hydrogen and helium atoms were formed by the attachment of electrons. After perhaps 20 million years — with the decline in the pressure of the originally high-energy light quanta and further cooling — the gas could condense through the force of gravity into clumps of matter and finally into galaxies, into presumably 100 billion Milky Ways, each with as a rule more than 10 billion stars.

There is still no explanation of what caused this concentration of matter into galaxies. There are better explanations of the following phases, which, to simplify, can be described like this. Gravitation made the clouds of gas condense into stars when they collapsed under their own weight. Nuclear reactions took place in these, which in addition to hydrogen and helium now also produced heavy elements such as carbon, oxygen, and nitrogen. Some of these stars became unstable over time, exploded, and hurled unimaginable masses of the newly created raw materials into interstellar space, where they again formed massive gas clouds; however, in time these also condensed into stars.

Only with these second-generation stars, which now also contained the heavy elements as well as hydrogen and helium, did our sun take shape in one of the outer arms of our spiral galaxy, which has a diameter of 100,000 light-years. This happened after around 9 billion years. It condensed matter into planets, which now likewise contained the carbon, oxygen, nitrogen, and other heavy elements that are absolutely necessary for life on earth. It was this second generation of stars with planets that was the basis for the development of life and consciousness.

In the course of billions of years radiation cooled, so that today there is only an extremely low cosmic background radiation close to absolute zero (-273.15° Celsius). By chance, in 1964 the American engineers Arno A. Penzias and Robert W. Wilson (who were awarded the Nobel Prize for physics in 1978 for their findings) discovered by means of noise-level measurements with a radio telescope that the cosmic microwave or background radiation they detected from all directions in the decimeter and centimeter range was none other than the residue of that originally very hot radiation bound up with the Big Bang. As a result of the expansion of the universe, this residual radiation turned into a very low-temperature radiation. Since the discovery and measurement of this cosmic field of radiation, the Big Bang model has been taken as standard.

Only after 13.7 billion years did human beings appear on the scene, consisting above all of atoms of carbon and oxygen, the chemical raw material of life, which had been incubated by the first generation of stars. As the poet Novalis put it, "We are stardust."

3. What Holds the World Together in Its Innermost Being?

Of course, even the standard model does not answer all the questions. What remains unexplained is why the distribution of matter was so homogenous and isotropic and why the equal distribution of matter led to the formation of structures, i.e., galaxies and clusters of galaxies. Be this as it may, the new physics amazingly succeeded, in a dramatic success story, in giving an exact empirical description of the beginning of the universe. No wonder some physicists are attempting to penetrate yet deeper into reality from such a high level of knowledge, in order to give a definitive answer to the question of Goethe's Faust: "What holds the world together in its innermost?"

Heisenberg and Quantum Theory

Albert Einstein rightly assumed that space and time did not come into being in an empty space, as it were, but in the Big Bang itself. Only with extended space-time could matter condense and galaxies and stars come into being. This whole event was determined by gravity. In a logical continuation of the theory of relativity, for decades after 1920 Einstein attempted to present a "unitary" field theory that was to embrace both gravity and electrodynamics. As we know, he was unsuccessful. At all events, he did not take account of the demands of quantum theory and elementary particle physics, especially the existence of such marked reciprocal effects as nuclear forces.

However, as early as 1900 the physicist Max Planck in Berlin had recognized that electromagnetic energy is radiated or absorbed only in quite definite discrete portions, in "packets" or quanta of energy. In this way quantum theory was born, the greatest change in physics since Newton: without it there would be no nuclear energy today, no atomic clocks and solar cells, indeed, no transistors and lasers. Whereas Einstein criticized Planck's ideas, in Copenhagen in 1913 the Danish physicist Niels Bohr made decisive progress with his atomic model — negatively charged electrons circulate around a positively charged atomic nucleus.

Only around a decade later, from 1925, did Bohr's German pupil Werner Heisenberg (1901-76) and the Austrian Erwin Schrödinger (1887-1961) propose a mature quantum theory independently of each other: this was further developed by Max Born (1882-1970) and the Briton Paul Dirac (1902-84). This quantum mechanics describes the mechanics in the world of the invisibly small atoms and molecules: it can embrace both the particle and the wave property of the smallest mass of energy that appears as a unit (quantum) and thus combine without contradiction the corpuscular and the wave theory. So quantum physics became the foundation of modern chemistry and molecular biology.

But as so often happens, new ignorance came in with the new knowledge: quantum physics is subject to the law of fuzzy or indeterminate relationship formulated by Heisenberg. If we know where an electron is (position), we cannot know what it is doing (momentum). However much one may measure and calculate, the position and momentum of a particle cannot be measured simultaneously, as the measurement becomes blurred and therefore "fuzzy." The stimulating discovery was that here there is no physical certainty but only statistical probability. The consequence is that if it is impossible precisely to measure the present state of an object (in the classical sense), its future cannot be precisely predicted either. Thus chance is an element necessarily bound up with quantum theory and cannot be eliminated by more precise observations.

For this reason, although Einstein had already anticipated quantum theory in 1905 with his brilliant light quantum hypothesis, he fought a stubborn battle against it: "Quantum mechanics is certainly imposing. But an inner voice tells me that it is not yet the real thing. Quantum theory says a lot, but does not really bring us any closer to the secret of the Old One. I, at any rate, am convinced that He (God) does not throw dice."[13]

The World Formula — a Great Hope

Nonphysicists may comfort themselves with a remark attributed to the Nobel Prize winner Richard P. Feynman, one of the fathers of quantum theory: "Anyone who claims to have understood quantum theory has not understood it." In fact, the fuzzy relationship does not fit into either Newton's or Einstein's model of the world, in which the whole universe from the planets to the smallest particles is subject to the same compelling laws. Since then, the efforts of physicists have been concentrated on the great task of combining the laws of gravity, which describe the world as a whole, and quantum physics, which explains the microscopic structure of matter, in a single theory. After all the previous sensational successes, such a comprehensive theory of the forces of nature or "world formula" seemed to lie well within the realm of the possible.

13. A. Einstein, letter to Max Born of 4 Dec. 1936, in Albert Einstein and Max Born, *The Born-Einstein Letters: Friendship, Politics, and Physics in Uncertain Times* (New York, 2005), 129f. (cf. also 118f.).

Einstein had already presented a first version of a world formula in 1923 — errors were demonstrated in it and also in later formulations. It was then above all Werner Heisenberg who after the Second World War attempted to develop such a unitary theory of matter: with the help of a quantum field theory, a world formula for all the elementary particles and their reciprocal effects. But even the "Heisenberg world formula" (1958) that was eventually discovered could not convince the physicists.

Finally, a new approach to solving the fundamental problems was promised by string theory, which regards the most elementary quantum particles not as points without extension but as tiny strings vibrating at different frequencies. However, in the attempt to quantify the theory it proved that a consistent mathematical description of these strings is difficult; scientists arrived at eleven or more space-time dimensions and a thousand different possible universes, without being able to explain why it was our universe in particular that became reality.[14]

Some physicists — not Heisenberg — influenced by this theory seemed to dream of being able to establish with a watertight supertheory that a creator God would have had no choice as to how he was to create the world. This would make God superfluous, or identical with the world formula that was sought. Consciously or unconsciously, such physicists are still thinking in the paradigm of a mechanistic-materialistic science that has been popular since the nineteenth century and is convinced that it can solve all the problems of science move by move. No one has made the ideological background so clear as the physicist who most recently worked on a grand unified theory (GUT) that would make a creator God (GOD) superfluous.

GUT instead of GOD? Hawking

It was the English physicist Stephen Hawking (born 1942) in Cambridge, rightly admired by many people (because of an incurable nervous disorder in his spinal cord, he can communicate with his environment only

---

14. For the criticism of the superstring theory and the "so-called Great Unified Theories," cf. M. Gell-Mann, *The Quark and the Jaguar* (New York, 1994).

by computer), who hoped in his investigations into the universe in the state immediately after the Big Bang to develop a "grand unified theory" (GUT) by fusing all known interactions. The theory was to explain what "holds the world together in its innermost." Whereas Heisenberg with quantum mechanics had already put forward a grand theory that had been empirically confirmed, and moreover showed a deep respect for the religious sphere, in his best seller *A Brief History of Time* (it has sold 25 million copies, though it is difficult even for scientists to understand) Hawking, full of the optimism of the Enlightenment, promised a single grand theory that would not only explain particular empirical data for us but would also enable us "to know the mind of God."[15]

That remark was made deliberately and meant ironically. For Hawking's view was that with such a unified theory of everything (TOE) the world would explain itself and God would no longer be necessary as creator. If the universe were completely shut up in itself, without singularities and limits, if it were described completely by a unified theory, then physics would have made God superfluous. However, an impressive acronym such as GUT or TOE could be found more quickly than the theory that would unite all physical forces.

In Hawking's notion of the world — a closed universe without limits or initial conditions — in contrast to the older Big Bang theory, there would be no "singularity" in which God would have had complete freedom to lay down the conditions for the beginning of the universe and its laws. "He would, of course, still have had the freedom to choose the laws that the universe obeyed. This, however, may not really have been all that much of a choice; there may well be only one, or a small number, of complete unified theories, such as the heterotic string theory, that are self-consistent and allow the existence of structures as complicated as human beings who can investigate the laws of the universe and ask about the nature of God."[16]

A "complete unified theory"? Hawking soberly stated that however ingenious the equations are for everything, the reality of everything is

15. Cf. S. Hawking, *A Brief History of Time: From the Big Bang to Black Holes* (London and New York, 1988), 175.
16. Hawking, *Brief History of Time*, 174.

still in no way given, and the question remains open why there is a universe at all: "Even if there is only one possible unified theory, it is just a set of rules and equations. What is there that breathes fire into the equations and makes a universe for them to describe? The usual approach of science of constructing a mathematical model cannot answer the question why there should be a universe for the model to describe."[17]

Nevertheless, Hawking clearly expressed his hope that a GUT could one day answer the question why there is a universe at all: "However, if we do discover a complete theory, it should in time be understandable in broad principle by everyone, not just a few scientists. Then we shall all — philosophers, scientists, and just ordinary people — be able to take part in the discussion of the question of why it is that we and the universe exist. If we find the answer to that, it would be the ultimate triumph of human reason — for then we would know the mind of God."[18] But things were to turn out quite differently.

The World Formula — a Great Disappointment

Hawking had thought that a complete formula of the laws of nature could be found, a series of rules that should enable us at least in principle to predict the future "to an arbitrary accuracy" and thus define the state of the universe precisely at a particular time. Classical physics had still assumed that if one knew the positions and velocities of all particles at a particular time, one could also calculate the positions and speeds for any other time. But quantum physics had shown that there are events that in principle are incalculable. Yet it was the aim of Hawking and those of like mind to find a comprehensive description of reality including quantum theory — with or without God.

Now came the great surprise: in 2004 Hawking remarked in a Cambridge lecture that in principle he had given up his quest for a "grand unified theory" forever.[19] He had concluded that hope of finding a complete comprehensive theory for knowing the world in its innermost

17. Hawking, *Brief History of Time*, 174.
18. Hawking, *Brief History of Time*, 175.
19. Cf. Hawking, "Gödel and the End of Physics," available at www.damtp.cam.ac.uk/strtst/dirac/hawking.

parts and thus also controlling it had been deceptive. It did not seem to him to be possible to establish a theory of the universe with a finite number of statements.

Here Hawking surprisingly referred to the first incompleteness theorem of the Austrian mathematician Kurt Gödel (1906-78), perhaps the most important logician of the twentieth century. This theorem from the year 1930 says that a finite system of axioms always contains formulas that can neither be proved nor refuted within its system.[20] The situation resembles the well-known example from antiquity where someone says, "This statement is false." If one presupposes that all statements are in principle either true or false (this would be the completeness of the system), then the statement made is true precisely when it is false. There is therefore a contradiction.[21]

Whether or not Hawking quotes and understands Gödel rightly, with all this he has only repeated the experience that leading mathematicians and theoretical scientists had decades before him. For already around 1910 the development of mathematics had led to a dispute about its foundations, a dispute that is still alive today, especially about the status of set theory and the principle of the excluded third.[22] Those who have concerned themselves as thoroughly with the results of scientific theory as I did as early as the 1970s[23] will not be amazed at Hawking's change of mind. So do we have GOD instead of GUT? I want to investigate this principle specifically, but only after I have considered the problems of the foundations of mathematics.

20. For those who know the subject, the precise formulation is: in any recursive-axiomatized formal system free of contradiction, which can be described in first-level logic and in which the natural numbers can be described with addition and multiplication, there are always formulae that can neither be proved nor refuted in this system.

21. The proof is given with the example of a formula that after appropriate number-theory deciphering asserts its own unprovability. I am grateful to Ulrich Felgner, the Tübingen Professor of Logic, the Foundations and History of Mathematics, for this reference and other valuable suggestions.

22. Cf. the survey of the debate in C. Parsons, "Mathematics, Foundations of," in *Encyclopedia of Philosophy* (London, 1967), 5:188-213.

23. Cf. H. Küng, *Does God Exist? An Answer for Today* (London and New York, 1978), A.III.1: "The Epistemological Discussion."

4. The Dispute about the Foundations of Mathematics

Since the beginning of modern times mathematics has constantly and inexorably developed hand in hand with physics, in a straight line. With its application to celestial mechanics, acoustics, optics, electricity, and finally to every branch of science and technology, it achieved one triumph after another. So wouldn't the dream of a mathematical universal science cherished by Descartes and Leibniz be realized? In this section I shall venture on a very difficult problem that possibly initially affects only those particularly interested in mathematics and logic but has considerable effects on the relationship between science and religion. Those who are less interested may happily skip the next pages.

Mathematics without Contradiction? Gödel

It was the very intention of making mathematics the basic and universal science that led to the crisis: as early as the second half of the nineteenth century, set theory, invented by the German mathematician Georg Cantor (1845-1918), threatened the unassailability of mathematics and its freedom from contradictions. It led to antinomies, paradoxes, and contradictions: statements that could be both proved and refuted mathematically at the same time. A famous example is the paradox of the "set of all ordinal numbers" (according to C. Burali-Forti): for every set of ordinal numbers there is an ordinal number that is greater than all the ordinal numbers occurring in the set. But any ordinal number that is greater than the "set of ordinal numbers" cannot occur in this set (because it is greater), yet — as can be proved at the same time — it must occur in this set (because otherwise we do not have the set of all ordinal numbers).

Thus coping with the numerous logical-mathematical and also linguistic (semantic and syntactic) paradoxes in mathematics produced a momentous crisis over its foundations. For the first time in the history of mathematics the problem of freedom from contradiction in a mathematical theory was posed. Attempts were made to master the problem by a variety of methods or ways of thinking. Finally three different standard interpretations, logical in themselves but contradicting one an-

19

other (at the same time, they were schools of mathematics), developed: logicism (F. L. G. Frege, B. Russell, A. N. Whitehead), intuitionism (L. E. J. Brouwer), and formalism (D. Hilbert). But neither logicism, which derives mathematics from logic, nor intuitionism (constructionism), which attempts to construct logic from certain fundamental mathematical insights, has been able so far to gain general acceptance. Nor has formalism, which regards logic and mathematics at the same time as a system of rules gained by a calculus of axioms (leaving aside all meanings).

Kurt Gödel's famous second incompleteness theorem of 1930 thus stands in a historical context. In it Gödel demonstrated that one cannot prove that a sufficiently complicated system is free of contradiction with means that are at one's disposal in the system itself, insofar as the system is generally free from contradiction. It follows from this that most systems of mathematical axioms are not in a position to prove that they themselves are free from contradiction. It was not possible to safeguard mathematical thought by finite, constructive proofs of freedom from contradiction in a way that was universally compelling. A bon mot circulates among mathematicians: God exists because mathematics is free from contradiction, and the devil exists because this freedom from contradiction cannot be proved (thus André Weil).

In his famous 1961 book *Enumerability — Decidability — Computability*, the mathematician and logician Hans Hermes observes that "in view of the important role which mathematics plays today in our conception of the world . . . it is of considerable interest . . . that the mathematicians have shown by strictly mathematical methods that there exist mathematical problems which cannot be dealt with by the methods of calculating mathematics."[24] Taking up Emil L. Post, Hermes speaks of a "natural law about the 'limitations of the mathematicizing power of Homo Sapiens.'"[25]

---

24. H. Hermes, *Enumerability — Decidability — Computability* (Berlin, 1969), vi. Here Hermes refers to Gödel's first principle of incompleteness. For the difficulties in the transition from everyday language to the formal language of mathematics and logic, cf. Hermes, *Einführung in die mathematische Logik. Klassischer Prädikatenlogik*, 2nd ed. (Stuttgart, 1969).

25. Hermes, *Enumerability — Decidability — Computability*, vi.

Thus mathematicians themselves want a mathematics without illusions. The judgment of the important American mathematician Morris Kline (1908-92) may seem to some of his colleagues exaggerated, even malicious, but it is understandable in view of the fundamental uncertainties of which many mathematicians seem to be little aware. This has become clear to me in conversations. In 1975, around a decade before Hawking's best seller, Kline wrote: "The present state of mathematics is regrettable. Its claim to truth had to be abandoned. The efforts to exclude the paradoxes and to emphasize the freedom from contradiction in its structures have failed. Everyone disagrees over the axioms to be applied. . . . We must abandon the claim to unobjectionable proof. Finally, the dominant concept of mathematics as a collection of structures, each of which is grounded in its own axiomatic state, is incapable of embracing all that mathematics should embrace."[26]

No Ultimate Theory of Everything

In everyday mathematical practice, however, questions about problems over the foundation of mathematics play a minor role. What is important for our topic is that a mathematician or physicist who aims "to know the mind of God" would perhaps have to grapple with philosophical and theological questions as seriously as with those of physics. If the foundations of mathematics are often unproven, shouldn't one then formulate universal claims of mathematical and scientific thought with more modesty and restraint?

Today Stephen Hawking sees this. "If there are mathematical results which cannot be proved, there are physical problems which cannot be predicted. . . . We are not angels, who view the universe from outside. Instead, we and our models are both part of the universe we are describing. Thus a physical theory is self-referencing, like in Gödel's theorem. One might therefore expect it to be either inconsistent, or incomplete."[27]

26. M. Kline, "Les fondements des mathématiques," *La Recherche* 54 (Mar. 1971): 200-208, here 208. Cf. Kline, *Mathematical Thought from Ancient to Modern Times* (New York, 1972).

27. See Hawking, "Gödel and the End of Physics," for this quotation and the three following.

But after the failure of his attempt at a unitary theory that knows the mind of God, Hawking ultimately concedes indirectly: "Some people will be very disappointed if there is not an ultimate theory that can be formulated as a finite number of principles." He says that he too belonged to this camp: "But I have changed my mind. I'm now glad that our search for understanding will never come to an end, and that we will always have the challenge of new discovery." So he makes a virtue of necessity and adds: "Without it, we would stagnate. Gödel's theorem ensured there would always be a job for mathematicians." And of course, also for physicists.

Occasion for Self-Critical Reflection

Thus the pretentious ambition of a physicist who wanted to subsume the whole world into a physical theory and was not afraid of deposing philosophy, theology, and anthropology has fallen to the ground of reality. And we can understand the commentary by John Cornwell, director of the Science and Humanity Dimension Project at Jesus College, Cambridge: "Hawking's fame," which produced no theory tested by observation at the level of Einstein, Bohr, Dirac, or Heisenberg, "was based on the notion that he was in a race against time to discover the ultimate truth of existence before his own death. With his admission that 'will always be something left to discover,' he now joins the ranks of lesser intellectual mortals. Indeed he may well concede, such as the brilliant British scientist J. B. S. Haldane, 'that the universe may not just be queer to imagine, but queerer than we *can* imagine.'"[28]

With his friend and colleague Roger Penrose, Hawking has shown that "Einstein's General Theory of Relativity includes the fact that space and time begin with the Big Bang and end in black holes."[29] But Hawking also had to correct his empirical views of black holes, enormous concentrations of extremely dense mass, which occur at the cen-

---

28. J. Cornwell, "Hawking's Quest: A Search without End," *Tablet,* 27 Mar. 2004.
29. Cf. "About Stephen — a Brief History of Mine," available at www.hawking.org.uk/text/about/about.html.

ter of our Milky Way and possibly also in the center of most galaxies.[30] A black hole — described and calculated long before by the German physicist Karl Schwarzschild (1873-1916) — comes about when a particularly massive star burns out and collapses, and under the pressure of its own gravity is condensed into an extremely highly-concentrated lump of matter, so that the laws of gravity and those of quantum physics can be applied to it. For example, our earth would be a sphere of less than a centimeter; the sun would have a diameter of less than three kilometers. According to Hawking's earlier theory of 1976, everything that transcends a certain limit, "the event horizon," is sucked into the black hole, a mass so dense that not even light can escape it. Hawking postulated pure radiation that contained no information. Indeed, in 1997 he made a widely publicized bet with American colleague John Preskill of the California Institute of Technology that the information swallowed up by the black hole remained hidden forever and would never be released.

However, in July 2004, at the Seventeenth Congress on General Relativity and Gravity in Dublin, Hawking stated that information could after all emerge through fluctuations at the edge of a black hole. He had lost the bet. At the same time, he revised the view he had put forward thirty years earlier that the alleged disappearance of matter and energy into the black holes was to be explained by parallel universes alongside our universe. The massive maelstroms that form when stars collapse did not send the energy and matter they had absorbed into a parallel universe. Everything remained in our universe and survived the dissolution of the black hole in a compressed form: "There is no baby universe, as I once thought."[31] He regretted very much that he had to disappoint the science-fiction community.

Moreover, according to the Vienna Professor of Scientific Computing, Rudolf Taschner, Gödel's first incompleteness theorem has the following consequences for computer experts: "There is no universal procedure that can be carried out by a calculating machine which

---

30. For what follows see the report in the *International Herald Tribune*, 17/18 July 2004: "Hawking Backpedals on Black Holes."

31. S. Hawking, communication from AP, 22 July 2004.

can decide for all computer programs whether these stop or whether they run without interruption in an endless loop. This is the redeeming message of the almost religious belief in the omniscience and omnipotence of the computer: however refined the conception of a calculating machine may be, there always remains a nut which it cannot crack, confronted with which all its arts fail."[32] Even before Taschner, Alan Turing had recognized and proved the insolubility of this "stop problem."

Isn't it time, I ask myself, for Hawking and scientists of like mind to examine not only fantastic speculations and certain empirical views but also the positivistic foundations of their scientific thought, which stem from the nineteenth century? However, this is no easy undertaking, as it affects the foundations of mathematics and logic. Positivism is more than a theory, it is a worldview. And some natural scientists do not notice that they are constantly looking at the world through positivistic spectacles. So I now have to shed critical light on the basic assumptions of this positivistic worldview.

5. The Inadequacies of Positivism

Stephen Hawking need only have consulted with his prominent British colleague Karl Popper (born in Vienna in 1902, died 1994), from 1946 Professor of Logic and Theoretical Science at the London School of Economics, to have been enlightened at an early stage about the fundamental limits of the natural sciences. In his youth Popper was close to the positivistic Vienna Circle of philosophers, mathematicians, and scientists around Max Planck's pupil Moritz Schlick.[33] The circle also included Kurt Gödel, and in 1922 it published a manifesto, "Scientific

32. R. Taschner, *Der Zahlen gigantische Schatten. Mathematik im Zeichen der Zeit* (Wiesbaden, 2004), 102.

33. Cf. M. Schlick, *Gesammelte Aufsätze, 1926-1936* (Vienna, 1938). For Schlick's complicated personality (he was not completely against metaphysics), cf. the commemoratory address by Friedrich Waismann reprinted as a foreword. In 1930 Schlick announced the "shift in philosophy," referring to Leibniz, Frege, Russell, and especially Wittgenstein.

View of the World,"[34] which asserted that only the statements of mathematics and logic, which are purely formal statements without empirical content, and statements of the empirical sciences that can be completely proved by experience, could be meaningful statements. So are all meta-empirical, metaphysical statements meaningless?

Rejection of the Meta-empirical? Popper

Logical positivism, which assumes something posited, a "given" in the experiential sense, as the ultimate foundation of its argumentation, no longer wanted to accept the experience of the senses as a starting point, as the older empirical positivism of the French philosopher Auguste Comte assumed: Comte had coined the term "positivism" in 1830. But the experience of the senses was to be the controlling authority for the correctness of all assertions; to this extent people talked of logical neo-positivism, or empiricism.

Deeply impressed by the "objectivity," "exactness," and "precision" of the natural sciences and mathematics, the neo-positivists, a century after Comte, also required an empirical examination of philosophy, a "verification" of all its statements. Only statements that expressed a state of affairs subject to direct observation or open to examination by experiments may be regarded as real and meaningful. It is clear that in such science and philosophy there is no reflection on the meta-empirical, religion, indeed "God." Philosophy seems to be reduced to logical and linguistic analysis; metaphysics is definitively superseded and theology is a priori meaningless.

However, all in all, isn't the positivist "recognition" that metaphysical problems are only "meaningless pseudoproblems" wishful thinking? That was Karl Popper's objection at an early stage:

> This wish . . . can always be gratified. For nothing is easier than
> to unmask a problem as "meaningless" or "pseudo." All you

34. In addition to Moritz Schlick, Kurt Gödel, and Rudolf Carnap, the main members of the Vienna Circle were Herbert Feigel, Philipp Frank, Hans Hahn, Victor Kraft, Karl Menger, Otto Neurath, and Friedrich Waismann (with a link to Hans Reichenbach in Berlin).

have to do is to fix upon a conveniently narrow meaning of "meaning," and you will soon be bound to say of any inconvenient question that you are unable to find any meaning in it. Moreover, if you admit as meaningful none except problems in natural science, any debate about the concept of "meaning" will also turn out to be meaningless. The dogma of meaning, once enthroned, is elevated for ever above the battle. It can no longer be attacked. It has become (in Wittgenstein's words) "unassailable and definitive."[35]

But the optimistic hope of Moritz Schlick, Rudolf Carnap, and others from the Vienna Circle that the future would belong to the disposition that above all aims at clarity was completely destroyed by Nazism and Fascism. As early as 1935 Carnap emigrated to the USA, in 1936 Schlick was shot by a former pupil, in 1937 Popper emigrated to New Zealand, and in 1938 the other members of the Vienna Circle, who were largely Jewish and therefore now banned, emigrated. However, precisely because of this, logical positivism now spread to the Anglo-Saxon world. That makes all the more urgent the critical question: Are there only meaningless pseudoproblems?

Only Meaningless Pseudoproblems?

It was the internal aporia that caused a crisis for the program of logical positivism, as the logicians finally themselves had to recognize. The objections to such a faith in science were numerous. Can the basic concepts of natural science such as the atom be clearly defined at all? Don't they perhaps depend more on research that constantly changes, so that while clarity of concepts is striven for, it cannot be attained? Hasn't the very word "atom" (= "the indivisible") been repudiated by science? In mathematical and scientific knowledge and research, can the subject, i.e., subjective conditions and presuppositions, standpoints, and perspectives, be completely excluded in favor of a pure objectivity? Must every science really adopt the mathematical-scientific method as the

35. K. R. Popper, *The Logic of Scientific Discovery* (1934; London, 2002), 29.

only legitimate leading idea? Hasn't the unitary scientific language that was striven for at that time and with it the unity of science meanwhile clearly proved to be an illusion?

But we will have to ask an even more fundamental question about meaning and meaninglessness. Is it legitimate to exclude particular questions a priori as "meaningless" if one cannot define what "meaning" is in empirical mathematical terms? With what right does one then make the empirical experience of the senses the criterion for meaning? Isn't one making a "metaphysical" and thus "meaningless" statement and at the same time declaring two thousand years of critical thought in metaphysics "meaningless"? Can an "overcoming of metaphysics by logical analysis of language," to use Carnap's phrase, be attained with such a move? Is any metaphysic really nothing but a figment of the imagination? Are metaphysical statements really only pseudostatements, concepts such as the absolute, the unconditional, the being of the entity, the I, only pseudoconcepts? Is the word "God" really no different from a meaningless invented word such as "babig," for which it is said that no criterion of meaning can be given?[36] Is the distinction between theism, atheism, and agnosticism already meaningless? Because of the success of mathematics and science, must we in fact end up with the "death of God in language"? I maintain the opposite: a modern logic and theory of science need in no way necessarily present itself as antimetaphysical and antitheological. Why?

The Impossibility of Proving
All Statements True, Even in Science

As early as 1935 in his influential book *The Logic of Scientific Discovery,* Karl Popper had acutely analyzed the rules for arriving at scientific hypotheses and theories and demonstrated the limitations of the inductive method in the empirical sciences. His question was: How does a researcher arrive at a theoretical system from individual pieces of experiences? How are new scientific insights ever achieved? Popper's

36. Thus R. Carnap, "Überwindung der Metaphysik durch logische Analyse der Sprache," *Erkenntnis* 2 (1931): 219-41, here 227.

perplexing answer was: not through verification and proof but through falsification and refutation.

The principle of verification that is central to logical positivism, namely, the radical demand for the verification of all human statements by the empirical, would not just do away with meta-empirical statements. At the same time, it would annihilate empirical hypotheses and thus the whole of scientific knowledge: "Positivists, in their anxiety to annihilate metaphysics, annihilate natural science along with it."[37] Why? Because most scientific statements cannot be empirically verified either, and so would have to be rejected as pseudostatements. "For scientific laws, too, cannot be logically reduced to elementary statements of experience." To take an example: were a statement such as "All copper conducts electricity" to be verified in experience, all the copper in the universe would have to be examined for this property, and of course, that is impossible. So no theory can be as reliable as the experiment on which it bases itself in its generalization.

Popper's opposing position was that natural laws, which should also make decisive predictions for the future possible, are by no means verifiable; they can only be falsified, refuted by the method of trial and error. To take another example: the statement "all swans are white" cannot be verified because no one knows all the swans in this world. But a single black swan discovered in Australia was enough to falsify the statement "all swans are white." That makes for modesty. "The old scientific ideal . . . of absolutely certain, demonstrable knowledge has proved to be an idol, or to put it positively: every scientific statement must remain tentative for ever. It may indeed be corroborated, but every corroboration is relative to other statements."[38]

So at the beginning of our knowledge there always stand only "conjectures," suppositions, models, hypotheses that are to be exposed to examination. That there is an ultimate foundation for the statements of science that cannot be criticized is for Popper a belief that ends in a hopeless trilemma. He develops this by starting from the philosopher Jacob Friedrich Fries (1773-1843): either the simple assertion of a dog-

---

37. Popper, *Logic of Scientific Discovery*, 13.
38. Popper, *Logic of Scientific Discovery*, 280.

matism or an infinite regression doomed to ever new reasoning or a psychologism that generalizes individual experiences.[39] None of these ways is viable.

What does that mean for the criterion of verification? Such a criterion may not be used as a positivistic criterion of meaning, as a rule for distinguishing between intrinsically meaningful and meaningless statements. It can be used only as a rational criterion of demarcation, for distinguishing between statements that are reliable or unreliable in logic, mathematics, and experimental science. Positively, that means that such a rational but not positivistic criterion of demarcation also leaves room for meaningful "nonphysical," "meta-empirical" statements that are "metaphysical" in the broadest sense, statements that extend beyond the scientific realm. The conclusion that Popper draws from this is that in principle a rational analysis of metaphysical questions is possible. These include above all "the problem of cosmology," in which "all thinking men are interested": "the problem of understanding the world including ourselves, and our knowledge, as part of the world."[40]

Thus, according to Popper, "it is a fact that purely metaphysical ideas — and therefore philosophical ideas — have been of the greatest importance for cosmology. From Thales to Einstein, from ancient atomism to Descartes' speculation about matter, from the speculations of Gilbert and Newton and Leibniz and Boscovic about forces to those of Faraday and Einstein about fields of forces, metaphysical ideas have shown the way."[41] What does all this mean for our knowledge of reality?

The Autonomy and Limits of Scientific Knowledge

Quite rightly, and with much success, scientists attempted to advance their knowledge to the point of mathematical certainty. The standard model of the Big Bang is an impressive example of this. The research in

---

39. Cf. H. Albert, *Traktat über kritische Vernunft*, 3rd ed. (Tübingen, 1975), 13-15: he varies this scheme to the "Münchausen-Trilemma": infinite regression–circular argument–breaking off the proceedings or dogmatism.

40. Popper, *Logic of Scientific Discovery*, xviii.

41. Popper, *Logic of Scientific Discovery*, xxiii.

branches of science from nuclear physics to astrophysics, from molecular biology to medicine, can be carried out with such a degree of precision that the greatest possible mathematical certainty is achieved. Thus mathematically orientated science is fully justified, independent, and autonomous. No theologian or churchman should put it in question with reference to a higher authority (God, Bible, pope, church). Confronted with attempts at control by religious authorities of a kind that even now are a constant threat in individual questions, a demarcation of mathematical scientific statements from meta-empirical philosophical and theological statements is in principle justified and necessary.

This demarcation does not just favor science; science favors the demarcation. If questions of science are rightly discussed in accordance with the method and style of science, questions of the humanities — i.e., questions of the human psyche and society; law, politics, and history; aesthetics, ethics, and religion — should also be discussed with a distinctive method and style that correspond to their object. For all the legitimate emphasis on the independence and autonomy of science, the problems of its foundation must not be passed over; the hypothetical character of its laws must not be overlooked; and its results must not be absolutized.

The most recent history of both physics and mathematics has produced admirable results, but it also shows fundamental limits to physical and mathematical knowledge. This must also be significant for biology, which builds on physics and mathematics, and especially for neurobiology.

- *Physics* came up against fundamental limits with quantum theory. The Heisenberg indeterminacy relation is one of its main principles: since the position and momentum of a particle cannot be measured at the same time, in principle certain atomic events cannot be calculated beforehand. The indeterminacy allows only statistical probability.
- *Mathematics* came up against fundamental limits specifically in the problems of its foundations. According to Gödel's second incompleteness theorem of 1930, no finite, constructive proofs can

provide a universally compelling guarantee that mathematical thought is free from contradiction.

All this means that along with the great possibilities of science, we must also note its limitations. There are limit questions at which the competence of mathematics and physics end. In the face of the threat of a control of human thought and action not only by religion but sometimes also by science, it has to be maintained that there is no mathematical or scientific criterion according to which meta-empirical philosophical-theological statements can be declared to be meaningless, "pseudoproblems." Mathematizability cannot be the goal for any science; it cannot be carried through in history, which has to do with singular events, and in psychology and philosophy too it clearly comes up against limits.

In any case, after the 1980s a shift of accent took place in mathematics from the questions about its foundations, which manifestly could not be given a definitive answer, to a more pragmatic attitude and the posing of concrete problems. Here the computer opened up unsuspected possibilities. But now I have every reason to turn back from mathematics to the universal philosophical questions that relate to reality as such.

6. The Questionability of Reality

I said by way of introduction that reality is everything real. So it is all that is, all entities, the totality of entities and in this sense the being that exists. But is that a definition of reality? No, reality cannot be defined a priori. The whole, the all-embracing, cannot by definition be defined, delimited. In just a few words I shall point out what I mean by reality, so that we are not talking in an abstract or empty way. This reality is not an a priori transparent, indubitable, unquestionable reality, but a reality that in many respects is questionable. Why?

31

Universe — Human Being — Self

Reality is in the first place our universe, the origin of which we have considered, our cosmos, the world and all that makes up the world in space and time, macrocosm and microcosm with their abysses; matter and antimatter, the protons and antiprotons, the elementary particles, fields of force and curved space, white dwarfs, red giants, and black holes. But reality is also the world in its history that has extended for around 13 billion years since the Big Bang, 5 billion years since the formation of the sun, and 3.5 billion years since the origin of life, and only around 200,000 years since the hominization of human beings. It is the world with nature and culture, with all its wonders and terrors. It is not a "whole world," but the real world in all its questionableness and fragility, with all its concrete dangers and natural catastrophes, its real misery and immeasurable suffering. It is animals and human beings in their fight for existence, in coming into being and passing away, eating and being eaten.

In the world reality is especially human beings, human beings of all levels and classes, all colors and races, nations and regions, the individual and society — the greatness and misery of the human race. It is the human being as a natural being, the object of science and medicine, and at the same time the human being as a free being, the object of the humanities, who cannot be calculated precisely and who often enough is a riddle to himself or herself. Human beings are responsible for vast technological progress, but also for an unprecedented destruction of the environment, the population explosion, the shortage of water, AIDS, and so on.

Reality is especially myself. I can become an object to myself as subject, and have self-awareness. Reality is myself with spirit and body, with disposition and behavior, with strengths and weaknesses, heights and depths, light sides and shadow sides. According to scientific insights, I am completely subject to material, biological causality: a causality apparently without any gaps. But in the indisputable experience of myself (and countless others, on which we can also reflect critically) I recognize that I am capable of knowing myself and deciding for myself, thinking and acting strategically. This already makes it possible to give a more concrete answer to the question I asked at the beginning: What is reality? Reality is not one-dimensional and on one level but is rich in facets.[42]

Multidimensional and Multilayered Reality

Scientific research is said to get to the root of things, the *radix*. But authentic thoroughness and radicality are not to be identified with one-sidedness and one-dimensionality. In the face of an absolutized rationality, in the face of the ideology of rationalism, we must reckon a priori with the multidimensionality and multilevel character of reality: the real can indisputably occur in very different ways; it can have a very different character. I recall visiting the National Museum in Athens with friends from the senior class of my Lucerne school. I was surprised that the reality of the same museum is one thing for the chemist, who notes above all the problems of casting bronze and other technical processes; another for the historian, who is interested in the development from archaic through classical to Hellenistic art; and something yet again for the art lover, who is fascinated above all by the aesthetics of the objects. The same gold mask of a prince of Mycenae can be described and assessed from extremely different perspectives. And it is important that every description and assessment, that of the chemist, the historian, or the art lover, can be true — depending on the perspective.

Evidently the same reality differentiates itself depending on the perspective and interest under which it appears to the observer. There is never reality "in itself," and there are many different aspects, dimensions, layers of reality. Among the great physicists, it was above all Werner Heisenberg (as early as 1942, during the Second World War) who in a "'theory of layers' in reality" spoke of a bottommost layer where the causal connections of phenomena and processes in space and time could be objectivized, and an "uppermost layer of reality in

---

42. The following sections also give an indirect answer to the materialistic or naturalistic monism put forward for example by the biologist E. O. Wilson, *Consilience* (New York, 1998).

which the view opens up of those parts of the world which can be spoken of only in parable": "the last ground of reality."[43]

For the practice of research, teaching, and living, that means there is not just one explanation, the physical one, for simple objects such as tables and bicycles, but several levels of explanation (including the functional). Absolutizing a particular aspect of reality cannot be recommended, for in that case one becomes literally blind to others. Among philosophers, theologians, scholars in the humanities generally, and also among mathematicians, physicists, neurophysicists, and all scientists, professional blindness can easily become blindness to reality. People no longer see how things really are but only what they want to see. This happens in the discussion of a "theory of everything" that, looked at closely, is a theory only for all that is physical and contributes little to the understanding of Shakespeare, Handel, or Newton. It also happens in the debate about the brain and freedom of will, as we shall see later.

Think especially of the great figures who gave impetus to modern science — philosophers such as Descartes, Spinoza, and Leibniz, but also Voltaire, Lessing, and Kant, and natural scientists such as Copernicus, Kepler, Galileo, Newton, and Boyle: Would they ever have succumbed to simply denying another dimension than that of mathematical scientific reason or dismissing it as meaningless? At least in this respect it is wrong to call the great rational thinkers "rationalists." They are not the representatives of an -ism and blind to other aspects of reality.

However, I must immediately guard against one misunderstanding. Though there are many levels of reality, one may never simply say that the different strata of reality are different realities. For all the multidimensionality of reality, one may not overlook the unity in the different dimensions. In all the different perspectives, dimensions, layers, aspects, and differentiations, there is the one reality that is split up by human beings, always at the expense of their full humanity in this world.

Therefore, at an early stage Descartes's dualism between subject and object, thought and being, spirit and matter, soul and body, human

43. W. Heisenberg, "Ordnung der Wirklichkeit" (1942), in *Gesammelte Werke*, ed. W. Blum et al. (Munich, 1984), vol. 1, sec. C, 217-306, here 294, 302.

being and animal was subjected to criticism. But also in the face of the dualism between reason and faith, philosophy and theology, the unity and truth of reality must time and again be expressed anew: the question posed by Greek philosophy about the unity and truth of being and the question of the ancient Hebrews about salvation and the meaning of the whole are thus by no means settled — they are closely connected. Here we should pause to reflect.

Reason, but Not Reason Alone

From the seventeenth century on — a time of great uncertainty caused not least by the new cosmology — human beings learned to find in reason a new basis of certainty *(cogito, ergo sum)* and learned to use reason ever more comprehensively in surroundings of doubt. In principle it was justified, indeed historically necessary, for human beings in the scientific Enlightenment to investigate without prejudice, in a rational and systematic way, nature and its laws, and finally also themselves and their social relationships in all their different aspects.

But human beings do not live by reason alone. Although independent reason and scientific knowledge are justified in principle and historically necessary, an absolutized rationality is to be rejected. Whether a physicist or a philosopher or whatever, every man or woman has to do with more than reason: with willing and feeling, imagination and disposition, emotions and passions that cannot simply be reduced to reason. Alongside methodical rational thinking, Descartes's *esprit de géometrie,* there is also intuitive holistic knowing, sensing, feeling, the *esprit de finesse.*

However, one could object: Isn't only the "objective" real? By no means; even scientific objectivity, which is so central to modern science, has undergone a history in modern times:[44] "objectivity" is not simply identical with "truth." Just as justice is far from exhausting the list of social virtues, so objectivity is far from exhausting the epistemological virtues. And just as in the concrete instance justice

44. Cf. L. Daston, "Can Scientific Objectivity Have a History?" *Alexander von Humboldt-Mitteilungen* 75 (2000): 31-40.

can come into conflict with benevolence, so objectivity can come into conflict with other dimensions of the truth; for however objective the formulas of physics, mathematics, or chemistry may seem, they are by no means the sole criteria for the real. Scientists, too, constantly have the experience that the colorful world of colors, tones, smells, indeed the whole sensual wealth of the world, is infinitely richer than all the physical and chemical formulas. And before physicists or chemists can perceive the colorless electromagnetic waves of varying length and frequency, they also see — with all the emotions bound up with the situation — red, yellow, blue, and green in their thousands of variations.

The reductionism of scientific knowledge by reason must be countered. Certainly, Kant is right in saying that a religion that unthinkably declares war on reason will not hold out against it in the long run. The Tübingen theologian Jürgen Moltmann has formulated the correct counterpart to that: "even reason, in its enlightening victory over what it called faith, could not hold out alone, but developed highly unreasonable forms of naïve credibility."[45] Indeed, the cult of the "goddess reason" did not prevent the terror of the guillotine in the French Revolution. Even science, which is so rational, often functions in a quite irrational way and sometimes leads to irrational results.

7. Science and Theology: Different Perspectives

Science has long lost the innocence of its beginnings. The euphoria over progress in the nineteenth century and first half of the twentieth century has evaporated. Over past decades it has become increasingly clear that scientific progress is far from always humane progress.

Science: The Foundation but Not the Totality

Almost all significant scientific and technological progress — nuclear technology, gene technology, intensive medicine, the "green revolu-

45. Cf. J. Moltmann, "Theology in the World of Modern Science," in *Hope and Planning* (London, 1971), 200-223, here 207.

tion," the automation of all production, the globalization of economics, technology, and communication — also has negative consequences that are unintended or simply taken into account. After the collapse of the bubble economy at the end of the twentieth century, even neoliberal economists no longer believe that the allegedly self-regulating markets are ruled by reason. That even in the third millennium billions are invested in the all-embracing armaments industry instead of in the fight against poverty, hunger, disease, and illiteracy goes against all reason. Indeed, the wars in Afghanistan and Iraq supposedly fought quite rationally at the beginning of the twenty-first century with their top-level technology, which have had devastating consequences for the countries concerned and the whole world, make many people doubt whether the human race has any reason at all. Certainly all this is not an argument against reason and science. But it is an argument against a credulity in science that absolutizes science and technology.

Science has rightly become the foundation for modern technology and industry, indeed, for the modern picture of the world, modern civilization and culture. But science will meaningfully do justice to this role only if the foundation is not made the whole building; if people see the relativity and provisionality, the social conditioning and ethical implications of every picture of the world, of all sketches, models, and aspects; if alongside scientific methods those of the humanities and social sciences are also allowed, and with them those of philosophy and — in yet another way — theology. In other words, science must not be made a worldview. Every science, however precise and penetrating, that absolutizes itself makes itself a laughingstock to all the world and easily becomes a common danger. And if it attempts to demystify all the others (one thinks of psychoanalysis), in the end it will be demystified itself. But here we need to make the opposite point.

Theology Too Needs Self-Criticism

The perspectives are different: scientists are more concerned with the analysis of data, facts, phenomena, operations, processes, energies, structures, developments — and rightly so. But theologians — and philosophers if they so want! — can just as rightly be concerned with questions of last or first meanings and aims, with values, ideals, norms, decisions, and attitudes. Today, too, it is welcome to see that many scientists acknowledge that they cannot offer any final, definitive truths. They appear more than ever ready to revise a standpoint once gained, indeed, in some cases to take it back again completely — by trial and error.

On the other hand, theologians and philosophers should also remain modest and self-critical in conversation with scientists. For while they too are concerned with the truth of faith by virtue of their profession, they do not possess these truths a priori and definitively. They must seek the truth time and again; like other people, they can only approximate to it; they must learn it by trial and error and be prepared to revise their standpoint. In theology, too, if it is to be a science and not sterile dogmatism, in principle the interplay of scheme, criticism, countercriticism, and improvement is possible and often called for. Theologians should not make the controversy easy for scientists by introducing into the discussion the argument from authority that at the latest from after the Enlightenment has been shown to be unscientific, and withdraw to the alleged infallibility of the Bible, of the pope, and of statements of the councils, which tolerate no further questioning.[46]

Indisputably German theology has a considerable need to catch up in its relationship to science. Members of Karl Barth's school were prevented from dialogue with scientists by a historically conditioned antipathy to any "natural theology." In Rudolf Bultmann's school there was a concentration on illuminating human existence with a complete neglect of cosmology. Catholic theologians were concerned only with working out the baneful Roman Catholic doctrinal documents and the rehabilitation of Galileo and Teilhard de Chardin.

Things have been quite different in the Anglo-Saxon sphere: here not only have theologians been deeply involved with physics, but physicists have been deeply involved with theology and have done important mediating work. For decades a number of scholars have been models, with nu-

---

46. This is attempted by the philosopher B. Kanitscheider, "Es hat keinen Sinn, die Grenzen zu verwischen," interview in *Spektrum der Wissenschaft,* Nov. 1995, 80-83.

merous publications: the American physicist and theologian Ian G. Barbour (Northfield, Minn.), quoted above;[47] the British theologian and biochemist Arthur Peacocke (Oxford);[48] and John Polkinghorne, professor of mathematical physics and a theologian (Cambridge).[49]

Here I am concerned less with a parallelism in method between science and theology and a unitary concept of science and rationality, of the kind John Polkinghorne attempted to work out in his early books. On the contrary, the methodological independence and autonomy of science and the humanities, especially of philosophy and theology, seem important to me: any defensive apologetic attitude is alien to me. Unlike the Anglo-Saxon scholars, I want to compare the results of science less with the "classic" Hellenistic dogmas of Greek patristics, which I have subjected to a thorough historical-critical investigation,[50] than with what is to be found in the Old and New Testaments, as shown by contemporary historical-critical exegesis.[51] Finally, in the comparison with science one does not keep simply to the "classical" theories of the great Newton, but grapples with the theory of relativity and quantum theory.[52]

---

47. Basic works were I. G. Barbour, *Religion in an Age of Science* (London, 1990), and the impressive synthesis already cited: Barbour, *Religion and Science.*

48. Cf. A. Peacocke, *Theology for a Scientific Age: Being and Becoming — Natural and Divine* (Oxford, 1990); Peacocke, *Paths from Science towards God: The End of All Exploring* (Oxford, 2001).

49. J. Polkinghorne, *Belief in God in an Age of Science* (New Haven, 1998), offers a new summary of his thought. See also Polkinghorne, *Science and Theology: An Introduction* (London, 1998). A. Dinter, *Vom Glauben eines Physikers. John Polkinghornes Beitrag zum Dialog zwischen Theologie und Naturwissenschaften* (Mainz, 1999), investigates Polkinghorne's early works between 1979 and 1990 that have an epistemological and ethical-ecological orientation.

50. Cf. H. Küng, *Christianity, Its Essence and History* (London and New York, 1995); Küng, *Great Christian Thinkers* (London and New York, 1994).

51. Cf. Küng, *On Being a Christian* (London and New York, 1977).

52. Here I am building on the methodological foundations already laid in my book *Does God Exist?* Cf. especially A.III, "Reason or Faith? Against Rationalism for Rationality," and G.II.2, "The God of the Bible: God and His World." The Tübingen postdoctoral dissertation by A. Benk, *Moderne Physik und Theologie. Voraussetzungen und Perspektiven eines Dialogs* (Mainz, 2000), offers a thorough critical discussion of the theory of relativity and quantum theory.

Physical Knowledge Cannot Transcend
the World of Experience

Immanuel Kant has often been confirmed in his insight that physical knowledge has to do with phenomena in space and time but not with the world "in itself," independent of our subjectivity. Physics has to do only with the world of "phenomena," the experiences in space and time that in principle it cannot transcend.

However, present-day physics will hardly agree with Kant on two points.

First, basic determinations of nature such as space, time, and causality are not to be understood as objective data but are only the aprioristic conditions of our knowledge. The world of experience is not grounded wholly in pure subjectivity.

Secondly, not only is the absolute preeminence of the pure subjectivity of science done away with, but the "thing in itself" that according to Kant "affects" us has become problematical. The formative consciousness is not a timeless authority, nor is objectifiable content a world "behind" the phenomena. To put it positively, the dimension of physics is a process that is not to be grounded either solely in the subject or simply in the world of things in itself, but forms a world of its own, what Walter Schulz calls "the world of physics."[53]

It follows from this that the classical self-understanding of science, that one can clearly describe the entity as it really is, i.e., as it is "in itself," can no longer be maintained today. Quantum physics and the discussion of the foundation of mathematics point to the incompleteness and ambiguity of human knowledge. Indeed, even if we could combine all the scientific theories with a limited sphere of validity, if we could bring them all together into a scientific picture of the world, the empirical reliability would not necessarily increase.

For the scientists who take the relativity of their perspective on reality seriously, on further reflection at a "higher" (as Heisenberg puts it) or, as I would prefer to say, a deeper level, the question arises, What holds the world together in its innermost? This is not just the question

---

53. Cf. W. Schulz, *Philosophie in der veränderten Welt* (Pfullingen, 1972), 114f.

of the strong force at work between the smallest particles (quarks) in the atomic nucleus (in 2004 D. J. Gross, F. Wilczek, and H. D. Politzer won the Nobel Prize for physics for this) but the question of the foundation and meaning of the whole of reality.

Today's mathematicians and astronomers will hardly still follow their predecessors Nicholas of Cusa, Kepler, Galileo, and even Cantor and Planck in assuming, along the lines of Plato and the Pythagoreans, that the mathematical properties of things are pointers to their divine origin. Yet, after the discussion on foundations, it must make us think more than ever that mathematics, which is an invention of the human spirit, and the world, which was not created by human beings, fit amazingly well together: they appear equally rational, ordered, and ultimately very simple. By now it must have become clear how I understand the relationship between science and religion.

A Model of Complementarity instead of a Model of Confrontation or Integration

This will be my method in the chapters that follow:

- *no model of confrontation* between science and religion: neither a model of fundamentalist premodern origin that ignores or suppresses the results of science or historical-critical exegesis of the Bible, nor a model with a rationalistic modern coloring that evades the fundamental philosophical and theological questions and declares religion a priori to be irrelevant;
- *no model of integration* with a harmonistic stamp, whether this is advocated by theologians who assimilate the results of science to their dogmas or by scientists who exploit religion for their theses;
- but rather *a model of complementarity involving the critical and constructive interaction* between science and religion in which the distinctive spheres are preserved, all illegitimate transitions are avoided and all absolutizings are rejected, but in which in mutual questioning and enrichment people attempt to do justice to reality as a whole in all its dimensions.

41

So in my reflections in the following chapters I want to penetrate not just to the mathematical structure of the physical world but more deeply to a basic meaning of all things in our phenomenal world that holds them together.[54] Here even for scientists without religious faith the question of the beginning of all things and thus the question of an absolute beginning poses itself unavoidably.

54. A similar approach to the problems of science and religion is attempted by K. Wilber, *The Marriage of Sense and Soul* (New York, 1998). The collection of texts edited by H.-P. Dürr, *Physik und Transzendenz. Die grossen Physiker unseres Jahrhunderts über die Begegnung mit dem Wunderbaren,* 7th ed. (Berne, 1994), is illuminating. Contributors include David Bohm, Niels Bohr, Max Born, Arthur Eddington, Albert Einstein, Werner Heisenberg, James Jeans, Pascual Jordan, Wolfgang Pauli, Max Planck, Erwin Schrödinger, and Carl Friedrich von Weizsäcker.

CHAPTER II

God as Beginning?

—◦◦◦—

For only 200,000 years humankind has been living on a very small planet at the edge of one of the perhaps 100 billion galaxies, each of which as a rule contains more than 10 billion stars. Our telescopes reach a long way, but they have limits. And even if we built telescopes that reached farther and farther, these would always remain limited by the cosmic horizon. There are galaxies that lie beyond our horizon: "Such galaxies are not only in principle unobservable now — they will remain beyond our horizon for ever," remarks Sir Martin Rees, British Astronomer Royal.[1] So human beings cannot grasp the greatest of all, cannot establish scientifically their limited cosmic horizon but, it seems, can at best transcend it in speculation.

However, in this second chapter I am less concerned with cosmological speculations than with philosophical-theological reflections. If we do not know or do not yet know how the four cosmic forces — electrodynamic, weak, and strong forces, and gravity — are connected, we can perhaps move forward to the question of how a beginning of all things could be, even without a "world formula" or physical "theory of everything."

---

1. M. Rees, "Andere Universen — Eine wissenschaftliche Perspektive," in *Im Anfang war (k)ein Gott,* ed. T. D. Wabbel (Düsseldorf, 2004), 47.

1. The Question of the Beginning of Beginnings

The question of the "beginning" (Greek *arche*) of all things was already a main philosophical problem for the ancient Greeks. The earlier Ionian natural philosophers at the beginning of the sixth century B.C.E. assumed a single primal principle from which all things arose: Thales of Miletus thought it was water, Anaximenes air, Heraclitus fire, but Anaximander thought it the "boundless" (Greek *apeiron*) and "divine" (Greek *theion*). Then among the later natural philosophers in the fifth century B.C.E., Anaxagoras opposed to the matter of the world the independent "spirit" (Greek *nous*) that ordered the world. Since then the divine has been present in Greek philosophy, whether it was conceived of by Plato in the fourth century as the idea of the good or by Aristotle as the unmoved Mover of the cosmos and the ultimate goal of all striving in reality. For the first Christian philosophers and theologians ("apologists") (who were also Greek), it was possible without any great conceptual effort to identify this divine and this spirit with the creator God of the Bible. But in present-day science the problem looks different.

The Singularity of the Beginning

Quite understandably, physicists do not like the unique, the singular, in nature. Rather, singularity prompts them to investigate whether this singularity does not dissolve into regularity, cannot be ordered within the structure of proven laws of physics. Their characteristic is not the individual instance but repetition. And such a dissolution of the singularity has been successful in many instances.

But the singularity of the beginning is something fundamentally different: it evades all the concepts and laws of physics. Only 100th of a second after the Big Bang, well-known laws of physics apply. But physicists are in some perplexity over the time 0 (zero) and the cause of the mysterious primal explosion: How are they to explain the fact that the whole potential for hundreds of billions of galaxies was contained in a tiny unit of infinite density, temperature, and initial thrust? Only if the conditions of the beginning can be explained can they explain the special character of our universe. But if physicists are not to refrain from giving an answer, mustn't they perhaps venture into the metaphysical or protophysical?[2]

Now, of course, it could be argued ad hominem: Is that really asking too much of human reason? One can also look at it the other way around: How much "faith" does the standard cosmological model ask of human reason? Did the billions of galaxies come into being from a tiny unit after the Big Bang? Isn't that a kind of "scientific belief in miracle"? At all events, that is what the American scientific journalist Greg Easterbrook thinks: for "sheer incredibility, nothing in theology or metaphysics could touch the Big Bang. If this description of the genesis of the cosmos came from the Bible or the Qur'an instead of the Massachusetts Institute of Technology it would certainly be treated as an exaggerated myth."[3]

Yet, of course, as an informed theologian, I too regard the standard physical model as well founded and at the same time hope that informed scientists too will not understand the "beginning" of all things as a random beginning: the Big Bang is no mere "beginning." After all, what we have here is not just an individual first moment (the first 100th of a second) within a series of many comparable moments of the beginning of a history of the world. What we have here is what makes a history of the world possible at all: not just a temporal beginning but the beginning of time. That means it is not a relative but the absolute first beginning, which cannot be a beginning within world-time or time-world. Indeed, without it world-time or time-world cannot be explained at all.

A beginning of the world that transcends time and space can also be expressed with the word "origin" (Latin *origo*). However, this "origin" must not be identified a priori with "author," with God in the Christian sense. Here theologians easily end up with fallacies. At all events, modern philosophical thought can no longer simply begin with God, as did

2. At a very early stage the physicist and scientific journalist H. von Ditfurth investigated all the questions that arise here in his books, which are serious yet easily understandable: *Children of the Universe* (New York, 1976); *The Origins of Life: Evolution as Creation* (New York, 1982).

3. G. Easterbrook, "Wissenschaftliche Wunderglaube. Die Theologie des Urknalls und die Frage nach dem Anfang des Kosmos," *Neue Zürcher Zeitung,* 23/24 Oct. 1999.

medieval or Reformation thought, but must begin "from below": for modern thought the beginning of knowledge lies in human experience.

The "Copernican Shift" in Philosophy: Descartes

The Copernican shift in astronomy was continued at a very early stage by a "Copernican shift" in philosophy. The foundation for it was laid by Galileo's contemporary René Descartes (1596-1650), the brilliant inventor of analytical geometry and the initiator of modern philosophy. In a new age of calculation and experimentation, of method and the exact sciences, he proclaimed the ideal of mathematic certainty. He no longer moved in a medieval way from the certainty of God to certainty of the self, but in a modern way from self-certainty to certainty of God. Theocentricity was replaced by anthropocentricity: a methodical beginning from the human being, the subject, his reason and freedom. In this way a philosophical basis can be laid for the autonomy of the sciences. Indeed, this is really a paradigm shift that is completed by the fundamental criticism of Immanuel Kant, whose critique of "pure" or theoretical reason culminates in a radical critique of the proofs of God.

Proofs of God — Doomed to Failure: Kant

It is not, as is often conjectured, resignation over the role of reason that lies behind the criticism of Immanuel Kant (1724-1804). Rather, this criticism is grounded in the conviction, which ultimately has an ethical and religious foundation, that limits must be set to reason and that the limits of reason are not identical with the limits of reality. That means that what reason does not know can nevertheless be real. Does that include God?

In the preface to the second edition of his *Critique of Pure Reason,* which he published in 1781 when he was already fifty-seven years old, Kant wrote: "I have therefore found it necessary to deny *knowledge,* in order to make room for *faith.*"[4] Even for the "critical" Kant, as for Rous-

4. I. Kant, *Critique of Pure Reason,* trans. Norman Kemp Smith (London, 1964), 20.

46

seau, whom he highly esteemed, faith is a truth of the heart, or better, of the conscience, beyond all philosophical reflections and demonstrations. As he himself attests at the end of his *Critique of Pure Reason:* "Belief in a God and in another world is so interwoven with my moral sentiment that as there is little danger of my losing the latter, there is equally little cause for fear that the former can ever be taken from me."[5]

But according to Kant, scientific proofs of God are not possible. God does not exist in space and time and therefore he is not the object of contemplation. Therefore no knowledge with the proof of science can be gained and no judgments made, since these are dependent on contemplation. The proofs of God, including those Kant himself put forward in his precritical phase, have in fact come to grief; they are theoretically impossible. According to Kant, the question of a beginning of the world in time cannot be decided either. Why not? "All those conclusions of ours which profess to lead us beyond the field of possible experience are deceptive and without foundation."[6]

Kant is convinced that reason spreads its wings in vain to go beyond the world of phenomena by the power of thought to the "things in themselves" (necessary for thought but not capable of being seen through) or even to penetrate to the real God. Human beings cannot build towers that reach to heaven, but only dwellings large enough and high enough for our business at the level of experience. There is therefore no proof of God that would find general assent even among believers. But that is only one side of the problem.

Counterproofs Also Fail

Kant rejects not only the proofs *for* God but also the proofs *against* God. Why? Because they too transcend the horizon of experience. The idea of God is not a contradiction in itself, and those who want to prove that God does not exist are even more wrong. According to Kant, "the same grounds" that prove the impossibility that reason can assert the existence of God are enough "to prove the invalidity of any counter-

5. Kant, *Critique of Pure Reason,* 650.
6. Kant, *Critique of Pure Reason,* 531.

assertions": "For from what source could we, through a purely speculative use of reason, derive the knowledge that there is no supreme being
as ultimate ground of all things?"[7] Kant is convinced that the idea of
God is a necessary theoretical limit concept that, like a distant star,
while not reached in the process of knowledge, can nevertheless be
steered for as an ideal goal.

To put it metaphorically: anyone who concedes that he cannot
glimpse beyond the curtain may not claim that there is nothing behind
it. Here atheism, too, is shown its limits. All proofs or demonstrations
by important atheists may be enough to make the existence of God
questionable, but they are not enough to put the nonexistence of God
beyond question.

It is regrettable how many misguided battles were fought between
belief in God and science, between theology and atheism in the nineteenth and twentieth centuries. And it is even more regrettable that even
in the twenty-first century many scientists are trapped in the arguments
of the atheistic critique of the nineteenth and twentieth centuries that
have long since been seen through, but on which they often do not reflect
much. Even today atheism has some prophets among the scientists.

2. Science Blocked by the Critique of Religion?

I need not go into the advocates of a "new materialism." Keith Ward,
Regius Professor of Divinity Emeritus at the University of Oxford, made
a detailed examination of the arguments of many of them, including
Stephen Hawking, Carl Sagan, and Jacques Monod, whom I discuss
elsewhere in this book. Ward writes:

> Regrettably, a form of materialism which is entirely hostile to re-
> ligion, and which mocks any idea of objective purpose and value
> in the universe, has become fashionable in recent years. Good
> scientists such as Francis Crick, Carl Sagan, Stephen Hawking,
> Richard Dawkins, Jacques Monod and Peter Atkins have pub-

7. Kant, *Critique of Pure Reason*, 532.

lished books that openly deride religious beliefs, and claim the authority of their own scientific work for their attacks. Their claims are seriously misplaced. Their properly scientific work has no particular relevance to the truth or falsity of most religious assertions. When they do stray into the fields of philosophy, they ignore both the history and the diversity of philosophical viewpoints, pretending that materialist views are almost universally held, when, in fact, they are held by only a fairly small minority of philosophers ("theologian," of course, is for them only a term of abuse). The form of materialism they espouse is open to very strong, and standard, criticism, particularly in respect to its virtual total inability to account for the facts of consciousness and for the importance of ideas of truth and virtue.[8]

Beyond question, the critique of religion offered by these "new materialists" does not remotely reach the depth of their classical predecessors.[9]

The Rights and Wrongs of the Critique of Religion: Feuerbach, Marx, Freud

Even those who believe in God should concede that the critiques of religion by the atheists Feuerbach, Marx, and Freud, who are representative of European modernity, were largely justified.

- Ludwig Feuerbach was quite right: beyond doubt religion, like all human believing, hoping, and loving, contains an element of projection. But did Feuerbach prove that religion is *only* projection? No, it can also be a relation to a quite different reality.
- Karl Marx too was quite right: religion can be and often is opium, a means of social soothing and comfort, of repression. It can be, but it need not be. Rather, it can also be a means of comprehensive enlightenment and social liberation.

8. K. Ward, *God, Chance, and Necessity* (Oxford, 1996), 11f.
9. H. Küng, *Does God Exist? An Answer for Today* (London and New York, 1978), C: "The Challenge of Atheism," 189-340.

- Sigmund Freud was also quite right: religion can be and often is an illusion, the expression of psychological immaturity or even neurosis, of regression. But again, it need not be. Rather, it can be an expression of personal identity and psychological maturity.

What are we to think of the psychological or social-psychological argument for religion as projection that is put forward time and again in a variety of forms? It is based on a postulate that has no methodological or substantial basis: Feuerbach's projection theory, Marx's opium theory, and Freud's illusion theory cannot prove that God is *only* a projection of the human, *only* a prevarication conditioned by a particular interest, or *only* an infantile illusion. So "only" statements or "nothing but" statements must be treated with mistrust (of course also among theologians).

For it has to be conceded that belief in God can be explained psychologically. Psychology or not psychology is a false alternative here: from the point of view of psychology, belief in God always displays the structures and content of a projection, is always suspect of being a projection. But the fact of the projection by no means decides whether or not the object to which it relates exists. A real God can correspond to the wish for God. And why may I not wish that everything does not end on my death? Why may I not wish that there is a deep meaning in my life, in human history, in short, that God exists?

The Death of God? Nietzsche

What are we to make of the argument for an end to religion, put forward in constant variations in the philosophy of history or culture? It is founded on an extrapolation into the future that ultimately has no foundation: globally speaking, neither the "abolition of religion" as a result of atheistic humanism (Feuerbach), nor its "dying out" as a result of atheistic socialism (Marx), nor its "replacement" by atheistic science (Freud) proved to be accurate prognoses.

Serious though the problem of theoretical and practical nihilism is today, even Friedrich Nietzsche's prognosis of the death of God proved to be wrong — one hundred years later. We see, on the contrary:

- Instead of religion being "abolished" by atheistic humanism, as was announced in Feuerbach's projection theory, despite all the secularization in many places, a new theoretical and practical humanism of religious people is coming into being. By contrast, atheistic humanistic belief in the goodness of human nature itself came under the suspicion of being a projection after the great atrocities of the twentieth century.

- Instead of religion "dying out" as a result of atheistic socialism, as was proclaimed in Marx's opium theory, there is often a new religious revival even in former socialist countries. By contrast, today, after the implosion of the Soviet Union, atheistic materialist belief in the rising socialist society seems to be a prevarication governed by particular interests, revolution as the opium of the people.

- Instead of religion being "replaced" by atheistic science, as is prophesied in Freud's illusion theory, despite all the hostility to religion in certain sectors of science, a new understanding of ethics and religion is coming about. By contrast, in view of the highly ambivalent results of technological progress, atheistic-scientistic belief in the solution of all problems by rational science has almost become an illusion for many people. But can science perhaps offer an alternative to atheism?

Science Must Leave God Out of Account

Those who believe in God should also understand that if modern science wants to proceed in an unobjectionable way, necessarily it should have left and has to leave God out of account. The statements of physicists all relate to the physical sphere (time, energy), to natural laws formulated in the language of mathematics. Questions of reciprocal effects that, as some think, lie outside this sphere, or more precisely outside the possibilities of physical measurement, cannot be answered meaningfully by physicists. To this degree the problem of the existence of God is not a question for physics.

Scientists should reflect that subject and object, method and object, are interwoven, and thus a distinction must be made between the phenomena that can be grasped by science and reality as a whole. No method, however certain, no scheme, however adequate, no theory, however precise, may be made absolute. The perspectivity and variability even of mathematical scientific methods in particular require us to be constantly aware of their limits in respect of reality as a whole, which is always greater. Aren't there perhaps entities, events, and reciprocal effects in our universe that do not take place in the physical sphere, and that therefore a priori evade the possibility of scientific knowledge?

Thus if science is to remain faithful to its method, it may not extend its judgment beyond the horizon of experience. Neither the stubbornness of a skeptical ignorance nor the arrogance of those who always know better befits it. In some circumstances, can't musicians, poets, artists, and religious people have an inkling of, glimpse, hear, see, and express in their works realities that burst physical space, the space of energy and time? Can, for example, Mozart's music, which is beyond doubt a phenomenon of physics, be grasped solely with physics? May the physicist qua physicist want to pass a *final* judgment on the *Jupiter* Symphony?

This applies even more to the question of an absolute beginning, an origin, what Kant called a "final ground of everything," a possible comprehensive very first and very last reality that human beings designate with the name "God" (though this is constantly misused), and that may not be observed, analyzed, and therefore manipulated. But the question arises in return: With reference to reality as a whole and to human beings in particular, may the question of first and last meanings and criteria, values, and norms, and thus a first and last reality, be rejected a priori? In principle openness toward the whole of reality is to be required of human beings, whether scientists, philosophers, or theologians. And even the theorists of science (cf. chap. I.5) today acknowledge beyond the sphere of scientific knowledge the more comprehensive "meta-empirical" question of what Wittgenstein called the "problems of life," Popper "cosmology," and T. S. Kuhn the "world."

Atheism Is Understandable but Not Necessary

The case of Galileo was a disaster, because it was unnecessary. For according to the views of the scientists of the sixteenth and seventeenth centuries, Christian theology and the church could have been allies of the new science.[10] Even in the light of biblical belief in God, it was in principle unnecessary for Christian theology and the church a priori to put themselves in opposition to the insights of rising natural science. At an early stage a distinction could have been made between the biblical view of the world and the message of the Bible, as Galileo and Descartes wanted, and the results of science and the scientists themselves suggested. But by their failure over science and new developments in philosophy, society, and politics, theology and the church essentially contributed to the establishment of scientific and political atheism: in the eighteenth century among individual forerunners, in the nineteenth century among a large number of educated people, and in the twentieth and twenty-first centuries finally also among broad strata of the population in East and West.

But the "case of reason" was also a disaster. For it was equally unnecessary that autonomous reason for its part should often have so absolutized itself in the form of modern science that there was no longer any room for the meta-empirical, and belief in God was in practice largely replaced by belief in science. We can hear Japanese Buddhists, for example, asking why modern science developed on the foundation of Jewish-Christian tradition in particular. And we will not go far wrong in assuming that in Descartes, Galileo, and Newton this also has something to do with belief in creation, which radically de-divinized nature, and with the idea of the two books of God, the book of the Bible and the book of nature, both of which were to be taken seriously.

Be this as it may: today, as I have already mentioned (chap. I.7), a confrontational model for the relationship between science and theology is out of date, whether put forward by fundamentalist believers and theologians or by rationalistic scientists and philosophers. But readers will certainly expect me now to go into the two basic questions I raised at the beginning (chap. I.1), which make up the riddle of reality: first the question of the conditions of the beginning of our universe and then the question of the beginning generally.

---

10. L. Châtellier, *Les éspaces infinis et le silence de Dieu. Science et religion, XVIe-XIXe siècle* (Paris, 2003).

3. Where Do the Constants in Nature Come From?

Let's not make things too easy for ourselves. Naive Christians have used the theory of "singularity" (the Big Bang) to prove the reality of a creation of the world: "And God said, 'Let there be light.' And there was light. . . . The first day." Some biblical believers joyfully hear the Big Bang sounding in this sudden act of creation. That is a fundamental misunderstanding of the saying about the creation of light in the Bible, which does not mean to offer a scientific "fact," as we shall see. But both believers and nonbelievers should beyond question reflect on the knowledge associated with the Big Bang.

A Universe Finite in Space and Time

If this universe owes itself to a point in time, then it is ultimately in time, as many scientists assume today. Our universe did not always exist and one day perhaps it will no longer exist. So the cosmos has a definite age, presumably 13.7 billion years, according to the most recent, 2001 measurements by the probe WMAP (Wilkinson Microwave Anisotropy Probe), which was launched from the Space Center at Cape Canaveral. Moreover, it has a definite future, about which astrophysicists dispute. Astrophysicists have been able to decipher quite a number of signals from distant stars and galaxies that have been on the way at the speed of light for millions and billions of years.

But is the universe to be regarded as open or closed? Is the cosmos infinitely great or does it have a finite volume? Is it finite in space? The new telescope in Arizona (LBT), the biggest in the world — two giant mirrors each with a diameter of 8.4 meters — can detect the light of a burning candle 2.5 million kilometers away, but not the limits of the universe. The question of the correct model of the world has probably not yet been finally answered. It still has not been clearly explained whether the expansion of the universe will go on permanently or will one day come to a standstill and revert to a contraction.

At a very early stage, for reasons of faith, advocates of dialectical materialism vigorously condemned Einstein's model of the world as "idealistic"; it did not seem to them to confirm their dogma of the infinity and eternity of matter. Similarly, but in a spiritualistic way, Giordano Bruno asserted the infinity of the universe because he identified it pantheistically with God. He was burned in Rome in 1600 in the Campo de' Fiori by the Inquisition (today the Congregation for the Doctrine of Faith) since — another fact that should not be passed over — the senate of the strictly Protestant Tübingen University had refused him a license to teach, and had expelled the heretic from the university.[11]

But back to the present. When around the middle of the twentieth century an attempt was made in apologetic Christian writings to identify the point in time of the Big Bang with a divine creation of the world, non-Christian Marxist scientists, according to the German astronomer Otto Heckmann, "disturbed about these theological tendencies, decided simply to put a stop to their cosmological source: they created 'steady state cosmology,' the cosmology of the expanding but unchangeable universe."[12]

This theory was put forward above all by Fred Hoyle (Cambridge, 1948/49), who in 1950 in a radio broadcast invented the term "Big Bang" almost as an insult. This theory claims that there is an eternal universe in equilibrium that extends without a temporal beginning and a temporal end and in which the density of matter remains the same as a result of the constant production of matter. But the thinning of matter as a consequence of continuous expansion must be balanced by a spontaneous production of matter. However, this contradicts the second law of thermodynamics, the entropy principle of the irreversibility of physical processes: without the introduction of energy to maintain the structure, a system always tends toward a state of higher disorder (for example, flowers put in a sealed container will die).

This theory reminds me of the centuries-long vain efforts of scientists to construct a "perpetuum mobile," a machine constantly in motion without the introduction of energy, although this contradicts the energy principle or entropy principle, the two main principles of thermodynamics. Energy cannot be produced from nothing, and time and

11. Cf. W. Jens and I. Jens, *Eine deutsche Universität: 500 Jahre Tübinger Gelehrtenrepublik*, 6th ed. (Munich, 1993).

12. O. Heckmann, *Sterne, Kosmos, Weltmodelle. Erlebte Astronomie* (Munich, 1970), 37.

again the patent offices have rejected ingenious apparatuses. Musicians find the perpetuum mobile easier: examples are the amusing pieces with this title by Paganini, Johann Strauss, and Carl Maria von Weber. After the discovery of background radiation and repeated confirmations of the standard model,[13] the steady state model is even more in disrepute, and today at best is argued for by outsiders.

But the Big Bang theory also raises basic questions to which so far only a few satisfactory answers have been found, and which scientists should not dismiss with a shrug. They relate both to the end of the world (to which I shall return in the epilogue) and above all to the beginning of the world.

Intellectual Helplessness in the Face of the Question of Origins

This applies even to some distinguished physicists when asked where the universe ultimately comes from. Thus Gert Binnig, who won the Nobel Prize for physics in 1986 (and was professor in Munich until 1995), explains: "Perhaps the whole thing came into being like this: by the reproduction of something (I don't know what) a vacuum was created or space. With this space the properties of space also came into being, e.g. its symmetries. And by the reproduction of these properties some forms of energy came into being, how, I cannot say."[14]

Or the American elementary particle physicist Steven Weinberg (born 1933, today at the University of Texas in Austin), who in 1979 was awarded the Nobel Prize with two other physicists for the unified theory of weak and electromagnetic interactions, and who remarks in his extremely instructive book *The First Three Minutes: A Modern View of the Origin of the Universe:*

13. The latest confirmation of the standard model was given at the Congress of the American Astronomical Society in San Diego in January 2005: two research teams working independently of each other demonstrated how with telescopes in New Mexico and Australia they had detected traces of sound waves that had been rolling through the universe since the Big Bang (*International Herald Tribune,* 30 Jan. 2005).

14. G. Binnig, *Aus dem Nichts. Über die Kreativität von Natur und Mensch* (Munich, 1989), 75-77.

It is even harder to realize that this present universe has evolved from an unspeakably unfamiliar early condition, and faces a future extinction of endless cold or intolerable heat. The more the universe seems comprehensible, the more it also seems pointless. But if there is no solace in the fruits of our research, there is at least some consolation in the research itself. Men and women are not prepared to comfort themselves with tales of gods and giants [the Edda saga], or to confine their thoughts to the daily affairs of life; they also build telescopes and satellites and accelerators, and sit at their desks for endless hours working out the meaning of the data they gather. The effort to understand the universe is one of the few things that lifts human life a little above the level of farce, and gives it some of the grace of tragedy.[15]

Can research and technology help us in this way to get beyond the meaninglessness of the universe and the tragedy of human life? Here one is tempted to present to such physicists the much discussed wager of the brilliant physicist, mathematician, and philosopher Blaise Pascal, which is not about black holes and white dwarfs or gods and giants, but offers the following basic alternative: *Dieu est, ou il n'est pas,* "either God is, or he isn't." But both possibilities are uncertain: "Reason can decide nothing here. What will you wager? According to reason, you can do neither the one thing nor the other; according to reason, you can defend neither of the propositions. Do not then reprove for error those who have made a choice; for you know nothing about it." That is the decisive point: one must wager. *"Il faut parier,* you must wager. *Cela*

---

15. Cf. S. Weinberg, *The First Three Minutes: A Modern View of the Origin of the Universe* (New York, 1977), 154-55. Remarkably, in his historical retrospect (chap. 6) and in his bibliography, while Weinberg mentions G. Gamow (1948), he does not mention the "father of Big Bang cosmology," G. Lemaître (1927), though the latter did not yet associate the early stage with the origin of the elements, as Gamow did. Cf. also Weinberg's scientific work *Gravitation and Cosmology: Principles and Applications of the General Theory of Relativity* (New York, 1962). For the problems associated with the origin of the universe, cf. also the following nontechnical works: H. von Ditfurth, *Im Anfang war der Wasserstoff* (Hamburg, 1972); O. Heckmann, *Sterne, Kosmos, Weltmodelle;* H. W. Woltersdorf, *Die Schöpfung war ganz anders. Irrtum und Wende* (Olten, 1976).

n'est pas volontaire, it is not optional. *Vous êtes embarqué,* you are embarked."[16] And what are the odds? By the nature of the alternatives (infinite, happy life or nothingness) and the magnitude of the stake (a finite stake for an infinite return) — this should be considered precisely — the odds for unbelief and belief stand at "zero to infinity." In any case, one loses nothing if one believes in God, but can gain everything.

To see the argument of the "wager" as a new proof for the existence of God with a mathematical orientation would be to misunderstand it. Prompted by the game of dice, which he played, Pascal indeed made use of the calculation of probability, but with his wager he wanted to make it clear that in the question of the existence or nonexistence of God, what is asked for is not a judgment of pure reason but a decision of the whole person, which cannot be proved by reason but can be made rationally responsible. So it is a calculable risk and a serious matter. Pascal thinks that for this fundamental decision human beings should use as much care as they do in a decision at the gaming table or in life generally.

In his last years, one who suffered more than others under the problem of atheism, the "Antichrist" Friedrich Nietzsche, clearly turned against the self-confident, optimistic atheism "of our lords the naturalists and the physiologists," which he could regard only as a bad "joke": "they have no passion about such things, they have not suffered. . . . One must have had experience of that menace directly and almost succumbed to it, to realize that it is not to be taken lightly."[17]

Where Do the Principles of Cosmic Order Come From?

At present astrophysics is concentrating above all on two topics: the origin of the first structures in the universe and the quest for extraterrestrial and extrasolar life, life on other planets. In this chapter I shall concentrate on the first.

If at the beginning there was only a primal fireball of the tiniest extent but of the utmost density and temperature, the question inexora-

16. B. Pascal, *Pensées,* 451.
17. F. Nietzsche, *Antichrist* (1888), trans. H. L. Mencken (New York, 1920), par. 8.

bly arises: Where did it come from? And what was the cause of the un-imaginably gigantic primal explosion? Where did the immeasurable energy of the cosmic expansion come from? What brought about its tremendous initial force?

That is the fundamental riddle of reality. First of all I shall define precisely the question of the initial conditions of the universe (see chap. I.1): What established in the earliest phase the conditions that guarantee that after 13.7 billion years the universe would still have the properties we observe today? Where do the fundamental universal constants of nature come from:

- basic atomic constants such as the elementary charge e, the mass at rest of the electron and the building blocks (quarks) of the protons and neutrons;
- Planck's constant h;
- Boltzmann's constant k; and also
- derived atomic constants and entities such as the speed of light c?

At some point someone will perhaps be able to explain the fine-tuning of the basic cosmic constants, these delicately balanced and only approximately symmetrical relationships of power and energy. But the question remains: Where did the minimal structure that already existed at the Big Bang come from? Certainly, the standard model of an inflationary universe solves fundamental difficulties (what physicists call the horizon problem, the homogeneity problem, the surface problem, and the dark mass problem). But mustn't this inflation model presuppose the validity, the correctness of fundamental laws of nature, indeed, principles of cosmic order?

In a joint colloquium in Tübingen between theologians and physicists in 1994, my physicist colleague Amand Fässler posed the problem mathematically. How precisely was the small surplus of matter over antimatter "calculated," how precisely was the tiny surplus of protons over antiprotons $(1 + 10^{-9} = 1.000000001)$ "reckoned," without which there would not have been a universe of radiation *and* matter and the perplexing relationship of 25 percent primal helium and 75 percent hydrogen, and consequently there would also not have been the formation of galaxies, stars, and planets stable enough for life in this universe?

The handbooks of astrophysics give no answer to the basic question of the origin of the cosmic principles of order; that is understandable. What is less understandable is that normally they do not even hint at such fundamental questions. The handbooks begin, if you like, with the second day of creation — or with the first 100th of a second after the Big Bang. Is it still true, as the American magazine *Time* stated after questioning the best-known astronomers of the United States in the 1970s, that most modern scientists remain silent over the ultimate question of what existed "before" the Big Bang?[18]

But care is needed: Is that a plea for "God" at the beginning of all things simply because there is a gap in our knowledge? No, it is not a plea for a "God of the gaps," some of which will certainly be closed. Rather, it is an invitation to reflect on the fundamental presuppositions of this model of the world that also, indeed particularly, concerns physicists. For here a remarkable phenomenon emerges.

Instinctive Opposition

In the last two decades the question of what special characteristics there were in the first hundredth of a second — some scientists even speak of the first billionth part of the first second — has become even more important, and the alternatives have emerged more clearly. A variegated cosmic fine-tuning was in fact necessary:

- *of energy and mass:* had the mass been just a little too small, the universe would have expanded too quickly and there would have been no condensation of matter and no formation of stars and origin of life. Conversely, had the mass been just a little too large, the universe would almost immediately have contracted;
- *of nuclear forces:* had the nuclear forces been weaker, the heavy elements necessary for life (carbon, oxygen, and nitrogen) would not have formed and the universe would consist only of hydrogen. Con-

18. *Time,* 27 Dec. 1976.

versely, had the nuclear forces been only a little too strong, there would be only heavy nuclei and no hydrogen;

- *of the force of gravity and energy through nuclear reaction* in our sun: had the force of gravity been somewhat greater, the stars would have incubated nuclear fuel much more quickly, their life spans would have been only very brief, and no life could have formed. Conversely, had the force of gravity been less, matter would hardly have held together so well.

The properties of the cosmos — and a large number of further details of the physical laws could be cited — are evidently so precisely tuned to one another that life is possible — indeed, human beings can exist on our small planet. In view of all these relations, constants, and laws that have existed from the beginning, it seems that physicists must draw obvious conclusions about the origin of the universe. But a doyen of American physics, Charles Townes, who together with two colleagues was awarded the Nobel Prize for the discovery of the laser in 1964, recently gave a precise description of the fine-tunings described above with their alternatives, and then — with unusual openness — noted an "instinctive opposition" among physicists: "Nevertheless the scientific community is in general instinctively opposed to the assumption that there was once some such unique period or situation in the universe. That seems too arbitrary and too improbable."[19]

It is amazing that here we evidently do not have rational, scientific arguments of the kind that would be expected from scientists, but a "feeling" — which otherwise they usually suppose to be mostly in the religious sphere:

This feeling led to a considerable effort to make a great detour round the special character of a Big Bang and the initial stage. As the evidence compellingly suggests that there was in fact an explosion, one possible way of dealing with this unique time is to assert that the universe will finally come to a standstill through

19. C. Townes, "Warum sind wir hier? — Wohin gehen wir?" in *Im Anfang war (k)ein Gott,* 29-44, here 29f.

the force of attraction exercised by gravity and will then contract and again collapse on itself. Although the universe is extending because of this explosion, it will again become a very small object. There will be another explosion and a further phase of expansion will be sparked off, so that our own period is not in fact unique but only one of many such cycles of the universe.

This is as interesting an idea as the perpetuum mobile mentioned above, but unfortunately just as unrealistic.

Townes then immediately adds, "At present we know no mechanism which would spark off a new explosion. Nor in the universe is there sufficient mass to slow down its expansion accordingly and bring about the subsequent contraction."[20]

4. Reactions to the Cosmic Fine-Tuning

We can be grateful to Charles Townes for openly addressing an emotional, "irrational," "religious" element in the discussion of physics that is usually taboo. I would like to analyze it more closely by describing two opposed reactions to the cosmic fine-tuning before developing my own answer: cosmological speculation and cosmological demonstration.

Cosmological Speculation: Alternative Universes

What is speculation? The Latin word *speculatio* means "spying out the land," "observing." For a long time it had good connotations in philosophy. It meant a way of thinking that transcends the immediate experiences of reality and attempts to investigate the ultimate foundations and principles of all reality. But it lost these good connotations when the heightening of the reference to experience in the wake of German idealism degenerated into extravagance and arbitrariness. Since then, "speculation" has often been used in a disparaging way — quite apart from talking about "speculation" on the stock exchange with a view to uncer-

20. Townes, "Warum sind wir hier?" 30.

tain future gains — to denote suppositions that go beyond reality as it can be experienced, hypothetically thinking through mere possibilities.

Mustn't one perhaps also ask whether cosmological hypotheses aren't sheer speculations, the thinking through of mere *possibilities* that aren't covered by empirical evidence? Couldn't this be said of the assumption that if instead of the Big Bang at the beginning of our universe convincingly described by research in physics during the twentieth century, there were various separate "Big Bangs": i.e., the postulate of the reality of completely independent structures of space and time beyond the horizon of our experiences, alternative universes, which perhaps follow completely different laws?[21]

I also think it possible for our real structure of space and time to extend quite considerably beyond our human horizon. The Hubble Space Telescope was the first instrument to show extremely sharp images of the fainter galaxies at greater distances, unaffected by the earth's atmosphere, and advanced astrophysics by light-years. What will future generations of such telescopes be able to show us? There are arguments that our universe extends at least 1,000 times farther than we can see. However, I don't call any of this "speculation," but calculations and reflections within the cosmos for which there is a broad empirical basis.

"Extracosmic speculations" that postulate completely separate structures of space and time, i.e., other "universes," indeed a "multiverse," without any empirical data from our universe, are a different matter. In the many-worlds theories no limits are set to speculative fantasy, and we are spoiled for choice:

- Should we follow Andrei Linde and Alexander Vilenkin in assuming an unlimited phase of expansion in which many universes grow from separate Big Bangs into separate universes or space-time structures?
- Or should we assume with Alan Guth, Edward Harrison, and Lee Smolin that a new universe can originate in a black hole that extends into a new realm of space and time and is inaccessible to us?

---

21. Up till now, significantly the word "universe" appeared only in the singular. Now the plural usage is quite common.

• Or should we conjecture with Lisa Rendell and Raman Sandrum that other universes could exist separately from us in dimensions outside space and could or could not mutually influence one another through gravity?

Sir Martin Rees, whom I quoted at the beginning of this chapter, and who as a pupil and like-minded contemporary of Fred Hoyle in Cambridge occupied himself intensively with this topic, describes the cosmological attempts already mentioned and wants to open up a "scientific perspective" for them by means of verification.[22] For he is aware that such notions of other universes have a "speculative, theoretical background" and remain "merely a mathematical construct" as long as they "cannot be applied to a phenomenon that we can observe."[23] Of course, he is right that such speculative theories are "never simply plucked out of thin air." Even the wildest speculations, say about telekinesis or telepathy, must display some real points of contact if anyone is to believe them. Of course, that is even more true of speculations about our universe as a small but fertile oasis in the middle of a gigantic "multiverse."

But what about the "observable phenomena" from which Martin Rees wants to argue for the reality of different universes?

Is Our Universe One among Many?

The comparison made by the British astronomer with astrophysicists' remarks about the interior of the sun, which we accept although we will never get inside the sun to see for ourselves, does not seem to me helpful. The existence of the sun and its effects are extremely real, and therefore the conclusions are empirically founded and completely legitimate. But the existence of a universe separate from our universe cannot be ascertained or proved; it is a pure conjecture, for which there is not the slightest proof. Mathematical aesthetics cannot replace physical reality in such extrapolations. While the Terrestrial Planet Finder planned by NASA for 2014 may lead to "worlds" like the earth, it will in

22. Cf. Rees, "Andere Universen," 45-48.
23. Rees, "Andere Universen," 49.

no way transcend the immense limits of our universe. Just as misleading is the comparison with the real atom and the conclusion based empirically on it that quarks are "building blocks of the atom." The legitimacy of the conclusion from our universe to other "universes" also presupposes such an empirical basis.

In view of such unhelpful comparisons, it is understandable that some physicists reject as meaningless the very question "What is outside the universe?" They say it presupposes that there really is an "outside" of the "whole." They say, mockingly, that to claim that outside the universe a giant hen is incubating another universe in the form of an egg would be just as unprovable and meaningless. Both are completely random hypotheses that cannot be proved or refuted and therefore are scientifically worthless. However, no more than 10 percent of physicists are said to advocate a many-worlds theory, and so renowned a physicist as Steven Weinberg indicates that he is "too busy to deal with rubbish like the many-worlds interpretation."[24] In a more friendly way, but no less clearly, the Göttingen physicist Hubert Goenner says of "the concept of the multiverse which is epistemologically suspect": "According to a theoretical notion the nucleation process of new part- 'cosmoses' will go on continually: 'parent' cosmoses form 'baby universes.' However, the origin of such 'baby universes' could not be observed by the parents, as no signal can leave them. Of course such scenarios are conceivable and imaginative, but if they cannot be tested in principle by measurements, they are not part of scientific cosmology."[25]

But in all seriousness, I am by no means in principle opposed to the possibility of other universes. I see no fundamental theological objections to a "multiverse." For an infinite God is in no way limited in his infinity by an infinite universe or even by several universes. I am opposed only to purely speculative hypotheses in physics that are scientifically decked out with mathematical calculations — one might compare

24. This is how he is quoted by the British physicist D. Deutsch, whose arguments for the existence of parallel universes tend rather to suggest the opposite. See *Spiegel-Gespräch* 11 (2005), "Die Welt ist bizarr."

25. H. Goenner, "Das Urknallbild des Kosmos: Beginnt die Zeit?" in *Kosmologie, Fragen nach Evolution und Eschatologie der Welt,* ed. H.-A. Müller (Göttingen, 2004), 24-38, here 34.

them to those economists in the USA who developed theories of the "new economics" with much theoretical and mathematical effort and propagated them with tremendous support from the media, as if the laws of classical economics no longer applied. And how many stock-exchange speculators, banks, and analysts thereupon promised a credulous public "mountains of gold," which proved to be the pseudo-products of a speculative bubble economy with losses of billions! So does this bubble physics stem from a fear of metaphysics? Andrei Linde of Stanford University speculates about cosmic "bubbles" separate from one another, constantly coming into being and passing away!

Of course, we could calculate one or two, twelve, a thousand or a billion other "universes," "cycles," "realms," "quantum worlds," or "quantum fluctuations" — which are certainly attractive mathematical constructions. But Martin Rees rightly says that a "logical description" of other universes is not enough; it would have to be "applicable to phenomena that we can observe."[26] Whether the examples cited (cosmic constants, black holes) are suitable for testing the many-worlds hypothesis is something I must leave to competent specialists. According to Rees, they would show only that some highly speculative assertions about other universes "could be" tested: "For them to be put on firm foundations we must wait [!] for a fundamental theory which tells us whether instead of just one Big Bang there could also have been many [!], and if [!] that is the case — what diversity they could produce [!]."[27]

My exclamation marks indicate that the language is constantly in the subjunctive, i.e., in the form of possibility, behind which there is something doubtful or even unreal. At any rate, a hypothesis does not become more certain if it is supported by an increasing number of hypotheses. A model can be extended at will if an empirical testing is a priori impossible. A house of cards is not built up by more and more cards but finally brought crashing down: *a posse ad esse non valet illatio* — "the argument from being possible to being is not conclusive." Those who know the history of philosophy are aware that the existence of such a being as God cannot be proved even by the famous idea of a "perfect"

26. Rees, "Andere Universen," 49.
27. Rees, "Andere Universen," 57.

or "absolutely necessary" being (Anselm of Canterbury's and Descartes's "ontological proof of God"). Far less is it possible to conclude the existence of a completely different universe from the idea of an incomplete universe.[28]

In all this one asks oneself whether it wouldn't be simpler and more plausible, instead of clinging to the utopia of "self-reproducing" universes along Fred Hoyle's line, to allow oneself to be challenged by the age-old view of a universe that does not create itself.[29] In short, I wish physicists would without prejudice face up to the real challenge of a real Big Bang without "instinctive opposition" and speculative "detours."

Happily Martin Rees gets down to talking about the basic question and rejects "chance" as an explanation "of a providence-like physics which has led to galaxies, stars, planets and the 92 elements of the periodic table." In a few words Rees arrives at creation as an explanation, saying that "our universe developed from a simple beginning — *one* Big Bang — for which quite a short recipe was normative. But this recipe seems to be a very special one."[30] Unfortunately, however, instead of grappling scientifically with the modern understanding of creation, he passes over the notion of creation without discussion to devote all his attention to the hypothesis of a "special universe belonging to an ensemble or multiverse."[31] Is this once again a case of "instinctive opposition"? Perhaps — may I allow myself this observation as an honorary doctor of the University of Cambridge? — as well as political correct-

---

28. As a methodological principle against wild speculations the scholastics developed the maxim *entia non sunt multiplicanda sine necessitate* — entities are not to be multiplied unnecessarily. And the new physics in particular was successful because it did not exclude phenomena or characteristics like the world ether, absolute contemporaneity, or the exact position of the electron from its process of theorizing. Well-founded scientific theories are always marked by a conformity of facts and experimental content that have been tested empirically — alongside rationality, simplicity, and explanatory power.

29. Perhaps a theologian should warn speculative physicists not to lose themselves in cosmological hypotheses as the speculative theologians of late medieval scholasticism once did, for example, discussing how many spiritual beings could stand on the point of a needle.

30. Rees, "Andere Universen," 51.

31. Rees, "Andere Universen," 52.

ness there is also something like scientific correctness that makes it difficult in a scientific community to discuss certain questions seriously although they are obvious. Or will a proof from physics appear? That seems to me questionable. But let's examine the opposite reaction to cosmic fine-tuning: instead of speculating and fantasizing, others want to offer strict proof, to demonstrate.

A Cosmological Demonstration: A Designer Universe

In the late 1960s Frank J. Tipler, professor of mathematical physics in New Orleans and author of the best seller *A Physics of Immortality,* attended two seminars with Steven Weinberg at the Massachusetts Institute of Technology (MIT). After the discovery of microwave background radiation, cosmic models were at the center of the discussion. According to Tipler, Weinberg is said to have remarked to his students: "Of the two cosmological models — the Big Bang theory and the steady state theory — I favor the latter because it least resembles the account in the book of Genesis. Regrettably this theory has been refuted by the discovery of cosmic background radiation."[32] Evidently a case of "instinctive opposition."

Thirty years later Tipler is still surprised that a physicist and later Nobel Prize winner such as Weinberg was ready at that time to put in question the validity of standard nuclear physics, the general theory of relativity, and quantum mechanics, simply so that as a confessing atheist he did not have to accept the narrative of the book of Genesis about the beginning of "heaven and earth." Now Weinberg's instinctive struggle in the face of the Genesis report may have to do not only with unenlightened criticism of religion, personal experiences, or his Jewish upbringing, but perhaps even more with overhasty exploitation of the Big Bang theory by fundamentalist Christian believers in the USA to prove that "the Bible is right."

However, Frank Tipler is anything but a fundamentalist who believes in the Bible. Rather, his view is "that the only rational way of proceeding is to accept the laws of physics and their consequences inde-

32. Cf. F. J. Tipler, "Ein Designer-Universum," in *Im Anfang war (k)ein Gott,* 72.

pendently of the report in Genesis or any other holy scripture. An established law of physics may be ignored only when an experiment shows that this law has limited application. A law of physics should never be rejected simply because of a religious objection to the consequences which follow from it."[33] Isn't he right here?

Thus against cosmic speculations by physicists that postulate an eternal chaotic inflationary universe or alternative universes, Tipler resolutely sets cosmological demonstration: strictly rational proof in the mathematical-scientific sense that is meant to compel intellectual assent. One simply cannot say no to Pythagoras's theorem or Newton's law of gravity. But is it true that one cannot say no to God?

If we accept the consequences of the known laws of physics, Tipler argues, we arrive at "a perplexing conclusion": "The universe has existed for a limited time, but over and above that the physical universe and the laws which govern it were called to life by a unity which does not underlie these laws and lies outside space and time. In short, we live in a universe that was planned and created by GOD."[34] Is Tipler also right here?

Can God Be Proved by Physics?

I must leave Tipler's cosmological demonstration, like the various cosmological speculations, to the verdict of experts. They may decide whether Tipler has in fact given a compelling rational proof:

1. "that the known laws of physics call for the existence of cosmological singularity";
2. "that this in fact displays all the characteristics which are traditionally attributed to the Jewish-Christian-Muslim God."[35]

However, I concede that the whole line of proof for a singularity at the beginning and a designer God hardly convinces me. I am already made mistrustful by the fact that Tipler uses as a first reference to an

---

33. Tipler, "Ein Designer-Universum," 72.
34. Tipler, "Ein Designer-Universum," 73.
35. Tipler, "Ein Designer-Universum," 73.

initial singularity the singularity theorems of Stephen Hawking and Roger Penrose (with whom he collaborated) — although the black-hole theoretician Hawking initially asserted that he had set aside singularity, but then lost his bet over black holes.[36]

I will not pass judgment on Tipler's individual arguments. I do, however, share the reservations of many physicists that in principle no physical law can imply the existence of an actual infinity. I do not dismiss this argument, like Tipler, as a "religious objection." On the contrary, I see in it an application of Kant's basic insight that theoretical reason is no longer competent outside spatial and temporal experiences and consequently that it cannot argue compellingly from the real finite to a real infinite.

A Questionable Basic Motivation

At a decisive point, though, I must concede that Frank Tipler is right: no physicist should prefer a scientific theory simply because it is easier to reconcile with his own atheistic conviction. Precisely because I argue resolutely against religious motivations as a basis for scientific theses, I must demand that rational questions be asked not only about Christian, Jewish, or Islamic faith but also about atheistic "faith," perhaps taken over unthinkingly for scientific political correctness. This is what I have done in my balanced criticism of religion.

I cannot judge which of the numerous theories (steady state theory,[37] string theory, superstring theory, or M theory) has been devel-

36. I have similar reservations about the very stimulating book by the German physical chemist Lothar Schäfer, *Versteckte Wirklichkeit. Wie uns die Quantenphysik zur Transzendenz führt* (Stuttgart, 2004). The professor of physical chemistry at the University of Arkansas attributes properties similar to consciousness to the quantum world, but these "must not be confused with physical properties" (61). From this he concludes "a principle of consciousness in the universe" that was there from the beginning, so that the background to reality has "spirit-like properties" (119). However, the author presupposes that there is no strict proof for the assumption of such transcendence: it is an occasion for trust and hope (cf. 152f.).

37. F. Hoyle, *Ten Faces of the Universe* (San Francisco, 1977), continued to support the steady state theory long after most of his professional colleagues had given it up again, because of his atheistic convictions.

oped above all with the aim of demonstrating that cosmic singularity is irrelevant as a way of evading the challenge of the book of Genesis and ignoring the question of God. There is even speculation about a "proto-universe" that preceded our actual universe and a "pre–Big Bang era," but without any evidence; in any case, its structure would have been destroyed by the primal fireball.

Stephen Hawking also postulated, with no empirical evidence, a grand physical theory of a universe completely shut in on itself, without periphery and without boundaries, without a beginning and end — and I must return to him. He openly concedes, "What place, then, for a creator?"[38] And in the preface to his book the American physicist and television author Carl Sagan (1934-96) points to its real theme: the absence of God. But if anyone wants to replace God, that can also have painful consequences, which the German physicist Ernst Peter Fischer acutely points out: the "bewitching maiden" with whom Hawking fell in love when his nervous illness was diagnosed thought on parting that she had to point out to her Stephen "that he is not God."[39]

At all events, it is surprising how in the question of the initial conditions of the cosmos cosmologists labor to overturn elementary philosophical statements such as *ex nihilo nihil fit,* "nothing comes out of nothing." Here some in all earnestness seek to avoid the problem of origins by creating a universe that functions as its own mother. "It created itself" (Richard Gott and Lin-Xin Li).[40] "How nice," one might exclaim. Faced with the self-confidence with which such theories are presented, I am reminded of the remark attributed to the Russian Nobel Prize winner for physics, Lev Landau (1908-68): "Cosmologists often err, but they never doubt."

A respected participant in the colloquium of physicists and theolo-

38. S. Hawking, *A Brief History of Time: From the Big Bang to Black Holes* (Toronto, 1988), 141.

39. E. P. Fischer, *Einstein, Hawking, Singh & Co. Bücher, die man kennen muss* (Munich, 2004), 28-35, here 34.

40. R. Gott and Li-Xin Li, "Can the Universe Create Itself?" *Physical Revue D* 58 (1998): 023501-2. The philosopher B. Kanitscheider, "Kosmologie zwischen Mythos und Physik," in *Kosmologie,* 153-68, engages in critical discussion with these speculations.

gians I organized in 1994 at the University of Tübingen, the theoretical physicist Herbert Pfister, ended his farewell lecture at the University of Tübingen on 14 February 2001 with this thesis: "At present theoretical physics is suffering from an excess of mathematical speculative constructs and a lack of innovative intellectual experiments," of the kind made by Einstein, Bohr, and Heisenberg. His comment was: "Today by contrast whole hosts of so-called physicists have already been working for more than ten years on e.g. 11-dimensional — or even higher dimensional — superstring theories, heterotic M theories or groups E8 × E8 and SO (32), without so far having produced a single datum that can be tested, let alone successfully tested."[41]

The testimonies of competent scientists to an "instinctive opposition" or a deliberate "avoidance" when faced with a singularity are too numerous for one to be able to neglect the question of the background motivation. And so finally, having investigated the question of the initial conditions of the universe, I must go into the core question of the beginning generally.

5. Why Isn't There Nothing?

John Archibald Wheeler of Princeton (I have fond memories of his visit to Tübingen), who had brought quantum mechanics from Europe to the USA, reduces the problem to the original formula, "it from bit": How does "it" (the world) come into being from a substratum of "bit" (information)? No "information-generating process" has so far been discovered. Can physics ever discover it? Or to put it more clearly: Isn't it asking too much of physics as the theory of basic structures and processes of change in matter and energy to venture to give an ultimate explanation of reality with its means, namely, observation, experiment, and mathematics? Isn't a kind of "meta-physics" called for when empiricism is definitively transcended and it has to be asked not only why the universe is as it is but also why it is at all? Or do people still want to

41. H. Pfister, "40 Jahre Faszination Physik" (farewell lecture, University of Tübingen, 14 Feb. 2001).

solve the "riddle of the world," as some scientists have attempted in their Sturm und Drang phase?

A Solution to the Riddle of the World

"The riddle of the world": in the nineteenth century the Berlin physiologist Emil Du Bois-Reymond, with his research into the electricity in the muscles and nerves of animals, elevated the natural sciences to the absolute organ of culture but in intellectual modesty spoke of seven last questions about the world that are raised by the constitution of the world but cannot be solved by human beings.[42] *Ignoramus et ignorabimus* — "we do not know and we shall not know." Here he was referring above all to the nature of matter and energy and the explanation of the simple sensations. But he also indicated doubt *(dubitemus)* about the ultimate explicability of the origin of movement, the beginning of life, purposefulness in nature, the derivation of rational thought and language, and the reality of the freedom of the will.

"The riddle of the world": it was then the zoologist and natural philosopher Ernst Haeckel of Jena who immodestly in his best seller, published at the very beginning of the twentieth century and translated into fifteen languages,[43] claimed to answer these basic human questions in terms of a monistic view of the world grounded on Darwin's notion of evolution. But today his atheistic confession, which thought it could explain the development of the world from the primal cloud to spiritual processes in materialistic terms and dismissed the spiritual-personal God as a "vortex made of gas," sounds rather naive even to scientists. For in some respects the mood in the natural sciences has also changed: instead of the earlier enthusiasm about progress that thought it could replace religion by science, today there is often a somewhat

42. Cf. E. Du Bois-Reymond, "Die sieben Welträtsel" (paper given in the Leibniz session of the Akademie der Wissenschaften on 8 July 1880), in *Vorträge über Philosophie und Gesellschaft,* ed. S. Wollagast (Hamburg, 1974), 159-87; in the same volume cf. his lecture of 14 Aug. 1872, "Über die Grenzen des Naturerkennens," 54-77.

43. Cf. E. Haeckel, *Die Welträtsel. Gemeinverständliche Studien über Monistische Philosophie* (Bonn, 1899).

comfortless acknowledgment of the godlessness and meaninglessness of the world and human beings.

No one disputes that in the twentieth century the natural sciences had a triumphant success and solved some riddles of the world that for a long time were thought to be insoluble. Yet despite all the imaginative progress in knowledge, the enigmatic character of the world has by no means disappeared — in the realm of the greatest any more than in the realm of the smallest. On the contrary, the impression is that the more deeply human beings penetrate into space and matter, the more inscrutable, the more enigmatic, reality becomes.

- An enigmatic *macrocosm:* the more astrophysicists know of the universe with the help of gigantic telescopes, a universe that alongside three-dimensional reality also contains a fourth dimension (and perhaps yet other dimensions), the more unimaginable becomes to us this space-time that (according to Einstein) is unlimited and has a finite warp, with its stellar systems expanding ever more quickly and the extremely strange objects such as pulsars and quasars that have been discovered only very recently.
- An enigmatic *microcosm:* the more elementary-particle physicists know of the atomic nucleus with the help of giant particle accelerators, a nucleus that in turn is composed of protons and neutrons, which in turn are made up of yet tinier subunits, the so-called quarks and gluons (= adhesive material), together with electrodynamics, weak and strong forces, and the force of gravity, which in turn perhaps also again have structures in common,[44] the less we can imagine what the primal material or primal force of the world really is. Some scientists therefore have the impression that the

---

44. In 1968 it proved possible to unite the electromagnetic and the weak forces into the electroweak forces, and this is the standard model in elementary particle physics. So far the grand unification, the explanation of the electroweak forces and the strong nuclear forces as a single power, has not been confirmed; this shows itself only with very high energies; with small energies this unity is broken. A consistent mathematical formulation of the unification of all forces including gravity has yet to be found. For this information and some other valuable suggestions, I am grateful to Amand Fässler, professor of theoretical physics in the University of Tübingen.

more they discover of the cosmos, the less they understand it. Those who know a great deal also know what they do not know — at least if they are wise.

Ignorance Also Grows with Knowledge

New results of research also raise new questions. We know more and more and we seem to understand the whole picture less and less. For it is becoming increasingly difficult to make a coherent picture of the cosmos. Infinitely much remains unexplained. Physical reality is largely inscrutable. Like the fascinating physical macrocosm, so the no-less-fascinating microcosm of subatomic particles can be depicted only vaguely with our terms. Both macro- and microcosm can ultimately be described only with images, ciphers, comparisons; with models and mathematical formulae.

Indeed, how am I to "imagine" the tremendously large world researched by astrophysics, in which space travelers, were they to succeed in finding a way into the middle of our own Milky Way and back again, would meet in relative youth a humankind that in the meantime had become around 60,000 years older? And how am I to imagine the unbelievably small processes discovered by elementary particle physics — in the order of magnitude of up to 10^{-15} centimeter = 1 million billionth of a centimeter (1 billion = 1 million million) and speeds of 10^{-22} seconds — 1 divided by 10 billion trillion seconds (1 trillion = 1 million billion)? Here even words such as "part" and "spatial extent" largely lose their meaning. The mode of reality of the building blocks of the core, the protons and neutrons, and even more of the quarks, their ups and downs, is totally unexplained. The "inventor" of quarks, Nobel Prize winner Murray Gell-Mann, has remarked that the "flavors" or "colors" associated with them were initially meant as a joke, but that at the same time they serve as a kind of metaphor.[45]

In particular the newest technology of all, nanotechnology,[46] has

45. M. Gell-Mann, *The Quark and the Jaguar* (New York, 1994), chap. 13.
46. Cf. W. Faul, "Einblicke in die Zwergenwelt — Warum die Nano-technologie im 21. Jh. eine Schlüsselfunktion hat," radio broadcast, SWR 2, 24 Oct. 2004.

penetrated into yet other spheres of the limit experience of the unimaginable. A nanometer (*nano* is Greek for dwarf) is a millionth of a millimeter = 10^{-9} meters. That means that a meter relates to a nanometer as the diameter of the earth to a hazelnut. The nano-particle, with which nanotechnology works successfully for novel chemical processes (e.g., as an additive to UV protection in paints, colors, sun-protection creams), is usually 5-100 nanometers big, that is, about 5,000 times smaller than the diameter of a human hair. This nano-world is unimaginable and yet real.

Many natural scientists also see it like this: their science sits on an island of knowledge and has only a limited picture of the cosmos. According to the most recent measurements of the space probe WMAP, mentioned earlier, which scanned the whole firmament for many months, which has calculated the age of the universe at 13.7 billion years and has thus completely confirmed the Big Bang model, it is certain that we know only 4 percent of the universe; only so much consists of ordinary, visible matter (stars, planets, moons). And what about the unknown "remnant" of 96 percent? It consists of:

- 23 percent *dark matter,* which is said to be fixed spatially by the force of gravity, so that the galaxies do not fly apart. Presumably this is a tremendous mass of invisible and inaudible elementary particles, for which various research teams have been looking feverishly for a long time. They are designated WIMPs (weakly interacting massive particles).
- 73 percent *dark energy* (according to Einstein, "cosmological constants"), which has not yet been fathomed. It is said to work as a kind of gravitational field, so that — as has been established to the great amazement of physicists — the universe can expand more and more quickly. "What this dark energy really is and how it fits in with the overall structure of the cosmos (and also of our physics) is largely not understood."[47]

---

47. S. Hüttemeister, "Der Aufbau des Kosmos: Seine Evolution und Eschatologie," in *Kosmologie,* 5-23, here 22.

"Dark matter," "dark energy": so for physics the greater part of our universe is still literally in the dark — despite the search all over the earth and in its depths (in mines and motorway tunnels). Will the gigantic particle accelerator that goes into service in Geneva in 2007 (Large Hadron Collider) produce the "neutralinos" that are being sought and have so far not been found on the shadow side of the cosmos?

At the beginning of modern science Blaise Pascal, who has already been mentioned, expressed his terror at the eternal silence of the infinite space of the macroworld. Couldn't one also be terrified at the abysses of a microworld that is infinitely small? This is the disproportion in which human beings have always stood, according to Pascal, *"la grandeur et misère de l'homme,"* the greatness and misery of human beings.

> For in fact what is man in nature? A Nothing in comparison with the Infinite, an All in comparison with the Nothing, a mean between nothing and everything. Since he is infinitely removed from comprehending the extremes, the end of things and their beginnings are hopelessly hidden from him in an impenetrable secret; he is equally incapable of seeing the Nothing from which he was made, and the Infinite in which he is swallowed up. What will he do then, but perceive the appearance of the middle of things, in an eternal despair of knowing either their beginning or their end? All things proceed from the Nothing, and are borne towards the Infinite. Who will follow these marvellous processes? The Author of these wonders understands them. None other can do so.[48]

Pascal rightly speaks not just of a "riddle" that surrounds us and could at some time be solved once and for all. He speaks of an "impenetrable secret," which can at best be talked of in images, figures, and comparisons. The enigmatic character of the world, which at the same time is full of wonder, is grounded in a mystery we can only approach. "The Author of these wonders understands them." What or who is meant by this "Author"?

48. Pascal, *Pensées,* 72.

Approaching the Primal Mystery

What takes place hour after hour is a dizzy "miracle": at about 1,000 kilometers per hour, dependent on the latitude, the earth circles around its own axis. And the earth circles around the sun at about 100,000 kilometers per hour. At the same time, our whole solar system circles around the center of the Milky Way at 800,000 kilometers per hour. This was not always the case, and probably will not always remain so. Here is a tremendous illustration of the nonnecessity, the contingency, the instability and relativity of humankind, our planet, a universe that is expanding . . . where to? At least the question "Where from?" needs to be clarified.

When we approach the ultimate questions of "Where to?" and "Where from?" don't we human beings, aware of our precarious situation in the universe and our extremely limited knowledge, need to have some intellectual modesty (and no false modesty) in making a decision? The theoretical scientific discussion (chap. I.5) has shown that whereas the arguments of physics, built up on observation, experiment, and mathematics, have a logically compelling character, the philosophical and theological arguments for the assumption of a meta-empirical reality can at best be a pointer and invitation. That means that in these ultimate questions there is no intellectual compulsion, but freedom.

At the same time, it has clearly emerged that the repertoire of scientific instruments fails when faced with the question of the ultimate origin of this enigmatic reality. The results at the point of time $t = 0$ are in principle inaccessible to physics. Nor can scientific methods help us to experience with constantly increasing breadth and refinement what was *before* this point in time. We saw that cosmic speculations about alternative universes prove to be hypotheses that are not backed by empirical observations. But cosmic demonstrations, too, did not prove to be a convincing way.

So what is the ultimate origin of the universal constants of nature that have been there from the beginning or — if a unification of forces is achieved — the one natural constant? What is the origin of the universe generally, which began with the Big Bang? This is not just a question about an initial event but the question of reality generally: Why is there something and not nothing? According to the great mathematician and philosopher Gottfried Wilhelm Leibniz, this is the basic question of philosophy, or according to the philosopher Martin Heidegger, the miracle of all miracles: "Why are there beings and not nothing?"[49] Indeed, this is the primal human question, which the scientist, who is not competent beyond the horizon of experiences, cannot answer. Here we do not have a God of the gaps. We do not have a "gap" but the absolute beginning. Here we come up against the primal mystery of reality. It is the question of the fundamental relationship of the world to a possible primal ground, primal support, primal goal of this reality, which poses itself not just to the scientist but to human beings as human beings.

However, often pseudomysteries — sometimes constructed by theologians or produced by popular piety, but hardly acceptable to scientists ("original sin," "immaculate conception," biological "virgin birth," "two natures" in Christ, "the mystery of Fatima") — conceal access to the true mystery. What I mean is the mystery in the strict sense, which appears as a great question on the extreme horizon of our experience in time and space, at the beginning as at the end, but also at the center of the world and human beings: that primal mystery of reality that Jews, Christians, Muslims, and believers of some other religions designate with the much misunderstood and much misused name of God.

So is "God" the "author" of everything? But is "God" more than a pious hypothesis, which the scientist does not need, as Laplace, the "French Newton," remarked to Napoleon? Scientists as such investigate so to speak the "grammatical" structure of reality, but at the same time of course the question arises of the "structure of the meaning" of reality, the great human questions of meaning and interpretation.[50] Basically the scientist is faced with the alternative of either capitulating in the face of these questions and abandoning questions about causes or embarking on the question of God. I would recommend to scientists that they should at least consider God as a hypothesis.

---

49. M. Heidegger, *Introduction to Metaphysics,* inaugural lecture, Freiburg im Breisgau, 1929 (New Haven, 2000), 2.

50. Cf. H. D. Mutschler, *Physik — Religion — New Age* (Würzburg, 1990), 25f.

God as Hypothesis

Simply to assert that there is no answer to the primal question of reality is a dogmatic evasion that amounts to a dismissal of reason. Here the scientist — if not as a scientist at least as a responsible human being guided by reason — should think more deeply, more subtly, as Werner Heisenberg thought. He dared to say: "If anyone wants to argue from the indubitable fact that the world exists to a cause of this existence, then this assumption does not contradict our scientific knowledge at a single point. Scientists do not have a single argument or fact with which they could contradict such an assumption, even if it was about a cause which — how could it be otherwise — would evidently have to be sought outside our three-dimensional world."[51]

However, "outside" must be made more precise: that our universe is probably finite in space and time, as the great majority of scientists assume today, is of considerable significance for our understanding of ourselves and the world — not least from a philosophical and theological point of view. It confirms age-old religious convictions of the finitude and transitoriness of all that is created, all that is.

But it should immediately be added that even the assumption of an infinite universe would not automatically "displace" the infinite God from the cosmos. For the infinite God, who is not a God of the gaps but all-embracing and all-permeating pure spirit, such a universe would not be a limitation of his infinity but confirmation of it. That means that belief in God is compatible with different models of the world. Moreover, both a beginning of time and an infinite duration of time are unimaginable: both are outside our sphere of experience.

Indeed, if God existed, then the key question of the beginning of all things would be answered, namely, why there is something and not nothing. So too would be the question about the basic cosmic constants that govern the development of the universe from the beginning. But does God exist? Does God really exist?

51. W. Heisenberg, "Naturwissenschaftliche und religiöse Wahrheit" (speech made at the Catholic Academy in Bavaria on receiving the Guardini Prize, 23 Mar. 1973), in *Schritte über Grenzen. Gesammelte Reden und Aufsätze,* 2nd enlarged ed. (Munich, 1973), 335-51, here 349.

God as Reality

How do I find access to the primal mystery? How do I become certain that "God" is not just a hypothesis, an "idea," but "reality"? It has already become clear that answers to the basic questions of reality are not to be sought on the level of pure theory but — and here in principle Kant is right — by way of practice that is lived out and reflected on. So answers are to be found not by the theoretical operations of pure reason, and not by irrational feelings and mere moods, but rather on the basis of a trusting, rationally responsible fundamental decision and fundamental attitude. I have always thought of this attitude of trust as being like learning to swim, which doesn't happen by standing on a riverbank, reading a textbook, or taking a dry swimming course, but rather by taking the venture, perhaps aided by others, of trusting oneself to the enigmatic water that not only supports those who trust in it and don't go rigid, but also moves.

In such an attitude of trust, despite all doubt, I can experience that reality as a whole is real — initially accepted as a matter of course, but philosophically often doubted. I can affirm the fundamental identity, value, and meaning of what is. And in such a rationally responsible comprehensive attitude of trust I can also accept that God is real — and no longer doubt that there is a primal ground of all that there is, which has an effect on my whole experience, behavior, and action.

Anyone who is interested in the theoretical scientific discussion (chap. I.5-7) will now be able to say precisely that both an inductive proof of God and a deductive derivation of God from the reality of the world and human beings as they are experienced are impossible through a theoretical reason that wants to demonstrate the reality of God by logical arguments. But an invitation that attempts to illuminate the experience of the questionable reality that is open to anyone in order to confront thoughtful and active people with a free but rationally responsible decision — as it were, along the line of "practical reason," or better, the "whole person" — is not impossible. This claims — like all deeply human hope, faith, and love — an openness of the whole person beyond pure reason.

If we want to apply a criterion of verification, it may not be as narrow as the empiricist criterion that allows only what can be experienced by the senses as real. But it may not be as wide as the purely hermeneutical criterion on the basis of which an uncritical attempt is often made to understand everything. All that is in question is an indirect criterion of verification that attempts to verify God by the experienced reality of human beings and the world. What is offered by the experience of the concrete reality of human beings and the world, accessible to all, can be deciphered intellectually and expressed in language. Statements about God should be proved and tested against the experiential horizon of our life and the fundamental existential questions: not by being persuasively derived from an allegedly evident experience that would make a human decision superfluous, but by clarification and illumination of ever-problematical experiences that call for a free human decision. Only if talk of God is backed up by the concrete experience of the reality of human beings and the world to which it is related, which is communicated with it, does it have a basic credibility.

An Archimedean Point

Questions about the whole and its primal mystery are by no means questions for the naive, for weaklings, what Nietzsche called "backwoodsmen," but for informed, committed people. They are not an evasion of action but a stimulus to it. The impossibility of answering these great questions makes many people dissatisfied with atheistic ideologies. By contrast I am convinced that to say yes to God makes possible a fundamental trust in reality with a rational foundation. Those who affirm God know the primal ground, the primal mystery of reality, know why they can fundamentally trust the reality of the world and human beings, questionable though these are. My trust in God as a qualified, radical fundamental trust can indicate to me the condition of the possibility of questionable reality. To this degree it shows a radical rationality that is clearly distinct from an ideological rationalism that absolutizes reason.

"Give me somewhere to stand and I will move the earth." With this remark the brilliant Greek mathematician Archimedes (285-212 B.C.E.) is said to have illustrated the principle of the lever, which he had proved. Those who believe in God have no automatic answer with which they can exert leverage on all the great questions of human life and human history. But they have an "Archimedean point," a firm standpoint from which they can approach the great (and sometimes also the lesser) questions.

Indeed, if God exists, then countless existential questions can be answered, at least in principle — if we link up with Kant's even more comprehensive questions:[52]

What can I know? Not just, why isn't there nothing, where does the universe come from and what is it for, but also, where do human beings come from and where are they going? Why is the world as it is? What is the ultimate ground and meaning of all reality?

What ought I to do? Why do we do what we do, and why and to whom are we ultimately responsible? What deserves unconditional contempt, and what deserves love? What is the meaning of loyalty and friendship, but also of suffering and guilt? What is the decisive measure for human beings?

What may I hope for? Why are we on earth? What does it all mean? Is there something that supports us in all the nothingness, that never makes us despair? Is there a constant in all change, an unconditional in all that is conditioned? Is there an absolute despite the relativity we experience everywhere? What remains to us? Death, which ultimately makes everything meaningless? What should give us courage to live and courage to die?

My answer, which will be developed further in the following chapters, is therefore: if God exists, then there is a fundamental answer to such questions: we can understand in depth why we are very finite, defective beings and yet have infinite expectations, hopes, and longings. In that case a basic answer can be found to the question where the basic cosmic constants, matter and energy, the cosmos and human beings come from. But we must examine human origins in the field of tension between creation and evolution.

---

52. Cf. Kant, *Critique of Pure Reason*, 635.

CHAPTER III

Creation of the World or Evolution?

—◦/◦/◦—

The human race always risks taking itself too seriously. Situated as we are on an insignificant star, just one of the billions of stars in our Milky Way, which itself is only one Milky Way among billions, we should be aware that in a world history of 13.7 billion years our planet earth has existed for 4.5 billion years, and complex forms of life for about 3.5 billion years. However, it was only 1.5 million years ago that the first early human being, the human being who walked upright *(Homo erectus),* appeared, and human beings such as us *(Homo sapiens)* appeared only 200,000 years ago. Thus the cosmos existed almost all the time without humankind, and of course it could go on existing without this humankind, which in its short history has even acquired the capacity to destroy itself.

1. The Beginning as the Beginning of a Becoming

In the nineteenth century the notion of the historical development of the world and humankind was in the air. In Germany the philosopher Georg Wilhelm Friedrich Hegel (1770-1831) had developed a tremendous encyclopedic system:[1] he saw the whole history of the cosmos as

---

1. Cf. H. Küng, *The Incarnation of God: An Introduction to Hegel's Theological Thought as Prolegomena to a Future Theology* (Edinburgh, 1987).

a history of God, the absolute Spirit, in the world. But this monistic system, constructed from "above," was soon done away with and surpassed by the progress on the one hand of history and on the other of the natural sciences, both of which began from "below," from empirical observation. Biology, the science of living things, which concerns itself with the phenomena and regularities of life (human beings, animals, plants), developed in the first half of the nineteenth century. But only in the second half of the century did the two great scholarly currents, nature and history, which had initially flowed completely separately, come together. It was then recognized that nature and history developed in a single powerful natural-historical process that over vast periods of time and by the tiniest of steps had produced the whole wealth of the world and the fullness of its living beings. The scholar who laid the foundations for a new view of the origin of the world and human beings with the principle of evolution was Charles Darwin.

Evolution of the Biological Species: Darwin

The son of a doctor, Charles Darwin (1809-82) first studied medicine and then theology, but finally turned to science. The turning point in his life was a five-year voyage around the world with the research ship *Beagle* (1831-36). But only in 1859, after numerous individual investigations in the two decades following his voyage, did he publish his epoch-making work *On the Origin of Species by Means of Natural Selection*.[2] Initially Darwin had been influenced by the enlightened natural theologian William Paley (1743-1805). Paley saw in the adaptation of living beings to their particular environments a proof for the existence of God as the constructor of nature, but at the same time he believed firmly in the assured constancy of species that was apparent from nature: cats always produce cats, and dogs dogs. Darwin's revolutionary theory of evolution put this very constant in question. It was based on two fundamental insights, already prepared for in early research and now thought through consis-

2. Cf. C. Darwin, *On the Origin of Species by Means of Natural Selection* (London, 1859).

tently, into the fact and nature of evolution that did not need an intervention from a creator: change and selection.

1. Change: *animal and plant species can change.* They were not created independently of one another, as is reported in the Bible. Consequently they are not unchangeable either, as the constancy theory assumes. Affinities of species and changes in species can be noted. As investigations both in the domesticated state and in the wild show, the species come from other species that usually become extinct, but some are still attested in fossils.

The Austrian Augustinian monk and abbot Gregor Mendel (1822-84) discovered how hereditary changes (mutations) came about. On the basis of crossings and artificial fertilizations (13,000 hybrid plants), he was able to form laws of heredity that have held since his time and have been named after him. But only through modern molecular genetics do we know more about genetic makeup: that the variability of life-forms is produced by a recombination of genes and by small mistakes in the "copying" of the gene.

2. Selection: *the struggle for life leads to a natural selection.* Only the strongest, the best, the best-adapted survive ("the survival of the fittest"). Small chance hereditary differences between living beings of one species result in different opportunities for survival and multiplication. Their variations are heightened and accumulated in accordance with the laws of heredity. The weaker and less adapted are "eliminated." This is the principle of life in nature. In a history of development extending over millions of years, it has developed according to purely causal-mechanistic laws without any presupposed aims and goals: from simple to ever more complicated forms, differing in form, magnitude, strength, color, armament, physiology, and behavior. Occasionally, isolated animals undergo their own course of development, so that they no longer procreate with members of their original state: the line of descent thus splits into two species.

As well as the developmental philosopher Herbert Spencer (1820-1903),[3] Darwin had been preceded above all by Thomas R. Mal-

---

3. Cf. H. Spencer, *The Principles of Psychology* (London, 1855); Spencer, *First Principles* (London, 1862), as vol. 1 of *A System of Synthetic Philosophy.*

thus (1766-1834), a pastor and national economist who was critical of progress. In his *Essay on the Principles of Population*,[4] Malthus had developed the theory of a discrepancy between population growth and the provision of food; this would inevitably lead to overpopulation and mass misery unless birth control was practiced by continence. A lack of food led to a fight for life.

Variation plus selection produces evolution. Darwin applied this theory to the whole plant and animal world and thus developed his idea of natural selection. What does this mean for human beings?

The Descent of Human Beings from the Animal Kingdom

Inductively and empirically, on the basis of his own observations, Darwin succeeded in making his theory of development clear and generally understandable with an impressive wealth of biogeographical, paleontological, embryological, and morphological material.

- *Biogeography* shows that closely related species appear particularly frequently in neighboring regions because they descend from common ancestors.
- *Paleontology* shows by means of fossils that closely related species are often to be found in neighboring strata as they are related to one another by evolutionary descent.
- *Embryology* shows similar phases of development in very different animals, because the embryo is the later animal in a less developed stage and this betrays the form of its ancestors.
- *Morphology* can classify animals by common anatomical features and differences in species, genres, families, orders, and realms. The new molecular biology confirms this: all living organisms contain two forms of a particular molecule (DNA and RNA) that fix the blueprint for all living beings.

4. Cf. T. R. Malthus, *An Essay on the Principles of Population*, vols. 1-2 (London, 1798).

Darwin's theory of evolution combined for the first time botany and zoology to form biology, a general science of life that can explain:

> how *in the earth's antiquity* first invertebrate animals, then land plants, and finally fish, amphibians, and insects arose from multicellular organisms;
> how *in the earth's middle ages* the conifers, the first birds, and the dinosaurs (which then became extinct) developed;
> how *in the earth's modernity* mammals and blossoming plants began to dominate, how in this period *Homo erectus* formed, from whom finally *Homo sapiens* emerged and spread from Africa all over the earth.

Of course, the whole explosive character of the theory of evolution became evident from its application to human beings, which Darwin describes in his late work *The Descent of Man* (1871).[5] Human beings, too, vary according to their build and embryonic development. They prove to be descendants of earlier and lower forms of life and are thus a natural product of biological evolution. They have simply done better in the fight for life by comparison with these. Through this insight and through his universal explanation of the development from the primal cell to the human being, Darwin had finally become the "Copernicus of biology." He became religious, the man who could never get over the death of his much-beloved daughter; toward the end of his life he was increasingly an agnostic.[6]

What about the reaction of theology and the church? Had people perhaps learned from the case of Galileo in the two centuries that had meanwhile passed?

---

5. Cf. C. Darwin, *The Descent of Man and Selection in Relation of Sex* (London, 1871).

6. For Darwin's theory as understood today, see E. Mayr, *One Long Argument* (Cambridge, Mass., 1991); Mayr, *Toward a New Philosophy of Biology* (Cambridge, Mass., 1988).

2. Theological Defense

In the nineteenth century the theory of evolution became a great ideological provocation and has remained so for some people to the present day. We know how conservative Christians, theologians, and ministers in the Anglican, Catholic, and Protestant churches protested and acted against the new theory, which was evidently contrary to the Bible and tradition.

Anglican Perplexity

In the seventeenth century, on the basis of a scrupulous investigation of the biblical chronologies, the Anglican archbishop James Ussher calculated the date of the creation of the world as 23 October 4004 B.C.E. Another Anglican bishop, Samuel Wilberforce, asked a famous question at a meeting of the British Association for the Advancement of Science in 1860 of the physiologist and embryologist Thomas Huxley, who understood himself as "Darwin's bulldog": Did he think he was descended from the apes on his grandfather's side or his grandmother's side? Huxley's answer is even more famous: he would prefer to have an ape as an ancestor than a bishop who was unwilling to look the truth in the face.

The chief argument against Darwin's theory of evolution then and often even now is that in the face of this revolutionary development theory one may not pass over the momentous consequences for faith and morals, indeed, for religion generally. Isn't the creation de-divinized so that it became a process without purpose, goal, or meaning? Isn't the human being dethroned as the crown of the creation, in the image of the apes rather than in the image of God? Isn't ethics also undermined: instead of human solidarity, a battle for survival with every possible means? In all this doesn't God become superfluous? Does God have any place in this world and its evolution?

As had already happened in the face of the new insights from physics and astronomy, once again, incapable of learning, people identified the message of the Bible with a particular scientific theory. Darwin's opponents stubbornly attacked the waves of pernicious "evolutionism" from the allegedly safe rock of a biblical and traditional faith — in favor of a "fixism" in accordance with Bible and tradition. The same weapons were used in the Anglican and other churches as were used against Galileo: books, pamphlets, articles, caricatures, and of course, sermons and religious instruction.

A Second Galileo Case for the Catholic Church

The treatment of the Darwin case in the Catholic Church was as symptomatic as that of the Galileo case. As early as 1860, a year after the appearance of Darwin's epoch-making work *On the Origin of Species,* in the year of the German translation, the German episcopate officially opposed the theory of evolution in the Particular Council of Cologne by declaring that the origin of the human body through evolution from higher animal species was contrary to Holy Scripture and had to be rejected as irreconcilable with the Catholic faith.[7] The majority of Catholic theologians and later also the Roman magisterium defended the same line. In view of this, it was understandable that in 1866 Darwin's most important follower in Germany, Ernst Haeckel, prefaced the two volumes of his great *General Morphology of Organisms* with Galileo's famous protest *"E pur si muove!"* as a motto on the title page.[8] The definition of papal primacy and infallibility came in 1870, Darwin's *Descent of Man* appeared in 1871: the way in which Rome had got left behind in the medieval antimodern paradigm could not be demonstrated more vividly.

In Roman Catholicism in subsequent decades, instead of serious scientific grappling with the completely new problems that had emerged, there were many acts of repression and inquisition. Under Pope Pius X (1903-14) theological deviants were intimidated, discrimi-

---

7. Cologne Particular Council of 1860, in *Collectio Lacensis* V, 292; cf. later the answer of the 1909 Pontifical Biblical Commission about the historical character of Genesis: *"peculiaris creatio hominis"* (Denzinger, *Enchiridion* 2123), and proceedings against individual theologians (unfortunately all the proceedings, which are scrupulously collected in the Vatican, are so far unpublished).

8. Cf. E. Haeckel, *Generelle Morphologie der Organismen. Allgemeine Grundzüge der organischen Formen-Wissenschaft, mechanisch begründet durch die von Charles Darwin reformierte Deszendenz-Theorie,* 2 vols. (Berlin, 1866).

nated against as "modernists," compelled to withdraw their books, and even deposed and silenced.

Only when forced, toward the middle of the twentieth century, did Rome yield to the increasingly oppressive power of scientific events and declarations. In 1941, almost a century after the publication of Darwin's *On the Origin of Species,* Pope Pius XII asserted in an address to the members of the Papal Academy of Sciences that the origin of human life from animal forebears was completely unproven, and — here one involuntarily draws a parallel with Paul VI's encyclical *Humanae vitae* on birth control (1968) — further investigations had to be awaited.[9] Only in 1950, in the encyclical *Humani generis* (which was reactionary all along the line), did Pius XII, under protest, graciously concede against the "errors of the time," in a statement full of warnings, that the still completely unresolved problem of an evolution of the human body might be investigated further by scientists and theologians — of course, on conditions. The direct creation of the human soul by God and the origin of the whole human race from a single human couple (monogenism) had to be maintained. Moreover, the judgment of the magisterium had always to be followed.[10] A few weeks later, on 1 November 1950, the pope solemnly proclaimed the "infallible" dogma of the bodily assumption of Mary into heaven — incomprehensible not just to scientists — which is attested neither in the Bible nor in the first Christian centuries. I have described in my memoirs the merciless purge of theologians that the same Pius XII, then much admired, carried out at the same time.[11] In this connection we shall have to talk later of Pierre Teilhard de Chardin.

---

9. Pius XII, *Allocutio ineunte anno Pontificiae Academiae Scientiarum* of 30 Nov. 1941 (Denzinger, *Enchiridion* 2285). Like others, this text, which is inconvenient for the present magisterium, has been suppressed in more recent editions of Denzinger; that is why I am quoting the "classical" edition (from the time of Pius XII).

10. Pius XII, *Litterae Encyclicae "Humani generis"* of 12 Aug. 1950 (Denzinger, *Enchiridion* 2327).

11. Cf. H. Küng, *My Struggle for Freedom: Memoirs* (London, 2003), chap. III, "Breakthrough to Freedom of Conscience."

Protestant Creationism

Just as the Roman Curia in the course of history acted time and again in public and even more in secret heresy processes, so did Protestant fundamentalism, which was widespread particularly in the American southern states. Those affected were above all professors in theological centers of education, and also teachers in church or state schools. The most famous example is the "monkey trial" in Dayton, Tennessee, in 1925, centered on the theory of evolution, which caused a dispute with American fundamentalists: the biology teacher J. T. Scopes was condemned for teaching, faithful to Darwin, the descent of human beings from the animal kingdom. But when in 1981 the U.S. state of Arkansas again introduced "creationism" into school by law, this law was abolished in a second "monkey trial." A similar draft law in Louisiana failed in 1987 before the U.S. Supreme Court.

Certainly now an increasing number of theologians have committed themselves to the development theory. But among the opponents since the beginning of the twentieth century the Roman Catholic integralists have increasingly been reinforced by these Protestant fundamentalists, who may be against the infallibility of the Holy Father but are for that of Holy Scripture. They too think that the picture of the world in modern science contradicts the picture of the world in the Bible in important respects and is therefore to be rejected: the traditional Christian picture of human beings was that they were created in the image of God, then fell, and were burdened with original sin. But according to the new theory, in the beginning there would have been only a primitive being descended from the apes, who did not know the one true God and was not capable of a primal and original sin. So in a way that was both defensive and offensive, the inerrancy of the Bible had to be defended against the threat from modern science, philosophy, and historical biblical criticism.

The present-day fundamentalists — of Protestant, Roman Catholic, or Jewish origin — reject the scientific ideas of origin and development as unverifiable and unprovable; they say there are missing links in the evolutionary chain. They equally strictly reject the modern historical-critical exegesis of the Bible: Moses as the author of the so-called Five

Books of Moses may not be put in question; the word of God may not be dissolved into different sources. Some of these fundamentalists still believe that the point of creation is to be put at 4004 B.C.E., calculated on the basis of the biblical genealogies; at best, they argue, the age of the earth and the universe extends to some 10,000 years.

The Protestant advocates of the doctrine of creationism — the creation of human beings directly by God — have disgraced themselves, just as the Roman Inquisition disgraced itself with processes against Galileo and many others. In view of the common resistance of fundamentalists of different religions, it is not surprising that the Darwin case still has not been settled in the twenty-first century. In thirty-one of the fifty U.S. states there is still a legal dispute as to how the history of development is to be taught in schools. It is an unending "monkey trial." According to a Gallup poll in February 2001, around 45 percent of adult Americans agree with the statement "God created human beings in their present form within around the past 10,000 years." But what is very much more effective than any processes, prescriptions, and bans? "Perhaps the most insidious effect of the campaign against evolution has been avoidance of the subject by teachers, who, whatever their convictions, want to forestall trouble with fundamentalist parents. Recent surveys of high school biology teachers have found this to be common among instructors throughout the United States."[12]

Is this just "American naïveté"? Far from it! According to a survey by the Swiss public opinion institute IHA-Gfk of November 2002, throughout the German-speaking world around 20 million people think Darwin's theory of evolution is worthless. The background is that millions of Americans and evidently also Europeans have apparently never seen a serious account of the theory of evolution either in biology lessons or in a book.[13]

Meanwhile, theology had withdrawn from asserting the direct creation of the whole world by God: first to the direct creation of the hu-

12. S. Jacoby, "How US Fundamentalism Survived," *International Herald Tribune,* 20 Jan. 2005.
13. These surveys are compared with the results of even more recent research in a survey article by D. Quammen, "Lag Darwin falsch? Nein! Die Belege für die Evolution sind überwaltigend," *National Geographic/Deutschland,* Nov. 2004, 86-119.

man body (not from the animal world); then to that of the human soul (in contrast to the human body). Finally — it seems today — a direct intervention in the development of the world and human beings is dispensed with altogether. The English philosopher Antony Flew was unfortunately right when he stated that through this constantly repeated strategy of protection and withdrawal with which we are familiar (and which for long decades kept young Catholics especially from the study of biology "which endangers the faith"), the hypothesis of God was being "killed by inches, the death of a thousand qualifications."[14] Is such an attitude credible belief in God? It isn't surprising that it is increasingly being put in question.

3. Evolution with or without God?

In his six-volume work *Cours de philosophie positive*,[15] the man who gave positivism its name, French philosopher Auguste Comte (1798-1857), who has been mentioned above (chap. I.5), attempted to depict world history not like the German philosopher Hegel, as a history of the absolute spirit, but as a history of humankind, which he saw as being at a new stage of progress.

Progress without God: Comte

According to Comte, the human race is developing toward positivity in three stages: from myth through metaphysics to science. Phase I: first of all there is the theological-fictitious formation of myths in a society governed above all by the military. Phase II: in a legally orientated society, abstract metaphysics develops. Finally phase III: in an industrial society we see the science of positive facts. So according to Comte, the traditional God is replaced: not, however, by "reason" in Robespierre's sense, the *raison* proclaimed as *"Être suprême"* in year II after the Great

---

14. A. Flew, "Theology and Falsification" (1950), in *New Essays in Philosophical Theology,* ed. A. Flew and A. MacIntyre (London, 1955), 96-130, here 97.
15. Cf. A. Comte, *Cours de philosophie positive,* 9 vols. (Paris, 1830-42).

Revolution, but by the *"Grand Être,"* humankind generally. God and his providence are now replaced by *l'homme* in his *grandeur:* this utterly modern human being sees in order to foresee; foresees in order to plan; and plans in order to master the world.

Auguste Comte, the proud proclaimer of the positivistic view of the world, ultimately saw himself even as the high priest of a new secular church. He strove for a new religion without God, whose organization, hierarchy, and ceremonial were to be modeled on the Catholic Church. From the beginning he was strongly influenced by the antidemocratic and authoritarian papal ideologist Joseph de Maistre, who had prepared the way spiritually for the definition of the two papal dogmas (primacy of jurisdiction and infallibility) at the First Vatican Council of 1870: *Les extrêmes se touchent* — "the extremes touch." However, apart from small positivist associations, Comte's church was never founded. And in other respects, too, this Catholicism without Christianity did not gain a following: only a couple dozen friends followed Comte to the grave after his death. Like those of Hegel, Comte's historical constructions with their forced systems were dismissed by the strict historical research of later times.

But the positive spirit continued to blow. More than Hegel, Comte proved to be the prophet of the new time by working out more clearly and systematically than others the positivistic foundations of the rising technocratic age: science and technology as the powers of history that would forcibly usher in the definitive progress of humankind and a new and better social order. However, this was less a view with a scientific foundation than a belief in science and technology (scientism), which in our days, as I described above in I.5, has been deeply shattered. In fact, what is responsible for the destruction of the foundations of human life is not "subdue the earth" (Gen. 1:28) — a commission to rule under divine law that is accompanied by the task of caring — as is asserted time and again, but the often unscrupulous exploitation of the earth brought about with the help of modern science and technology. Be this as it may: in the age of crises over oil, raw materials, nuclear weapons, and the environment, only the naive believe in an eternal progress of humankind through technology regardless of anything. This at the same time puts in question that sociological positivism of

Comte aimed at mastering the world, which also did not stop in its logical variants, as we saw in connection with the Vienna Circle.

Thus happily in the twentieth century thinkers emerged, particularly from the spheres of mathematics and the natural sciences, who developed alternatives to science without religion and progress without God. They wanted to see God in the midst of progress, indeed even as himself an ongoing process. The French Jesuit Pierre Teilhard de Chardin developed his vision of progress in diametrical opposition to the high priest of French positivism, as in another way did the British scholar Alfred North Whitehead.

Evolution to God: Teilhard de Chardin

The evolution of nature and the cosmos was the field of work of the important geologist and paleontologist Pierre Teilhard de Chardin (1881-1955). He saw his life's work as harmonizing the insights of science with theological ideas. To this thinker, who was strongly influenced by the vitalistic spiritual philosophy of Henri Bergson (1859-1941) and his notion of creative evolution *(élan vital),* nature seemed to be a giant process of development that, groping forward step by step over billions of years, matures toward its fulfillment by ever more marked complexity and internalization of matter. For him God is not only the origin and goal of creation but is himself involved in this evolution; he goes along with it, from the elementary particles and the immeasurable expanses of the cosmos through the biosphere of the plant and animal worlds to the noosphere of the human spirit.

In Teilhard's view of the world, human beings, too, are not yet complete. They are coming into being: becoming human, anthropogenesis, is not yet complete. It presses on toward Christogenesis, and Christogenesis finally presses on toward its future fullness, its *pleroma* (Greek: fullness) in the Omega Point, where the individual and collective adventure of human beings finds its end and consummation, where the consummation of the world and the consummation of God converge.

This "pleromatization," this coming to fullness, this development of the cosmos and human beings forward and upward, culminates in the universal cosmic Christ, who for Teilhard is the unity of the reality of God and the world in person. Of course, for him all this is a vision not of pure reason but of knowing faith. In his *How I Believe* he formulates his creed: "I believe that the universe is an evolution. I believe that evolution proceeds towards spirit. I believe that spirit is fully realized in a form of personality. I believe that the supremely personal is the Universal Christ."[16]

Teilhard is a mystic who assumes the evolutionary cosmic significance of the incarnation of God in Christ. Most scientists would not follow him in such bold scientific hypotheses. Theologians find some of his theological views often formulated in an extremely one-sided way, exaggerated or — in respect of Jesus' life and cross — defective. And possibly today both sides would reject above all his optimism, belief in progress, and orientation on the "Omega Point," which reflects too little on the problem of suffering and evil. Be this as it may: Pierre Teilhard de Chardin cannot be praised highly enough for being the first to combine theology and science in a brilliant way and bringing together scientists and theologians provocatively to reflect on the whole set of problems. He was concerned with the religious significance of evolution and the evolutionary scope of religion. He was by no means naive; he did not want any superficial "concordism" between Bible and science as favored by Rome. He firmly rejected "certain childish and immature attempts at reconciliation, which confuse levels and sources of knowledge and have led only to incomplete, monstrous formations."[17] But he did want a "coherence" with a deep foundation so that a positively "through-constructed whole" would become visible "in which the parts support and enlarge one another in a better and better way."[18]

As a result of a static interpretation of creation by God, Rome and its governors had been stuck for many decades in the ideology of a "creationism" that over against Darwin's theory of evolution advocated a "fixism" and "concordism." This is expressed throughout the multivolume *Dictionnaire de la Bible*. So it is not surprising that in 1926,

16. P. Teilhard de Chardin, *How I Believe* (1934; New York, 1969), frontispiece.
17. Teilhard, *How I Believe,* frontispiece.
18. Teilhard, "Comment je vois" (1948), in *Oeuvres de Pierre Teilhard de Chardin,* vol. 11 (Paris, 1969), 182.

under pressure from Rome, Teilhard, who entered the Jesuit Order in 1899 at the age of eighteen, was removed by his superiors from his chair at the Institut Catholique in Paris. Subsequently they suppressed all his philosophical and scientific writings, and in 1947 they instructed him not to discuss any more scientific topics. Teilhard became totally isolated: in 1948 he was forbidden to accept a call to the Collège de France; in 1951 — when Pius XII's encyclical *Humani generis* was "executed" — he was banished from Europe to the research institute of the Wenner Gren Foundation in New York. In 1955, the year of his death, he was forbidden to take part in the International Congress for Palaeontology. Only a few people who happened to be present followed his coffin when he died on Easter Day and was buried in the cemetery of a Jesuit college on the Hudson River, about 160 kilometers from New York; I had great difficulty in finding his grave when I was spending a guest semester in New York in 1968.

The list of Teilhard's works produced by C. Cuénot contains 380 titles. However, Teilhard could himself publish only purely scientific treatises. He did not see a single one of his main works published during his lifetime. They were published by an international committee because Teilhard had bequeathed the rights to a colleague instead of to the Order.

However, on 6 December 1957, two years after his death, the Holy Office (now the Congregation for the Doctrine of Faith) issued a decree that Teilhard's books should be removed from libraries, that they should not be sold in Catholic bookshops, and that they should not be translated into other languages.[19] The ancient Romans called this *damnatio memoriae* — deleting a name from the records and thus banishing it from memory. Only since the Second Vatican Council have Teilhard's writings also in fact gained the recognition they deserve in the Catholic Church and theology. But no pope has uttered his name. The church authorities have still not thanked Teilhard for his work of

19. I was helped in surveying the problems associated with Teilhard de Chardin (as later those associated with Alfred North Whitehead) by a paper given by Professor Karl Schmitz-Moorman, a contemporary of mine who sadly died young, at a study day of our Tübingen doctoral seminar on these two authors; he did lasting work on the German editing and translating of the writings of Teilhard and the French edition of Teilhard's diaries.

reconciliation. Even the Second Vatican Council could not resolve on a clear rehabilitation of his name or that of Galileo, acknowledging that they had been wrongly condemned, persecuted, and calumniated.

So the history of the suffering of this theological thinker, too, remains a shameful testimony to a poverty of spirit that manifests itself in the persecution of dissidents that has still by no means disappeared from the Roman system; in some respects it is not unlike that in the Soviet system (think of Sakharov!). But neither the "political theologian" J. B. Metz nor the critical philosopher Jürgen Habermas dared to tackle the head of the Congregation of the Doctrine of Faith, Joseph Ratzinger, in public over this deeply unchristian phenomenon (the most serious recent case is the dismissal of the chief editor of the respected Jesuit journal *America,* Thomas Reese).[20] I am glad now to turn to one who had a happier life.

God in Process: Whitehead

In Cambridge the great mathematician, logician, and philosopher Alfred North Whitehead (1861-1947), with his pupil Bertrand Russell, published the monumental *Principia mathematica;* he then turned to epistemology and finally, as professor in Harvard, to sketching out a comprehensive metaphysical system, a process philosophy.

Like Teilhard de Chardin, Whitehead, who was strongly influenced by Hegel's philosophy, understood the whole of nature as one giant process in which infinitely many very small units — not "entities" but a chain of "events" or, as he later says, "actual happenings" — enter into an active relationship with others and grow together in infinitely many small processes of coming into being (to a "concrescence of prehensions"). From him, too, in a completely new way we have become aware of the dynamism of nature: we take seriously the reality of time (the theory of relativity), the possibility of the new, the dynamic character of humanity generally, quite differently. But unlike Teilhard, who regarded this dynamic of nature as a series of different phases, as a cumulative

---

20. Cf. the headline in the *National Catholic Reporter,* 20 May 2005, "The Big Chill."

evolution running in a line "upward," Whitehead understood it as a life pulsating in every possible form. It is a process without a goal: a creative movement forward, certainly, but infinite time without a climax.

Whitehead's complicated philosophical system is described in his main work, *Process and Reality*. He works with forty-five categories understood in a very arbitrary way: eight categories of existence, nine categorical duties, twenty-seven categories of explanation, and one category of the last. In so doing he makes impressive use of numerous insights from mathematics and physics, Greek and modern philosophy.

However, the criticism is that Whitehead does not assume any fundamentally different species of entities in the world — organic and inorganic, spirit and body — but the same general character for every entity. Therefore he can use psychological terms such as "feeling" and generalize them also to explain biological, indeed physical processes: accordingly in his system even stones are given feelings. In doing this he does not want to assert any "panpsychism," any "all-ensouling." However, is it illuminating that all the different experiences — physiological, psychological, and also moral, aesthetic, and religious — are manifestations of the same basic principles, from protons to persons, a continuum of events without essential differences, at best differences of degree?

Whitehead does not want ultimately to make the concept of God comprehensible for today in a "metaphysical rationalization": he is rightly dissatisfied both with the East Asian concept of an impersonal order (absolute immanence) and with the Semitic concept of God as a personal being (absolute transcendence), as also with the pantheistic concept of the world as a phase of the being of God (extreme monism). Moreover, all three notions have been rejected by Christianity.

Whitehead wants to understand God essentially as God in process; not just to assert a becoming of God but to justify it rationally. Therefore he sees God's nature as "dipolar": a conceptual-ideal "original nature" and a physical-real "subsequent nature" of God. In the "end" God is "the realization of the actual world in the unity of his nature."[21]

---

21. Cf. A. N. Whitehead, *Process and Reality: An Essay in Cosmology* (1929; new ed. New York, 1960), 524.

For years I too have been advocating a dynamic understanding of God instead of the rigid natural immutability of the Greek-scholastic deity,[22] but I ask myself: Can the problem of God and the world in fact be resolved by regarding God and the world as entities eternally related to each other and ultimately interchangeable, so that finally "it is as true to say that God creates the world as that the world creates God"? In the exaggerated "antitheses" in which Whitehead sums up his understanding of God,[23] many critics see the compulsion to form a system that also seems to determine Whitehead's aversion to the concept of the creator, which in no way means irrationality, change, and arbitrariness. His assertion of an original nature of God without any consciousness is probably likewise grounded in this — though it can hardly explain the origin of consciousness in the world. Finally, the neglect of a real consummation of the world in the future, which is what the biblical message of the kingdom of God (quoted by Whitehead, but very selectively) really means, is also related to it. Whitehead rightly rejects the concept of a divine tyrant, but the beautiful picture of a compassionate God, "the fellow sufferer who understands," transcends any philosophical insight.

American process philosophy (represented especially by Whitehead's pupil Charles Hartshorne) and process theology (represented outstandingly by John Cobb and Schubert Ogden) have done well to learn from Whitehead. But his system as such can hardly be accepted without qualification. Rather, his concern must be taken up in a different form. So I do not want to content myself with historical reminiscences but to put to myself without prejudice the question: Can scientists today still use the word "God" at all? And as people of the twenty-first century, how are we to picture God, or better — since God cannot be "pictured" — how are we to think of God?

---

22. Cf. Küng, *The Incarnation of God,* excursus IV: "Is God Unchangeable?"
23. Cf. Whitehead, *Process and Reality,* 528.

4. How Are We to Think of God?

Many surveys of belief in God among scientists tell us little because they are framed in too sweeping a way. There are, for example, the surveys of the psychologist James H. Leuba of 1914 and 1933, which ask about a belief in God that can communicate with God through prayers, but at the same time about an immortality of the soul. It is difficult to answer such questions with a simple yes or no, any more than it is possible to answer the question "Are you for or against France?" And one cannot overlook that in some universities "political correctness" requires that one should not take a public position on basic religious issues. So what does it mean when an evolutionary biologist at Harvard University surveys his colleagues and states that they are all atheists? Here it would have been more accurate to ask how scientists imagine the God they reject or, perhaps in another form, accept. Some in fact are rejecting not God but a caricature of God in which no believers with any degree of education would recognize their God.

An Alternative to the Word "God"?

Many scientists, too, understandably jib at the word "God." Certainly one can also speak of the "Godhead" or the "Divine" instead of "God." The name God is often misunderstood anthropomorphically and misused for political, commercial, military, and ecclesiastical ends. But are we simply to drop it because of all the misuses and lack of credibility by so many official representatives and institutions of the faith?

I am often asked: "How can you bring yourself to say 'God' time after time? How can you expect your readers to accept the word in the meaning you want it to have? What human word has been so misused, so tainted, so violated as this?" Wouldn't it be better to keep quiet about God?

The Jewish philosopher of religion Martin Buber answered this very question:

> Yes, it is the most loaded of all human words. None has been so stained, so torn to pieces. Precisely for that reason I may not dispense with it. The generations of human beings have foisted the

burden of their tormented lives on this word and pressed it into the ground; it lies in the dust and bears all their burdens. The generations of human beings with their religious parties have torn the word apart; they have killed for it and they have died for it; it bears all their fingerprints and all their blood. Where would I find a word like it to designate the Most High? Were I to take the purest, most glittering concept from the inner treasury of the philosophers, I could catch in it only a voluntary image of thought, but not the presence of the one whom I mean, the one whom the generations of human beings have honoured and humiliated with their tremendous living and dying.

Hence his conclusion:

We must respect those who make it taboo, because they rebel against the injustice and the mischief which are so fond of calling for empowerment through "God"; but we may not surrender it. How understandable it is that some people propose that we should keep quiet for a while about the "last things" so that the misused words may be redeemed! But they may not be redeemed like that. We cannot wash the word "God" clean, and we cannot make it whole; but we can raise it from the ground, stained and torn to pieces as it is, and set it up over an hour of great anxiety.[24]

That is also my conviction: instead of ceasing to talk about God, or simply talking about God as before, today especially it is very important for philosophers and theologians in particular to learn to talk anew about God in a guarded way. This would also be good since one can hear scientists in particular saying: "I'm not a materialist. There must be something other than matter: spirit, transcendence, the holy, divine. But as a scientist I can't cope with the personified God who is up there or out there." No one should be put off by inquisitorial "representatives

---

24. M. Buber, "Gottesfinsternis. Betrachtungen zur Beziehung zwischen Religion und Philosophie," in *Werke,* vol. 1, *Schriften zur Philosophie* (Munich, 1962), 505-603, here 508-10.

of God" from trying out new ways of talking about God, so that a child-like faith can grow up. So first the question:

God — a Being above the Earth?

The sciences demand some hard thinking of the theologian. I ask myself whether conversely theology may not also require a little thinking from the scientist, when it is about central issues.

There are physicists who use "God" as a metaphor for the worldly. "If you are religious, this is like looking at God," remarked the American astrophysicist George Smoot when he announced the fluctuations in the background cosmic radiation (an echo of the Big Bang). This sounds pious, but it is superficial. Here God is a metaphor for the secular, for nature. So too the Nobel Prize winner Leon Lederman with his book title *The God Particle*.

Rather, we should maintain that God is not identical with the cosmos. And Einstein would not have had such insuperable difficulties in accepting quantum theory had he not identified God with nature or natural laws like his "house philosopher" Spinoza. So God is not a being within the earth, not a "thing" in this world; he does not belong to "factual reality," nor can he be observed empirically. God is not a "worldly being," and that means he is no "Father" or "Mother" in the human/all-too-human sense.

So is God a being above the earth? No, he is not a superterrestrial being above the clouds, in the physical heaven. This naive anthropomorphic notion is obsolete: God is not a "supreme being" who is in a literal or spatial sense "above" the world, in a "world above."

So is God an extraterrestrial being? He is not that either. God doesn't live beyond the stars in a metaphysical heaven. The enlightened deistic notion is also obsolete: God is not an existing, objectified, reified other, in the spiritual or metaphysical sense "outside" the world in an otherworldly beyond, a "hinterworld."

But what then can be said about God at the level of today's scientific awareness — in the face of our new vision of the unimaginably broad, deep, and ultimately not fully comprehensible cosmos and the billions of years of the evolution of the world and human beings?

Space-Time, Embraced by Eternity and Unfathomability

What is fundamental is that God is in this universe and this universe is in God. At the same time, God is greater than the world. We could follow Augustine in comparing the world with a sponge, supported and swimming in the eternal, infinite sea of the deity. And even if there were several worlds, according to Christian tradition God is *semper maior,* ever greater, and Muslims too express this in the formula *Allahu akbar* — "God is greater!"

God is not isolated in this universe. His immeasurability embraces space; it cannot be localized. He is present everywhere, omnipresent:

- God is immanent in the world: from within he permeates the cosmos and influences it. At the same time, he participates in its fate, has a share in its processes and suffering.
- And at the same time, God transcends the world: permeating the cosmos, at the same time he transcends it. In his infinity he embraces all finite beings, structures, and processes. He is the all-embracing, transempirical reality of relationship.

Transcendence need not be excluded when Goethe writes:

What kind of God would push only from outside,
letting the cosmos circle round his finger?
He likes to drive the world from inside,
harbours the world in Himself, Himself in the world,
so all that lives and weaves and is in Him
never wants for his power or his spirit.[25]

This infinite God is not static. His eternity embraces time: this eternity is not timeless, but rather is contemporaneous with all parts of time. God is not an unchangeable idea of the good (as Plato thought) without reference to human beings and the world in their historicity. Nor is he an "unmoved mover" (as Aristotle thought) or an unliving pri-

---

25. J. W. von Goethe, "Gedichte," in *Sämtliche Werke* (Zürich, 1950), 1:409.

mal One (as Plotinus thought). Nor does he intervene miraculously in history from a realm above history. He is not a magician who uses tricks. No, God is the dynamic himself; he creates the world in itself; he holds and moves it invisibly from within.

In this way God is conceivable in the context of a modern unitary and dynamic understanding of reality: God is not a (supreme) finite alongside the finite as part of reality. Rather, he is the intangible "infinite dimension" in all things. Not just the invisible mathematical dimension, though, but the real dimension of the infinite. The infinite in the finite, but with which one can reckon in principle as in mathematics, even the reckoning must not be included in everyday equations.

We can formulate the relationship between God and the world, God and human beings, only dialectically: God is transcendence, but in immanence. He is an eternity, but in temporality; immeasurability, but in space. So God is the absolute in the relative, the primal mystery in the reality of the world and world history — no more detectable than the architectural formula that supports everything in the bridge that spans the abyss. Can this infinite God still be called person?

Is God a Person?

This is a question that cannot be answered in a sentence. I shall answer it in three steps.

First, God is *more than a person*. Albert Einstein's objections to a personal understanding of God are to be taken seriously. If he speaks of cosmic reason or if Eastern thinkers speak of the "One" *(tad ekam),* of "nirvana," "void" *(Shunyata),* "absolute nothingness," "shining darkness," then we must understand this as the often paradoxical expression of reverence before the mystery of the Absolute. This cannot be grasped either in concepts or in notions — that has to be asserted over against all-too-human "theistic" notions of God, which is why even the name "God" is rejected by Buddhists.

It is true that God is certainly not a person as the human being is a person: the all-embracing and all-permeating is never an object from which human beings can distance themselves to say something about him. The abyss, primal support and primal goal of all reality, which for the believer determines every individual existence, who is nearer to me than my neck vein, as the Qur'an (sura 50.16) says metaphorically, is not a limited individual among other persons. God is not a superperson and a super-ego. So even the term "person" is only a cipher for God: God is not the supreme person among other persons. God explodes the concept of person: God is more than a person.

But a second thing is also true: *God is not less than a person*. Precisely because God is not a "thing," precisely because, as is emphasized in Eastern wisdom, he cannot be understood, seen, manipulated; because he is not at our disposal, he is also not impersonal, not subpersonal. God, who makes possible the coming into being of the personal, also explodes the concept of the impersonal: God is not less than a person either.

Spinoza's identification of God with nature and the laws of nature does not solve any problems. Rather, belief in the necessity of all natural processes would lead Einstein astray into dogmatically rejecting the indeterminacy relation of quantum physics a priori. But an unfeeling geometry or harmony of the universe in the necessity of natural laws such as physicists are tempted to assume on the basis of their particular and limited method cannot explain the whole of reality. According to Muslim tradition, God, the one, has a hundred names, the last of which is known to him alone.

This is not just the view of the Bible and the Qur'an; most Buddhists also accept an Ultimate Reality. And this is more than the cosmos: more than a universal reason or a great anonymous consciousness. It is more than the supreme idea (Plato) or a thinking related to itself and thinking itself (Aristotle). It is more than the pure beauty of the cosmos or the blind justice of history. The Ultimate Reality is not indifferent to us and does not leave us indifferent, but is our "ultimate concern," as Paul Tillich put it in a liberating and demanding way: omnipresent to us yet at the same time withdrawn from us. In the Hebrew Bible God appears as the hidden God who is nevertheless so near to the people that he enters into a covenant with them, becomes involved with the individual.

But how are the personal and nonpersonal to be bound together coherently? Certainly by transcending both concepts. But in the end, can theologians achieve what the physicist cannot, namely, to "know the mind of God"? While they certainly may not find the "world formula," can they find a "God formula" that resolves the mystery of God and the world?

Here we need to be cautious, and that is the third point. Theologians can certainly find a word that transcends the concepts of personal and nonpersonal, and they will then speak of "transpersonal" or "superpersonal." But with such a formula, would they have grasped the spirit of God? With this concept, would they have understood God? With this definition, would they have defined God? No, for had they understood him, had they defined him, this would not be God, who is and remains the Invisible, the Incomprehensible, the Indefinable. *Coincidentia oppositorum* — "the coming together of opposites" — is how the Renaissance thinker Nicholas of Cusa (1401-64) put it: as maximum also the minimum and thus transcending both minimum and maximum.[26] God is the "wholly other" and yet *interior intimo meo,* "more inward to me than my innermost part," as Augustine remarked.

Now people will use more personal or more nonpersonal concepts or metaphors depending on the concrete situation of the individual or the community; this depends on the context. Nonpersonal images (sea, horizon, sun) can in some circumstances say as much as personal, anthropomorphic images (father, mother). Friedrich Nietzsche's parable of the "madman" who in the brightness of noon lit a lantern to seek God (unsuccessfully) and therefore proclaimed the death of God is well known. In three impressive, powerful images he describes what is difficult to render in concepts: "How could we drink up the sea? Who gave us the sponge to wipe away the entire horizon? What were we doing when we detached the earth from its sun? Whither is it moving to now? Whither are we moving? Away from all suns? Are we not plunging continually?"[27] However, the Bible uses more anthropomorphic concepts and images. They include the term "creator God."

---

26. Cf. Nicholas of Cusa, *Of Learned Ignorance* (London and New Haven, 1954), I, chap. 26.

27. F. Nietzsche, *The Gay Science,* ed. Walter Kaufmann (New York, 1974), 181.

5. Bible and Creation

"Creation" in the narrower biblical sense means the creation of all that is by the one God, but also the created world itself, the cosmos. Creation in the wider transferred sense means all ideas of the world and its development. Ideas of the origin of the cosmos (cosmogony) that often precedes the origin of the gods (theogony) in the history of religion are almost too many to survey. There are cosmogonies according to which the world and human beings owe their existence to the movement of impersonal forces. There are others in which several deities or the one God created everything. In one way or another the creation story is not an end in itself; rather, it is meant to help to locate human life in a cosmic order and so make it possible for human beings to live an authentic life in harmony with the world.

Creation Myths of the World Religions

Three great religious river systems can be established on the primal ground of the tribal religions that still exist in Australia today (though these have often been developed further) (to set "natural religions" against "cultural religions" would be a false opposition, as tribal religions have usually shaped rich cultures). For millennia, despite all revolutions (paradigm shifts), they have persisted to the present day, and each has developed its own myths of origins. There are:

- the religions of *Indian origin,* Hinduism, Buddhism, Jainism, Sikhism, whose basic type is the mystic or guru: mystic religions that tend toward the unity of God and the world, God and human beings.
- the religions of Far Eastern, *Chinese origin,* above all Confucianism and Daoism, the basic type of which is the wise man: wisdom religions that start from a harmony of heaven and earth.
- the religions of *Near Eastern origin,* Judaism, Christianity, and Islam, the basic type of which is the prophet: prophetic religions that are governed by the opposition between creator and creation, holy God and sinful human beings. Their holy scriptures are the Hebrew Bible, the New Testament, and the Qur'an. All three have an idea of

creation by the One God that differs considerably from the myths of the other religions.

According to the myths of *the original inhabitants of Australia,* the Aborigines, the great ancestor spirits of the primal time formed the earth. They did not come from heaven but from the earth, in human or animal form. On vast wanderings they shaped the formless, monotonous earth into a landscape: hills, ways, watering places, mountains. They also created sun, moon, and stars, and from preformed masses human beings, tribes, and clans along with animals and plants. So human beings have the obligation to preserve the earth in the form and purity shaped by the ancestors: it is hallowed land.

The *Indian tradition* has from of old known many kinds of images and models of the origin of the world. For example, the Rig-Veda, India's earliest literature, speaks of a craftsman or artist who measures out the space of the world and shapes the world from primal matter in different ways; we read of a procreation and bearing of the world by the firstborn "world parents" heaven and earth; of a world egg, the "golden embryo," produced from the primal waters and the fire, from which the world then came into being. Finally Purusha, a cosmic primal being like a human being, is worshiped; it is said once to have produced heaven, earth, gods, and creatures in a cosmic sacrifice. In later "classical" Hinduism there are references back to these old ideas: they are integrated into comprehensive concepts such as the notion of numerous world ages following one another in a cycle. When this has run its course, the whole universe comes into being anew time and again thanks to the great classical Hindu gods (Vishnu, Shiva).

Siddhartha Gautama, the *Buddha,* is said constantly to have emphasized that it is meaningless to ask when and how the world once came into being and what will become of it in the end. However, this did not stop his pupils and the great Buddhist tradition from speculating time and again on the beginning and end, the essence and structure of the world. Essentially, here they resorted to the classical Indian myths, cosmogonies, and pictures of the world; in part they developed them further and finally interpreted them in the light of Buddhist ideas of salvation and redemption.

Chinese religion, too, underwent a mythical phase of dreams, heroes, and heroic acts, and early Chinese society also had a religious character. However, Chinese historiography began amazingly early, three thousand years ago, and Chinese mythology has been preserved only in fragments. These include the myth of the world egg from which heaven and earth were made. The Chinese picture of the world has always embraced three levels: below, the kingdom of the dead; above it, the earth as the abode of the living; and finally above, the heaven, the place of ancestors and nature gods, who have above them the one supreme God, called "Lord" *(di)* or "Lord on high" *(shangdi).* This is a humanlike (anthropomorphic) being but one who is remote and transcendent, perhaps the creator God; however, he receives no sacrifices. Later, heaven *(tian)* comes into the foreground, which is increasingly understood as an invisible cosmic-moral power of order.

The *old Germanic* sagas of gods and heroes were preserved on the remote island of Iceland. They were collected in the thirteenth century in the *Edda* as a textbook for the Skalds (the Nordic poets). Here the beginning of the world is connected with nothingness, an icy world in the north and a fiery world in the south, from which the giant Ymir and the cow Audhumla arise.

Isn't it amazing at the beginning of the third millennium that the Nobel Prize winner for physics, Steven Weinberg, who has already been mentioned, refers back to the *Edda* — instead of the Bible? As we heard, at all events he wants to avoid the challenge of the biblical creation narratives in the book of Genesis: "Some cosmologists are philosophically attracted to the oscillating model, especially because, like the steady-state model, it nicely avoids the problem of Genesis."[28]

A Need for Information?

Is one completely wrong in getting the impression that here some physicists simply lack the necessary basic information for a rational judgment, which in the sphere of religion no less than in the sphere of phys-

---

28. S. Weinberg, *The First Three Minutes: A Modern View of the Origin of the Universe* (New York, 1977), 154.

ics must extend beyond what was learned in childhood? American political theorists claim that in politics the majority of voters decide on the basis of a "low-information rationality," i.e., more instinctively, in a gut reaction. Small personal details or interests are often more important to them than the major points of a program. One might think that in science things would have to be much better than in politics. But on the other hand, it can be noted — unfortunately even more in Europe than in the USA — that the interest of scientists in religious matters is limited. Particularly in respect of their own tradition — usually Jewish or Christian — which they think they know adequately, decisions are often likewise made on the basis of a low-information rationality.

An outstanding instance to the contrary here is the physicist and philosopher Carl Friedrich von Weizsäcker. In his imposing life's work this pupil of Heisenberg and Bohr labored to reconstruct the unity of physics as a fundamental science in the framework of a unitary understanding of reality.[29] He attempted to bring together external nature and human beings, the physical-scientific and the metaphysical religious spheres. Here he raised the question: "Do we think of atoms and the space of galaxies correctly if we imagine them in accordance with the structures of our narrow existence which can be perceived by the senses?" His answer: "Perhaps structures with which we describe what can be perceived by the senses designate only the surface of a deeper reality. The real world of the senses already contains yet other qualities than these mathematical structures: perhaps it also in part conceals or reveals other forms. The boundary between this world and the beyond is again becoming permeable."[30]

As early as 10 December 1974 he wrote to me against the background of nuclear rearmament about the relationship between Christians and scientists: "Christians must ask scientists whether they are aware of the criminal irresponsibility of many of their activities, and scientists must ask Christians whether they realize that for centuries their

29. Cf. C. F. von Weizsäcker, *Zum Weltbild der Physik* (1943), expanded by many further articles, 13th ed. (Stuttgart, 1990); von Weizsäcker, *Die Einheit der Natur* (Munich, 1974); von Weizsäcker, *Aufbau der Physik* (Munich, 1985); von Weizsäcker, *Zeit und Wissen* (Munich, 1992).

30. Von Weizsäcker, *Zeit und Wissen,* 585.

awareness has lagged behind modernity. This is perhaps an indication of the direction in which I would like to go on asking questions."[31] And in his lecture on the 500th anniversary of the University of Tübingen in 1977, von Weizsäcker declared: "In truth science in its attitude and its themes cannot avoid confrontation with the attitude and the themes of religion. And it seems to me that religion may not tolerate the semblance of neutrality which has been produced by science. It must ask science: do you know what you are doing?"[32]

Both sides must carry on the discussion between science and religion in the present state of knowledge. So here I want briefly to offer some important information on the biblical accounts of creation in the light of extremely complex modern biblical research, which should make a rational, well-founded judgment in the question of God easier.

The Magna Carta of the Jewish-Christian Worldview

The historiography of the people of Israel — understood in the broadest sense — began around the same time as Chinese historiography: in the time of King David, around 1000 B.C.E. In indefatigable research, the Christian exegesis of the last two centuries has been able to establish a critical distinction between the different levels of sources in the Pentateuch (formerly called "The Five Books of Moses") into Elohist, Yahwist, Priestly Writing, and Deuteronomy, and also to elucidate the meaning of the stories of the creation of the world and of human beings. The process of the composition of the first book of Moses, Genesis,[33] must have covered five hundred years. In it, it becomes clear how people accepted the then state of knowledge of the world to proclaim the message of the one God and his creation. The two accounts of creation have shaped the worldview of Jews and Christians in a unique way.

---

31. Von Weizsäcker, *Lieber Freund! Lieber Gegner! Briefe aus fünf Jahrzehnten,* ed. E. Hora (Munich, 2002), 103f.

32. Von Weizsäcker, "Gottesfrage und Naturwissenschaften" (lecture given in Tübingen in 1977).

33. A whole library of commentaries and monographs has been written on the book of Genesis: the commentaries by H. Gunkel, G. von Rad, R. de Vaux, C. Westermann, and E. A. Speiser are outstanding.

The *first account of creation* (Gen. 1:1–2:4), from the source called the Priestly Writing (P) because of its style and terminology (God is called "Elohim"), was written after the Babylonian exile around 500 B.C.E. Evidently it uses material about the origin of the world already collected in Babylon in the sixth century B.C.E. and divides it into four periods of divine revelation: creation, Noah, Abraham, Moses. It is important that the biblical narrative presents itself here as an antimyth to the Babylonian myth. It does not have the world proceeding from a battle between the gods but from God's sovereign action. Certainly there is much in common with the Babylonian myths, for example, the notion of the heavenly ocean whose waters are prevented by the firmament from descending on the earth as a flood. But what is decisive for us today is the characteristic of this first biblical account of creation. For in a unique way it emphasizes:

- the *transcendence of God:* God, elevated over the world, creates the world solely by the word. The stars are not manifestations of the divine, but created lamps in heaven.
- *human dignity:* human beings are not created as servants of the gods but in the image of God; as his trustees and not as tyrants and exploiters, they are set above the rest of creation.
- *the order and unity of creation:* this differs from the chaos as cosmos; it is a well-ordered, structured, harmonious whole with numerous reciprocal dependencies. The one God creates "heaven and earth," the whole universe.

The Priestly Writing does not report a creation from nothing but a creation of order out of chaos. God stands at the beginning of all becoming, including the original chaos, which he put in order afterward. The universalism is manifest: the transcendent God has created everything: the cosmos, nature, and humankind. He continues to keep them alive. At the same time, we are told how heaven and earth came into being. But here what stands in the foreground is less the chronological sequence than the poetically shaped structure of the creation in six "days": the twice three "days" do not describe periods of the world but, first, three spheres of life that are then adorned on the following three "days." On the first day there is "Let there be light," and on the fourth day the adornment of the firmament with sun, moon, and stars. Thus the classes of being that fill the three spheres are depicted in a concrete way according to species, magnitude, genre, form, and sex. So this is more a phenomenology of the cosmos than a cosmology. With the "and God said" on each day is associated the formula of completion, "and it was so," and finally the formula of approval, "and God saw that it was good." All in all, this is a grandiose, comprehensive view of the whole cosmos created good by God and not wrested from a satanic counterpart.

The *second account of creation* in the book of Genesis (2:4-25) is some centuries older: it was written or edited around 900 B.C.E. by an unknown predecessor of the Elohist whom scholars call the Yahwist (the letter *J* is used to denote him because the sources were identified by a German scholar who used the spelling "Jahwist") because he constantly introduces the divine name Yahweh into the text long before the revelation of the name of Yahweh in Exodus 3:15. In his work, too, the creation takes place by ordering what is formlessly present. Here the impressive narrative concentrates on the creation of the first human couple. What is meant to be depicted here pictorially is not *how* God created man and woman but *what* man and woman are — with spirit and body in the image of God, and the woman, made of the same substance, the helpmeet of the man. "Subdue the earth" does not mean (as first became possible in modernity) "exploit the earth," but "cultivate it and look after it." "Rule over" the animals means taking responsibility for them as being in the image of God: "giving them names" means becoming familiar with their nature.

Neither the first nor the second account of creation speaks of a "creation from nothing" *(creatio ex nihilo).* That view, which does not presuppose any matter, was developed much later in the Jewish communities influenced by Hellenistic thought. It is first demonstrable in 2 Maccabees, which covers the years 175-135 B.C.E. and was originally written in Greek. But the real language of the Bible, the "Old Testament," is Hebrew. However, even where the Bible remains metaphorical, it has important things to convey.

A Metaphorical Language

At a central point in the Bible there is no process of change — despite all the further development of the understanding of God. God can be addressed — this is a biblical constant. Here "spiritualization" would be a dilution; it would remove the foundation from real prayer and worship. However God is spoken of in the Bible, whether mythically or unmythically, metaphorically or conceptually, in prose or in poetry, the relationship to God as one who can be addressed, as a Thou — one may call this person, personal, suprapersonal, transpersonal, or whatever — is a basic constant of biblical faith that cannot be given up, though it has to be constantly reinterpreted.

However, neither Christians nor Jews need believe that the Bible is proclaimed from heaven as the direct word of God — as is expected by Muslims in respect of the Qur'an; at any rate, according to the traditional Muslim understanding, the Qur'an was dictated word for word for human beings and therefore every sentence is infallibly true. But the Bible understands itself as the word of God in human words. For it shows everywhere that it has been collected, written down, worked on, and developed in various directions sentence by sentence by human beings. As a human work, it is therefore not without defects and contradictions, concealments and confusions, limitations and errors. At all events, it is an extremely varied collection of clear and less clear, stronger and weaker, original and derived testimonies of faith. This historical character of the scriptures not only makes biblical criticism possible but even requires it. Serious biblical criticism is indispensable, so that the biblical message of God does not remain shut up in a book by people of past times but is proclaimed again with new life in every age.

Thus the Bible is not simply God's revelation but human testimony to it — in a language of images and parables that have their own *Sitz im Leben* (e.g., in worship, the ordering of the community, and so on). In images and parables the Bible answers questions that concerned people already at that time, but are also still important for people of today: on the first pages the questions of the beginning and nature of the world and human beings. And how could prescientific human beings describe God's creation other than by metaphors and analogies taken

117

from the sphere of human activities, of which the philosophy of the Greeks and their descendants also made use?[34]

This is expressed particularly in the Psalms: God has "founded the earth" like the builder of a city or a palace. Like a tentmaker, he has "stretched out the heavens like a tent." Like a builder, he has "made firm" the roof, driven the "great waters" from the sphere of life, "made the firmament" and "the two great lights." The effective images and the living metaphors are not proof of a "cosmic designer or architect." They are an invitation to believing trust in the one invisible God who cannot be seen or described directly, who created and sustains the universe and whom one is not to paint nor form images of.

No Harmonization or Mixing

The Bible does not describe any scientific facts but interprets them, also for our present-day human life and action. Both levels of language and thought need always to be neatly separated if the fatal misunderstandings of the past on both sides, science and theology, are to be avoided. Scientific language and religious language are no more comparable than scientific language and poetic language. That means that the Big Bang theory and creation faith, evolutionary theory and the creation of human beings, do not contradict each other, but they are not to be harmonized either. The "scientific" interpretation of Genesis as creation in six million days or as flood geology in H. Morris and J. Whitcomb, *The Genesis Flood* (1961), leads us astray.

Our biblical interpretation does not have to work out a core of what can be proved by science, but what is indispensable for faith and life. Science does not have to "prove" the existence or superfluity of God. Rather, it has to advance the explicability of our universe by physics as far as possible and at the same time leave room for what in principle cannot be explained by physics. That is what the Bible talks about.

So there must be no mixing of the two languages: the language of the Bible, as the physicist Werner Heisenberg puts it, is a kind of lan-

---

34. Cf. B. H. F. Taureck, *Metaphern und Gleichnisse in der Philosophie. Versuch einer kritischen Ikonologie der Philosophie* (Frankfurt am Main, 2004).

guage "which makes possible an understanding about the context of the world that can be detected beyond the phenomena, without which we could not gain any ethics or scale of values. . . . This language is more closely related to the language of poetry than to that of science, which is orientated on precision." Therefore the words in the two languages often mean different things:

> The heaven spoken of in the Bible has little to do with the heaven into which we see airplanes or rockets take off. In the astronomical universe the earth is only a tiny speck of dust in one of the countless Milky Way systems, but for us it is the centre of the world — it is really the centre of the world. Science attempts to give an objective meaning to its terms. But religious language must avoid splitting the world into its objective and its subjective side; for who could assert that the objective side was more real than the subjective side? So we may not confuse the two languages; we must think in a more subtle way than was customary before.[35]

Moreover, answering the basic human questions is a matter of basic personal attitude:

- The Soviet cosmonaut Yuri Gagarin, the first man to orbit the earth on 12 April 1961, proclaimed afterward in accordance with Marxist materialist dogma: "There's no God to be seen up here." Later he explicitly took up religion.
- The American commandant of the Apollo spacecraft, Frank Borman, who was the first astronaut to orbit the moon, on Holy Saturday 1968, fascinated by the beauty of our blue planet and grateful in the darkness of the universe for the gift of light and life, read out the first verses of Genesis: "In the beginning God created heaven and earth. And the earth was without form and void. And darkness

35. W. Heisenberg, "Naturwissenschaftliche und religiöse Wahrheit" (speech made at the Catholic Academy in Bavaria on receiving the Guardini Prize on 23 Mar. 1973), in *Schritt über Grenzen. Gesammelte Reden und Aufsätze,* 2nd enlarged ed. (Munich, 1973), 335-51, here 348.

lay on the deep, and the spirit of God hovered over the waters. And God said, Let there be light, and there was light."

- The German physicist and astronaut Ulrich Walter, who took part in the German space shuttle mission D-2 in 1993, saw under the blazing sun our blue-white planet, and faced with the otherwise impressively monotonous black depths of the universe that were hostile to life, had similar experiences of solitude to those of Blaise Pascal: "the Copernican revolution which I experienced quite personally."[36] He himself believes in a creator God, though not one who corresponds with the notions and dogmas of the church: "Does a space flight bring a person nearer to God or not?" His answer was: "That depends on the individual."[37]

Indeed, here the biblical testimony calls for a decision.

6. The Testimony of Faith to the Ultimate Origin

Science can neither confirm nor refute what the two accounts of Genesis proclaim as their clear message: in the beginning of the world is God. So it is not "in the beginning was the Bang," but "in the beginning was the word, the will, and there was light; there was energy, matter, space and time."

Creation of Space and Time from Nothing

Here we are speaking only in an inauthentic way of a "before" the creation of the world. What was God doing before he created heaven and earth? Augustine in chapter 11 of his *Confessions* already gave a precise answer to this question, which he regarded as impertinent. He was brief and terse: the question was meaningless; the question about the "before" was superfluous. Why? Because the world was not created in

36. U. Walter, ". . . weil euer Gott im Himmel ist!" in *Im Anfang war (k)ein Gott,* ed. T. D. Wabbel (Düsseldorf, 2004), 246.
37. Walter, ". . . weil euer Gott im Himmel ist!" 247.

time, but with time; to this degree Einstein agreed with him. So only the creator is "before" the cosmos, only eternity is "before" time; here Augustine goes further than Einstein and addresses God: "Furthermore, although you are before time, it is not in time that you precede it. If this were so, you would not be before all time. It is in eternity, which is supreme over time because it is a never-ending present, that you are at once before all past time and after all future time."[38] Thus from a theological perspective the act of creation is a timeless act; it comes about through time. And time is created time, created time-space, created space-time.[39]

Now what does it mean to talk of creating the world "from nothing"? In the Bible, as I have said, this is only a later notion, the fruit of Hellenistic reflection. It does not mean the nothing becoming independent, as it were an empty black space before or alongside God. Nothingness must not be confused either with the "vacuum" of modern particle physics, whose "fluctuations" perhaps stand at the beginning of our universe, and which is in no way a nothing, but a something. What is meant rather is absolute nothing, which excludes any material cause in the act of creation. Creation "from nothing" is the philosophical and theological expression of the fact that the world and human beings along with space and time owe themselves solely to God and not to another cause.

But God does not owe himself to any cause. One may not even call God *causa sui* (cause of himself), as Descartes and Spinoza did. He is not caused at all. He is by definition the uncaused reality, because it is eternal and perfect: *Id quo maius cogitari nequit* — "that than which nothing greater can be thought" (Anselm of Canterbury, Descartes). The Bible does not philosophize about this. But it does express the conviction that the world is radically dependent on God as the author and sustainer of all being yet also remains independent of God. Christian theology has maintained that creation continues: *creatio continua*. For our present understanding, only in this way is the coming to being of

---

38. Augustine, *Confessions* 11.13.

39. For the history of the concept of time, cf. K. Mainzer, *Zeit. Von der Urzeit zur Computerzeit* (Munich, 1999).

the world as an ongoing process in time possible as a process that does not exclude the origination of new structures but includes them.

Creation from nothing and ongoing creation must thus be seen as a unity — both are the condition of the possibility of physical processes generally: *"Creatio continua* and *creatio ex nihilo* would simply be two names for one and the same creative activity of the eternal God, itself timeless and at the same time appointing time. And this one and the same creative activity of God would not lie beyond in a singularity billions of years away, but would be strictly present to us, beyond our control, but nearer to us than we are to ourselves."[40]

What Is the Meaning of Belief in Creation Today?

In images and parables of their time the biblical accounts of creation answer simple basic questions that also arise for human beings of today and that science cannot answer with its method and language. What are answered in the Bible are not purely theoretical questions but elementary existential questions:

- What was at the beginning? The good God, who is the origin of each and all.
- Is anything else (star, animal, or human being) God alongside God? No, there is no God but God.
- But aren't a good principle and an evil principle obviously fighting one another in world history? No, God is the good God who is not in competition with any evil or demonic counterprinciple.
- Isn't part of reality of a lesser quality: matter as compared to spirit, sexuality as compared to spirituality? By no means, the world of the good creator God, and thus also matter, the human body, and sexuality, is fundamentally good. "God saw all that he had made and it was very good" (Gen. 1:31).
- What is the goal of the process of creation? The human being — not

40. U. Lüke, "Schöpfung aus den Nichts oder fortlaufende Schöpfung? Zum Verhältnis von creatio ex nihilo und creatio continua," in *Kosmologie. Fragen nach Evolution und Eschatologie der Welt,* ed. H. A. Müller (Göttingen, 2004), 39-52, here 50.

isolated but in the midst of the cosmos — is the great goal of the process of creation. According to the Bible, it is not first a redemption but already the creation that represents God's gracious concern for the world and human beings. The preservation of the world can be seen as continued creation and evolution.

We can ask ourselves: Is it pure chance that modern science could develop in particular against the background of the Jewish and Christian doctrine of creation? Two basic insights that the Qur'an also stresses were beyond doubt helpful presuppositions here:

- The world is not God; it is created and not holy in itself; it has been put at the disposal of human beings.
- The world is not chaos but ordered, cosmos; it may be used, built on, investigated by human beings.

So what sense can it still make today in respect of the beginning of the world not only — scientifically — to speak of a Big Bang, of models of the world and theories of the cosmos, but also with full justification — theologically — to speak of a God who has created the cosmos, as countless people from the Hebrew Bible on, Jews, Christians, and Muslims but also many others, have confessed time and again?

Belief in creation adds nothing to the instrumental knowledge that science has so infinitely enriched; it does not offer any scientific information. But creation faith gives us an orientating knowledge — particularly in a time of rapid scientific, economic, cultural, and political revolutions and therefore of uprooting and loss of orientation. It allows people to discover a meaning in life and in the process of evolution, and may provide them with standards for behavior and an ultimate security in this unimaginably great universe. Even in the age of space travel, when they reflect on the amazing results of astrophysics and as always look out at the starry night sky, people will ask themselves: What does it all mean? Where is it going? Does nothingness explain anything? Is reason satisfied with that?

The only serious alternative, one pure reason, like so much else, cannot prove because it transcends its horizon of experience, yet for which there are good reasons, an answer that is thus completely rational, is that the whole does not come from a Big Bang but from an origin. It comes from that first creative ground of grounds that we call God, the creator God.

Even if I cannot prove it, I can still assert it with good reason: in that enlightened trust in which I have already affirmed the existence of God, which is so rational and so tested for me. For if the God who exists is truly God, then he is not just God now, for me here and today, but God already in the beginning, God from all eternity. Only in this way, it seems to me, does the universe become plausible to us in its existence as cosmos, in its mathematically ordered, highly complex, and tremendously dynamic nature. And in the face of the magnitude of our universe and the complexity of science, many scientists have shown feelings of amazement, of reverence, of joy, and even of terror and thus have also asked whether this universe does not embrace more than the apparent — a question that cannot be answered by science but only by a rational trust that has its grounds and that we call faith.

So believing in the creator of the world today does not mean believing in some myths, nor does it mean imagining God as creator in the way in which for example the incomparable Michelangelo as an artist painted him in a completely human way on the ceiling of the Sistine Chapel. Here all notions come to an end. Nor does believing in God as the creator of the world mean deciding for this or that one of the changing models of the world that great scientists have worked out. And this is not because here the issue is one of presupposing all models of the world and the world itself. Even an eternal world of the kind assumed for example by Aristotle would be compatible with belief in God. This was the view of Thomas Aquinas, though on the basis of the Bible he was convinced that the world had a temporal beginning. That the eternal God is before all time does not mean a temporal but an ontological priority.

Today, to believe in the creator of the world against the horizon of scientific cosmology means to affirm in enlightened truth that the ultimate origin of the world and human beings does not remain inexplicable; that the world and human beings have not been senselessly thrown from nothing into nothing; but that as a whole they are meaningful and valuable, not chaos but cosmos, because they have their primal ground, their author, a creator, a first and last security in God.

Once again it must be emphasized that nothing compels us to this faith. We can decide for it in complete freedom. Once we have decided for it, however, this faith changes our position in the world, our attitude to the world. Anyone who believes in God as the creator can with good reason also fully affirm the world and human beings as God's creation. The person can:

- above all, respect *human beings* as our fellow human beings (and not as lesser beings);
- but also respect and cultivate nonhuman nature, particularly the *animals,* as our *environment and the world with which we live* (and not as our born enemies, not as material to be used at random).

It is not although I am God's creature, but because I am God's creature, and because my fellow creatures and my environment are God's creatures, that I, my fellow human beings, and also — for all the difference — animals receive a dignity that has to be respected. The "Fill the earth and subdue it" of the creation story (Gen. 1:28) cannot be understood as carte blanche for unscrupulous exploitation and destruction of nature and the environment, certainly not in an age when we soberly contemplate the "limits of growth." Believing in the creator God allows me to take my responsibility for fellow human beings and the environment and the tasks imposed on me with greater seriousness, with more realism and hope.

"In Light Inaccessible"

The primal ground of grounds cannot be fathomed. But one thing is certain for the Jewish-Christian-Muslim tradition: God is not an abyss of darkness — darkness cannot bring forth light. Rather, he is the fullness of light, who alone makes the "Let there be light" in the cosmos possible.

In all religions light is an excellent metaphor, an old pictorial word for the supreme reality, for God — and modern scientific research into light helps us to a deeper understanding of the religious and symbolic significance of light. For what is light? An electromagnetic wave that spreads at maximum speed — a reality that is still mysterious even to physicists, which seems to have contradictory properties, showing itself sometimes as a wave and sometimes as quantum particles. As we saw, this is a *concidentia oppositorum:* two different images at the same time, that of the wave and that of the particle, which are mutually exclusive and yet supplement each other. As is well known, the great Danish nuclear physicist Niels Bohr, the teacher of Heisenberg and a whole generation of physicists ("the Copenhagen interpretation"), introduced the term "complementarity" for this: we need both contradictory images to explain the mystery of light. And such complementarity of opposite images and concepts is also needed to describe the mystery of God.

The nature of light is constantly being further explored, and perhaps one day it will be possible to explain the mystery of light. But the mystery of God remains: God remains the infinite, immeasurable, unfathomable, and unites in himself opposites such as eternity and temporality, distance and nearness, justice and mercy, anger and grace. He is as hidden in the cosmos as in my heart, decidedly more than a person and yet capable of being addressed at any time. We cannot penetrate God's spirit any more than we can penetrate the sun: "How great you are," we read in Psalm 104:1-2, "you veil yourself in light." Or in the New Testament: in us and around us is darkness, but God dwells "in light inaccessible" (1 Tim. 6:15f.): "God is light, and in him there is no darkness" (1 John 1:5).

So God is the primal light that sends out its illuminating, warming, and healing power into the cosmos. "Let there be light. And there was light." I began my introduction with these statements from the book of Genesis. "And God saw that the light was good." Good for the world and good for human beings. Verses from Ingeborg Bachmann's poem "To the Sun" express this and may speak to both scientists and theologians in the same way:

Much more beautiful than the fiery display of a comet
And so much more beautiful than any planet,
Because your life and my life depend on it daily, is the sun. . . .

Beautiful light, which keeps us warm, sustains and marvelously
ensures
That I see again, and that I see you again!

Nothing more beautiful under the sun than to be under the sun.[41]

Moreover: "If we become increasingly humble about how little we
know, we may be more eager to search." Thus Sir John Templeton, who
has done more than others for an understanding between science and
religion.[42] This builds the bridge to the fourth chapter, about a further
basic question, now well prepared for, in which research likewise has
made tremendous progress: the question of the beginning of life in the
cosmos, of the chance and necessity of a development that has amazingly been followed and leads up to the mind, the human being.

41. I. Bachmann, "To the Sun," in *One Hundred Great Poems of the Twentieth Century*, ed. Mark Strand (New York: Norton, 2005), 58-59.
42. J. Templeton, *John Templeton Foundation* (Radnor, Pa., 2004), 9.

CHAPTER IV

Life in the Cosmos?

—⟨⟨⟋⟍⟩⟩—

The Bible and science agree on at least one thing: at the beginning of the history of our planet there was no life. The European space probe Huygens has shown how "without form and void" the earth was shortly before the origin of the first life around 3.5 billion years ago. After a seven-year journey of 3.2 billion kilometers, on 14 January 2005 with amazing accuracy it landed on Titan, one of Saturn's moons — the only moon with an atmosphere. This was a triumph for science, which emphasizes the question: If according to the theory of evolution the history of our earth from beginning to end is a calculable, coherent, and successful development, if everything stands under the law of cause and effect — within the world — and if every step clearly follows from the previous one, where is there room for a special intervention of God? In the origin of life or later in the creation of human beings? This chapter will discuss the origin of life (biogenesis), and the next chapter the origin of human beings (hominization).

1. How Long Has There Been Life?

Both scientific research and biblical criticism have made it increasingly plausible that the paradise tradition about Adam and Eve and their fall (Gen. 1–3; Rom. 5:12-21) is to be understood as a symbolic narrative of human beings as such (Hebrew *adam* = the human being, or human beings = collective). It does not offer any historical accounts of a concrete human couple; the "monogenism" — the descent of all men and women from Adam and Eve — still propagated by Pope Pius XII — is hardly still advocated today, even by Catholic theologians. The first chapters of the Bible are not concerned to make scientific statements but to give a religious interpretation of the basic human situation from the beginning.[1]

Time and again theologians have attempted to introduce decisive breaks, before the history of human origins and the miracles of the Old Testament, where the causal course was interrupted and allegedly a direct "supernatural" intervention of God was needed in the otherwise undisturbed course of history. But after all the theological rearguard actions, theologians today must at least concede that both the cosmos as a whole and human beings have developed "naturally," at least in their bodies. Life developed about 3.5 billion years ago on our earth, and there have been human beings for about 200,000 years. So not only theologians must ask: Is it right still to insist that life, and even more the human spirit ("soul"), came into being by the direct intervention of the creator? But first comes the question: Can life be defined, distinguished from the inanimate? What is "life"?[2]

What Is "Life"?

Aristotle, the founder of scientific biology, postulated as the characteristic of all life the capacity for self-movement or its own dynamic. Here he already distinguished three forms of life:

• vegetative plant life with the capacities for nourishment, growth, and multiplication;

1. Cf. H. Haag, *Biblische Schöpfungslehre und kirchliche Erbsündenlehre*, 4th ed. (Stuttgart, 1968); U. Baumann, *Erbsünde? Ihr traditionelles Verständnis in der Krise heutiger Theologie* (Freiburg im Breisgau, 1970).

2. Cf. the popular accounts by S. E. Luria, *Life — the Unfinished Experiment* (New York, 1973), chap. 11, "Mind"; H. von Ditfurth, *Der Geist fiel nicht vom Himmel. Die Evolution unseres Bewusstseins* (Hamburg, 1976); B. O. Küppers, ed., *Leben = Physik + Chemie? Das Lebendige aus der Sicht bedeutender Physiker* (Munich, 1987).

- sensitive animal life with the capacities for perception, movement, striving;
- the rational life of the spirit: an *anima* (principle of life) not only *vegetativa* or *sensitiva* but *rationalis* with the capacity for knowledge and freedom of decision, the basis for the experience of morality, beauty, and meaning. Augustine, and even more resolutely Thomas Aquinas, later put forward the view that every human spiritual soul was directly created out of nothing by God (creationism) and not produced by procreation from parents (generationism).

Present-day biologists refrain from giving a philosophical definition of life because of the metaphysical implications and because of the countless transitions from the inanimate to the animate even at the level of physics and chemistry. They content themselves with describing the minimum demands, necessary structural and dynamic properties. Today there may be said to be a consensus that all living beings have three main dynamic characteristics:

- capacity to generate organisms of the same species: *reproduction;*
- hereditary changes as a presupposition for the origin of a diversity of living beings: *mutation;*
- the guidance of the change of material so that it accepts and replaces energy and material from the environment: *metabolism.*

The living is always individual: living beings are structures marked off from the environment, the smallest unit of which is the cell. So just as exciting as the question of what defines "life" is the question of where "life" exists. One much-discussed question is: Are we alone in the universe?

Are We Alone in the Universe?

To put it directly: Is there elsewhere in the universe life, on other planets of our solar system or on other stars of our Milky Way, which is 10 billion years old? I am aware that science fiction films and literature have done more to shape the ideas of many people about the "extraterrestrial" than any serious science. And why not devise hypotheses and models for oneself? The possibility of life elsewhere is not to be excluded a priori. However, one would in fact have to find somewhere in the universe a planet with similar physical conditions to those prevailing on earth: the right distance from the sun and the right temperature, the necessary elements in the right proportions. . . . All this doesn't seem too difficult, for it has been ascertained that the clouds spun off in past stellar explosions show a wealth of molecules of interstellar matter such as carbons, silicates, water, and so on that are necessary for the development of life.

Up until the 1960s there was speculation — and not just in the New Age and esoteric scene — about UFOs, unidentified flying objects. Such disc- or cigar-shaped "saucers" have not been demonstrated anywhere; they were recognized as natural or artificial phenomena or even unmasked as deliberate hoaxes. And how could they have flown through hundreds of thousands of light-years (one light-year = 9 billion kilometers) without then landing among us visibly?

Stimulated by an article by the physicists Giuseppe Gocconi and Philip Morrison in the journal *Nature,* a conference was held in 1960 in Green Park, West Virginia, under the title "Search for Extra Terrestrial Intelligence." As early as 1962, in the National Radio Astronomy Observatory, a radio telescope was set up that had a reflector with a diameter of 91.5 meters, though it was to collapse twelve years later.

It was here that the young astronomer Frank Drake (born 1930) was the first to search the universe systematically for soft extraterrestrial radio signals. In 1961 he had apparently put forward well-founded calculations and conjectures about the rate of production by which stars form, about the number of stars with planets, and about the number of planets on which life could exist. On the other hand, he also produced figures about the average age of technological civilizations (high cultures). With this logic he arrived at a figure of about 10,000 civilizations in our Milky Way that should be capable of interstellar communication. In subsequent years he looked for their radio signals in space.[3]

---

3. Cf. F. D. Drake, *Intelligent Life in Space* (New York, 1962). Since 1964 Drake has been a professor at Cornell University.

Life in the Cosmos?

From the beginning Drake was efficiently supported in the dissemination of his ideas by the equally young Carl Sagan (1934-96), who, like Drake, was called as an astronomer to Cornell University in the 1970s and became famous far beyond the USA as the author of a major television series about the cosmos.[4] Sagan increased the estimated number of extraterrestrial civilizations in our Milky Way to a million. He was intensively involved in the preparation of the NASA space expeditions and the unmanned space probes Mariner, Viking, and Voyager. He saw to it that Voyager was given a message about humankind for the other civilizations in space: a gold-plated aluminum plate (around 14 × 23 centimeters) containing drawings of the situation of the sun and planets and two human beings, man and woman, with a scale comparison to the solar antennae of the probe.[5]

More and more astronomers are now accepting the view that isolated civilizations exist all over the universe between the glowing "fixed stars" on planets dispersed from one another like grains of sand. Indeed, a whole science and industry developed on the basis of this impulse to make contact with one of the supposed extraterrestrial civilizations. Countless films (such as *ET*), TV shows, popular publications, and scientific enterprises of all kinds were produced on the basis of this hypothesis — not to mention all the attempts to trap radio signals from possible planets of other stars or to send out signals of their own. What was the result?

A Vain Quest

What has been discovered after all this tremendous scientific, financial, and journalistic expenditure of billions on life in the universe? So far virtually nothing. All the attempts were unsuccessful. No one from a distant planet has made any contact with us earth dwellers that is scientifically demonstrable — not to mention hostile or peaceful extraterrestrial visitors on our earth. Rather, the most recent space research has shown the opposite: complex life on other planets and their moons is

4. Cf. C. Sagan, *Cosmos* (New York, 1980).
5. Described in Sagan, *Murmurs of Earth* (New York, 1978).

highly improbable, at least in our solar system. Indeed, in February 2004 a report appeared in the *New York Times* under the headline "Maybe There Isn't Anyone 'Out There': After Years of the Quest for Extraterrestrials We Are Perhaps Alone in the Universe."[6]

The article refers to the most recent astronomical publication with the provocative title *Rare Earth*, written by Peter Ward, a paleontologist and specialist in the mass extermination of species (especially the dinosaurs), and Donald Brownlee (likewise of the University of Washington, Seattle), a well-known astronomer and chief scientist for the NASA Stardust project for collecting interplanetary and interstellar stardust. Their conclusion is that all the environments surrounding our earth in the universe are terrible for life; only on a "paradise garden" such as our earth could life arise. Not only Mars but also all the larger planets discovered thus far outside our solar system are completely unsuitable for the development of complex life.

So the theoretical physicist Harald Lesch of the University of Münster openly stated in 2005: "We have searched and searched but nothing has emerged. Nothing at all. Possibly we will have to listen to the universe for thousands of years to find any signal from an extraterrestrial civilization. This was at least the view of some experts who after 20 years of vain efforts thought that possibly we would have to look for 5,000 to 6,000 years by our reckoning until we had a reasonable chance of finding the others. Be this as it may — nothing has been discovered."[7] And according to Lesch, that isn't all that surprising. Why? In fact, an extraordinarily large number of difficult conditions had to be fulfilled for life to be possible on Earth. Such a planet had to have a mean temperature of around 15° Celsius. So it could not be like the glowingly hot Venus (450° Celsius surface temperature), which orbits closer to the Sun, or, farther out, like the ice-cold Mars (-70° Celsius mean temperature), where there can be no flowing water. Such a planet should not turn too quickly on its own axis to avoid stormy winds (here

6. W. J. Broad, "Maybe There Isn't Anyone 'Out There,'" *New York Times/International Herald Tribune,* 9 Feb. 2004.

7. H. Lesch, "Begegnungen mit der dritten Art — Gibt es ausserirdische Intelligenz?" radio broadcast on SWR 2, 16 Jan. 2005; Lesch, *Physik für die Westentasche* (Munich, 2003).

the Moon acts as a brake on our earth). At the same time, it should be protected as far as possible from the impact of great lumps of stone (large, heavy Jupiter on the outermost planetary orbit keeps a long way from our earth). Indeed, the more one reflects on the conditions for life on a planet, the less probable the existence of extraterrestrials appears in our broader environment.

The six *Star Wars* films of George Lucas with their noble space travelers, extraterrestrial wizened gnomes, slapstick robots, and the tragic demonic darkling Darth Vader are therefore — some of the countless fans may be disappointed to realize — pure mythology with no empirical basis. Of course, no one can theoretically exclude the possibility that somewhere far out in the universe there is life, and theology too has nothing to fear from such discoveries. But for us human beings on planet Earth whose elementary basis of life is being threatened, it may be as relevant as the sensational news that went through the media in 2004: a European satellite had recorded one of the greatest collisions in the universe. But where did the thousands of galaxies clash? According to information from the observatories, 8,000 million light-years away! So we needn't worry: these hurricane-like conditions are far away in the universe when one thinks that the diameter of our Milky Way alone, a disc galaxy, is "only" 100,000 light-years, which means that a light signal takes 100,000 years to travel from one end to the other. The nearest great Milky Way, the Andromeda Nebula, is already 2.2 million light-years away. What we can see today in the large photographs of the Hubble telescope in fact took place in the Andromeda Nebula 2.2 million years ago. So the collision of galaxies reported in 2004, 8,000 million light-years away, does not represent the slightest danger for humankind; it is no reason for alarmism or even expensive armament in the universe.

The most recent results of the Mars probes suggest that while there is rich carbon material on the Red Planet with its thin atmosphere, there is no flowing water and consequently no complex life, i.e., no more than bacteria and viruses. On Saturn's moon Titan, according to data from the Huygens probe, there are only similar geophysical activities to those on earth; we have indications of clashes, erosion, and flows. But the chemical processes are fundamentally different on this cold and alien moon: at -170° Celsius there is no water, but only fluid and gaseous methane. That makes all the more urgent the question:

2. How Did Life Arise?

Very much more relevant for our present than news of distant galaxies is the indisputable insight that all life on our earth appears interrelated. It is characterized by anticlockwise molecules (there are no clockwise molecules) that presumably all have the same origin. Above all, though, living beings are made up of genes that demonstrate the same four basic building blocks. For us human beings today a third question is more important than the concern to define life, more important too than a quest for life outside our planet: the question of the origin of life.

The Vehicles of Life

In this question in particular the biology of recent decades has sensational successes to record, so much so that Darwin's theory of evolution may now be regarded as grounded in physics and proved experimentally, not only at the level of the living cell but even at the level of the molecule. Darwin already expressed the hope that one day the principle of life would be recognized as part of or the consequence of a universal law. But what seemed a dream only a few decades ago has now become reality: molecular biology, since the middle of the twentieth century something like the new basis of biology, has discovered this law. James D. Watson and Francis H. C. Crick were awarded the Nobel Prize in 1962 for their double helix model of the structure of hereditary matter. This revolutionized biology, just as physics had been revolutionized a little earlier by quantum mechanics.

What was discovered about bacteria and viruses also applies to higher organisms and presumably to all life on this planet: the elementary vehicles of life and its basic characteristics are two classes of macromolecules, namely, nucleic acids and proteins, which have the form of a double spiral staircase, one inserted in the other, the famous double helix (Greek *helix* = spiral). In brief, it functions like this:

136

The vehicles of the hereditary properties of organisms are chain molecules of nucleic acids of the type DNA, which consist of long specific sequences with four different members (adenine, cytosine, guanine, and thymine) and occur primarily in the nucleus of the cell. The blueprint of the living being lies in the sequence of members, so to speak enciphered in the genetic code. These sequences are reproduced by a kind of printing process and thus hand on equal inherited substance from cell to cell and from generation to generation. But errors in reproduction can cause mutations and thus lead to organisms with changed hereditary characteristics.

How does the inherited substance DNA guide what happens in the cell? Primarily by the copying of sections of the DNA. The proteins function as catalysts for the change of material. They take over the "information" from the nucleic acids and carry out the functions of the living cell transferred to them through this arrangement of structure and function. That is how life functions and propagates itself: a "wonderworld" at the most elementary level, wherein the smallest space molecules often undergo their changes in a millionth of a second.

One instinctively asks: Is there perhaps a mysterious act of creation behind the origin of life, which so orders the individual atoms, for example in the formation of crystals, that life can come about? But individual atoms also find their way to their precise position amazingly quickly without a specific act of creation. Why not also in the origin of life? Is a creator or at least an organizer really needed?

Matter Organizes Itself

We still do not know for certain how life first arose from the inanimate. We do not know for certain what precise events introduced biogenesis. But we do know one thing: however this transition to life is explained in detail, it rests on biochemical regularities and thus on the self-organization of matter, the molecule. And just as ever more complex molecules and systems formed from the primal matter through electric charges, so life based on carbon formed from nucleic acids and proteins.

But why does evolution ascend to the higher species without being compelled or guided by external factors? That is the great discovery: the principle of natural selection and the survival of the fittest that Darwin first established in the plant and animal world holds even at the level of the molecule. This tendency toward "fitness" drives the development inexorably upward at the expense of less fit molecules. This leads to the development of unicellular and then of multicellular living beings, and finally of higher plants and animals.

There are still large gaps in our knowledge of the early stages and especially the beginnings of life on earth, but some broad features are emerging. In what follows I shall go by the scenarios that the longtime director of the Tübingen Max Planck Institute for Developmental Biology, Alfred Gierer, has summed up.[8]

In an early phase 3 billion years ago there was still no life on earth. But there were chemical conditions for the formation of nucleic acids of the RNA type with purely fortuitous sequences of their members. Here quite by chance, however rarely, RNA molecules formed that in a folded state themselves accelerated the synthesis of the nucleic acids as a catalyst: the same self-multiplication in conjunction with the change of matter and mutability was the starting pistol for life, so to speak. From there through the extension, mutation, and selection of RNA sequences there was an "invention" of fundamental biochemical processes and structures, above all the RNA-guided protein synthesis. From the RNA the role of the inherited substance could pass over to the DNA, which was closely related chemically, but had a double strand, and this dramatically increased the accuracy of the reproduction of the inherited substance.

Later, cells developed the capacity for photosynthesis: sunlight became directly usable as a source of energy for the change of matter and thus enriched the acid, which initially did not exist. Single cells arose with ever more complicated structures and functions: mechanisms for movement and stimulation, ion channels in the cell membranes that had already formed earlier; this made possible the extraordinarily rapid transfer and assimilation of electrical signals that were decisive for the later development of nerve cells of animals. Moreover, the possibilities

8. Cf. A. Gierer, *Biologie, Menschenbild und die knappe Ressource Gemeinsinn* (Würzburg, 2005), 15-22.

and speed of evolution were increased by mechanisms of the sexual, two-gender multiplication of cells.

A further essential step was the evolution of multicellular living beings and a differentiation of cells that through a complicated network of gene manipulation made possible cells with the same inherited substance and different stable conditions, such as muscle or nerve cells. With the help of ever new "discoveries" (for example, of "repair enzymes"), ever higher levels of complexity developed that finally allowed a reliable copying of sequences of billions of blocks of DNA. This was absolutely necessary for the inherited substance of mammals and human beings.

The evolution of multicellular organisms finally led to the formation and structures of higher plants and animals, which in each generation developed in an extremely impressive process from the egg cell after being fertilized: "Just as our senses are impressed by the beauty of biological forms, so our mind is fascinated by the subtle forms of animal behaviour. Their rich repertoire of behaviour is the result of the evolution of the brain. Behaviour is based on the incorporation of information into the network of neurons, in the form of chemical, and above all also electrochemical, signals."[9]

In the case of human beings, I shall investigate the philosophical and theological problems presented by the brain. It is certain that according to the most recent results of biochemistry it is impossible to see that this highly complex process needed a special intervention of the creator God. On the given material presuppositions and despite all the still unanswered questions, the origin of life is an event that can be understood by physics and chemistry. But is pure chance dominant in all this?

3. Chance or Necessity?

Decades ago there was a vigorous dispute between vitalism, which assumed a nonbiological element, a creative life force, indeed primal

9. Gierer, *Biologie,* 19.

force, that guided biological forces (Henri Bergson called it *élan vital*)[10] to explain life, and materialistic mechanism, which attempted to explain life in accordance with purely mechanical laws.[11] In some respects both were right: there is both law *and* chance, structure *and* novelty. Here the same problems emerge as in quantum mechanics: an indeterminacy, vagueness, chance element in the individual processes. Beyond doubt the overall course of biological evolution is necessary, guided by laws. Nevertheless, the higher development time and again stood at a crossroads, and often nature took both ways: for example, toward the insects and the mammals at the same time. And often it went no further: some species arose that later degenerated or completely disappeared again, dead ends in evolution.

The Primacy of Chance?

The temporal sequence of individual events is in fact undetermined: the ways of evolution in detail are not established a priori. The abrupt, microscopically small hereditary changes (mutations) from which by avalanche-like growth or swings sudden undirected changes and new phenomena result in the macroscopic sphere are fortuitous. But perhaps both change and necessity prevail together. The Greek philosopher and atomist Democritus (ca. 470-380 B.C.E.) had already written: "Everything that exists in the universe is the fruit of chance and necessity." Under this motto the French molecular biologist Jacques Monod of Paris, who in 1965 was awarded the Nobel Prize for the development of the genetic guidance of the enzyme and virus synthesis, wrote his well-known book *Chance and Necessity*. But he firmly accorded the precedence to chance: "pure chance, not as the fortuitous, but absolute, blind freedom as the basis for the miraculous edifice of evolution."[12] So

10. Cf. H. Bergson, *Creative Evolution* (1907; New York, 1944).

11. Cf. L. Büchner, *Kraft und Stoff* (Leipzig, 1855; 21st ed. 1904); J. Moleschott, *Der Kreislauf des Lebens* (Heidelberg, 1852).

12. J. Monod, *Chance and Necessity* (London, 1972); German, *Zufall und Notwendigkeit. Philosophische Fragen der modernen Biologie,* preface to the German edition by M. Eigen, 5th ed. (Munich, 1973), 141. Cf. Luria, *Life,* 120: "Man is but one product, albeit a very special one, of a series of blind chances and harsh neces-

is everything chance, and simply by virtue of that is there no need for a creator and sustainer of this edifice? Monod is right in two respects.

A confessed atheist, Monod rightly attacks the assumption of an evolutionary force or energy given a priori that is to explain the rise of evolution and lead to an Omega Point. According to Monod, this "force" or "energy" of the "vitalists" that comes from nineteenth-century belief in progress and is also held by Teilhard de Chardin represents an "animist projection" that is scientifically illegitimate.[13]

Monod, a former communist, also rightly attacks a purely materialistic biology that attributes an unknown and unknowable force to matter. According to Monod, this too is an "animistic projection" and an "anthropocentric illusion" that is "incompatible with science" and clearly signals the epistemological collapse of dialectical materialism.[14]

But the question is whether Monod is also right to attack a creator God whom he wants to exclude with his theory as radically as dialectical materialism. We need to investigate this question more closely.

Natural Laws Guide Chance

In his book *The Game* (1975), the German physical chemist Manfred Eigen of the University of Göttingen, who had been awarded the Nobel Prize in 1967 for his investigations of the kinetics of very rapid chemical reactions, formulated the counterthesis to Monod that today is largely shared by biologists: "Laws of nature direct chance"[15] is his programmatic subtitle. Or as Eigen writes in his preface to the German edition of Monod: "However much the individual form owes its origin to chance, the process of selection and evolution is absolutely necessary.

---

sities." However, the basic attitude of the American cancer researcher and Nobel Prize winner is not existentially pessimistic, like that of Monod, but quite optimistic in an American way; cf. 7, 148-60. But isn't the "Genesis prophecy" ("You will be like God and know what is good and evil"), which Luria sees fulfilled in the progress of science, a saying of the serpent's!

13. Cf. Monod, *Chance and Necessity,* 40.

14. Cf. Monod, *Chance and Necessity,* 46, 48.

15. Cf. M. Eigen and R. Winkler, *Das Spiel. Naturgesetze steuern den Zufall* (Munich, 1975); E. Schoffeniels, *L'anti-hasard* (Paris, 1973), is one-sided.

Not more! So there is no mysterious 'vital property' inherent in matter which would finally also determine the cause of history. But at the same time not less — not *just* chance."[16] "So does God play dice?" the Viennese biologist Rupert Riedl also asks: "Certainly, but he follows his own rules. And only the span between the two gives us meaning and freedom at the same time."[17]

Does that, we may ask, also apply to what physicists today in a dramatic way (which is open to misunderstanding) call chaos? Certainly. Even "chaos" is not outside the laws of causality. The Greek *chaos* originally meant empty space, the formless primal mass, but today in everyday language it usually means complete confusion. However, in physics chaos means a hypersensitive complex system of the kind that is evident, say, in the weather, in which extremely small causes have great effects. A much-quoted example is that the flapping of a butterfly's wing in the Caribbean could produce a whirlwind in the USA. In fact, such a system, in which solutions are irregular and periods cannot be established, can be predicted at best in the short term and in the long term not at all. The network of causal partial systems is so complicated that the resultant pattern of movement seems to be "chance." Chaos theory[18] nevertheless now attempts with the help of computers to give a mathematical and physical description of such dynamic systems (for example, in fluid mechanics, electronics, or quantum mechanics) characterized by a determined chance behavior and the formation of chaotic structures. All this means that causal connections remain even in "chaos," and order can be established even in chaotic disorder.

So for the explanation of evolution, chance or necessity, indeterminacy or determinacy, indeed materialism or idealism are false alternatives. But assuming that God plays dice within the rules, the question still remains: Is it really God who is playing dice? Don't self-organizing matter and self-regulating evolution make God superfluous?

16. Eigen, preface to *Zufall und Notwendigkeit,* by Monod, xv.

17. R. Riedl, *Die Strategie der Genesis. Naturgeschichte der realen Welt* (Munich, 1976), 122.

18. Cf. A. Kunick and W.-H. Steeb, *Chaos in dynamischen Systemen* (Mannheim, 1986); the work was revised and expanded in 1989, and "written for students who have heard introductory lectures on physics and mathematics."

Is God Superfluous?

Monod is certainly not alone among biologists in his negative view. How are we to respond to it? I would like to make a distinction. It is an unfounded assumption — here I would agree with Monod — to postulate the existence of God on the basis of the transition from the inanimate world to the biosphere or even on the basis of the molecular indeterminacy; this would merely be a pernicious God of the gaps. Here the biologist Eigen agrees with the biologist Monod.

> The "origin of life," i.e. the development from macromolecule to micro-organism, is just one step among many like that from the elementary particle to the atom, from the atom to the molecule ... or also from the single cell to groups of organs and finally the central nervous system. Why should we regard this particular step from the molecule to the single cell with greater reverence than any of the others? Molecular biology has put an end to the creation mysticism which has been maintained for centuries; it has completed what Galileo began.[19]

Biologists dispute whether the step from the macromolecule to the first cell must not be regarded as very much more important. For us, however, the central question arises: Must the rejection of a "creation mysticism," as Monod thinks, at the same time entail the rejection of God as creator and governor of the world?

By no means, since the assumption that the existence of God is to be excluded on the basis of the evidence of molecular biology is also unfounded. Here, moreover, the biologist Eigen rightly contradicts the biologist Monod: "In Monod's demand for an 'existential attitude to life and society' we see an animistic revaluation of the role of 'chance.' It largely leaves the complementary aspect of the regular out of account. Criticism of the dialectical over-valuing of 'necessity,' which to my mind is justified, should not lead to the complete denial of its influence, which is quite manifestly present."[20] It follows from this that

19. Eigen, preface to *Zufall und Notwendigkeit*, xv.
20. Eigen and Winkler, *Das Spiel*, 13, 197.

"ethics and knowledge may not stand side by side without any relation between them." Eigen agrees with Monod here, but by this he understands "more a task for the great religions and not at the same time their condemnation. . . . The scientists no more produce a proof of God than they postulate that human beings do not need a belief in God. And ethics — however much it must accord with objectivity and knowledge — should orientate itself more on the needs of humankind than on the behaviour of matter."[21] I can only agree with Eigen: the rejection of a creation mysticism by no means excludes a creator and governor of the world.

An Existential Alternative

Manfred Eigen told me in a conversation that there are as many different opinions on the question of God among biologists as among people generally. At all events, the opposed positions of two leading biologists mentioned above make it clear that, like anyone else, biologists, if they reflect deeply enough, see themselves confronted with the existential alternative: Is the evolutionary process meaningless and a last abandonment of the human, or not? To put it succinctly, what makes itself felt in the infinitely many individual variations of concrete life?

Either one says no to a primal ground, primal support, and primal goal of the whole evolutionary process, in which case one must take account of the meaninglessness of the whole process and the forsakenness of the human being. To quote Monod once again: "If he [the human being] accepts this message in its full significance, man must at last wake out of his millenary dream and discover his total solitude, his fundamental isolation. He must realize that, like a gipsy, he lives on the boundary of an alien world: a world that is deaf to his music, and as indifferent to his hopes as it is to his suffering or his crimes."[22] I concede that for me this is neither a hopeful nor even a rational prospect.

21. Eigen and Winkler, *Das Spiel*, 13, 197.
22. Monod, *Chance and Necessity*, 160.

Or one says yes to a primal ground, primal support, and primal goal. In that case, while one may not base the fundamental meaningfulness of the whole process and one's own existence on the process itself, one may trustingly presuppose it. Eigen's question would then be answered: "The recognition of connections still does not produce any answer to the question asked by Leibniz: 'Why is there something and not nothing?'"[23] This is the question I have attempted to answer (cf. chap. II.5).

Perhaps there are more biologists than one thinks who have the courage, like Rupert Riedl, in the face of the numerous "postmodern" prophets of godlessness and meaninglessness, to acknowledge the perplexity of science and the need for a trusting Yes:

> Even the atheist, mechanist, monist of our day needs only to consider the question of the causes of this world before the Big Bang to have to concede that with all our knowledge he is in the same perplexity which he may foolishly have ridiculed as the cause of the bear cult. — No one, I assert, can think without metaphysical premises. One cannot be aware of them, that is certain. But one cannot take a step into the unknown without including expectations which are metaphysical, which lie beyond the things we already know. Faith and its children religion, philosophy and world-view are indispensable to any culture. — Faith is the irreplaceable framework for the inexplicable.[24]

But we must penetrate even deeper.

4. Why a Universe That Is Friendly to Life?

Evolution took around 3.5 billion years to bring life to its present wealth of forms and modes of behavior and finally even to produce life with a mind. This is an astonishing development.

23. Eigen and Winkler, *Das Spiel,* 190f.
24. Riedl, *Die Strategie der Genesis,* 194f.

Evolution toward Human Beings

Think of all the things that had to "fit" after the Big Bang 13.7 billion years ago for such life to be able to arise! We may remind ourselves of the cosmic natural constants: the charge of the electron e, Planck's constant h, Boltzmann's constant k, the speed of light c. . . . All had to balance precisely in the cosmos (and by no means always symmetrically) for life to be able to arise after billions of years: the fine-tuning of energy and matter, of nuclear electromagnetic forces, of the force of gravity and energy through nuclear reaction in our sun.

So did all this develop toward life, toward the human being, utterly by chance? The most amazing thing of all is that finally, after billions of years on our earth, even life with mind could develop from the animal kingdom: the human being. If we speeded up time so that the 13.7-billion-year history of the cosmos was a single year, then more complex life (algae) developed only at the beginning of the tenth month, and human beings only in the last hours of the last day of the year. So is the whole development of the cosmos in 13.7 billion years focused on us? Sometimes one hears people say, "The universe knew that we would come." But does the universe know anything? Did the Big Bang know what it was sparking off? That's a comic notion. But in that case who knew that we human beings would come? The question that remains unavoidable in face of this tremendous development is: Does everything perhaps follow what Martin Rees calls a "very special recipe" for a universe friendly to life and the spirit?

The "many-worlds theories" certainly offer an intellectual way of avoiding such consequences. But as such speculations about imaginary alternative universes are pure hypotheses without empirical support, as I have already said, the question arises with even greater urgency: Is everything really pure chance? But is pure chance any explanation for this central problem of cosmology?

And if not chance, what then? Perhaps one day a genius could discover the mathematical structure of the basic laws of physics that make life on our planet possible. Why not? Since so far all efforts by physicists to find a world formula have come to grief on Stephen Hawking's insight that such a formula is impossible on the basis of Gödel's incompleteness theorem, biologists, too, are not left with much hope for a future fundamental solution. And why shouldn't other cosmic solutions have been possible in 13.7 billion years that led to life, or specifically to life with mind? It must be difficult to exclude this in principle and a priori. But in that case, what explains our development?

An Anthropic Principle?

On the one hand one cannot in any way argue from the physical principles of the beginning and the basic laws to a development toward life, and indeed toward human life; otherwise one might exclude chance as an empty principle of explanation: Could so many "chances" be chance? In the face of this dilemma some physicists and biologists are asking themselves whether there isn't something like a "metalaw" behind all the fine-tunings and natural laws, something like a "superlaw" above all laws of nature that guided the development of the cosmos through 13.7 billion years to the origin of life and finally human life. But no vitalistic force nor any consciousness of matter given from the beginning can be proved. Far less can proof be given of any providence of a governor of the world, thought of in anthropomorphic terms, who had worked out a detailed anthropocentric plan for the world.

In concrete this question has been discussed since the 1970s in the English-speaking world: quite a few cosmologists, physicists, and biologists accept a so-called anthropic principle[25] that guarantees that the initial conditions and natural constants of our universe are a priori so created that an "observer," i.e., life and intelligence, can arise. This was first formulated in a "soft" way by the distinguished American physicist Robert H. Dicke of Princeton in 1961. He did not argue that it *had* to arise, as did the British physicist Brandon Carter of the observatory of Meudon, Paris, in the "strong" sense. This latter argument holds that the cosmos was from the beginning so established and created in its basic constants and laws that at some point life and intelligence inexora-

---

25. R. Breuer, *Das anthropische Prinzip. Der Mensch im Fadenkreuz der Naturgeschichte* (Vienna, 1981), gives an excellent introduction to the problem (with the necessary bibliographies). Cf. also J. D. Barrow and F. J. Tipler, *The Anthropic Cosmological Principle* (Oxford, 1986).

bly had to arise. Thus the Australian physicist Paul Davies even wants to recognize a mind of God in evolution, though he leaves the judgment to personal taste.[26]

A strongly formulated anthropic principle seems to me an all too anthropomorphic and anthropocentric notion of the relationship of the creator to his creation. Wouldn't it be enough to understand the principle in the soft sense: That in retrospect one recognizes how the cosmos is in fact as it is so that life and life with mind became possible? Even such a principle would certainly not be a scientific proof that God had willed human beings. But it would have to be an unmistakable indication that the whole of the evolutionary process is not meaningless, but has a meaning at least for the human being, the first being capable of reflection.

So at all events it would be more understandable why human beings and they alone were capable of working out mathematical formulae with their reason and then of establishing that nature itself is composed in the language of mathematics, which they can very slowly decipher. Any change in the cosmic numerical values would have produced another universe, in which the development of life, especially spiritual life, would have been improbable or even impossible.

But there is the difficult question: How could science provide the basis for such a metanatural law? Or must it simply accept it as a fact? At all events, theological fallacies are to be avoided.

No Ultimate Foundation

Alfred Gierer, who has already been quoted, also regards the many-worlds theories as "intellectual constructions" that "fall short of the clarity of modern science, which began with Kepler's planetary orbits and Galileo's laws of gravity." To him, as to some other scientists, "the anthropic principle of a meta-natural law — 'the ordering of the universe makes possible life with mind' — seems the better alternative." But according to Gierer, whether "a mathematical logical basis for that exists" remains open. It is probable "that the anthropic meta-natural

26. Cf. P. Davies, *The Mind of God: The Scientific Basis for a Rational World* (New York, 1992).

law — if we suppose its validity — like the well-known basic laws of physics can be recognized only by its effects, and an ultimate grounding is impossible."[27]

On the basis of my epistemological remarks (chap. I.7), I have to confirm that in this question that transcends the whole empirical realm, in principle science cannot offer a "final explanation." A meta-empirical law of all laws of nature, philosophy, and even more, religion, is competent to provide this "recipe" for a genesis of this world. It may recognize and interpret the great connection that exists between the different levels of our world — the connection of the microcosm with the elementary particles, atoms, and molecules through the various forms of life, cells and organisms, to the macrocosm of the planets, stars, and the universe as a whole.

I feel that my view is confirmed by the astrophysicist Gerhard Börner of the Max Planck Institute in Garching, Munich, who remarks on the many studies of the "anthropic principle," that one cannot "argue from this to the 'principle' of a goal-orientated creation, to the 'deliberate' development of human beings." One cannot draw such conclusions within science, but one may allow oneself to be "stimulated towards such thoughts by the cosmological picture of the world."

If we want to interpret the origin of the cosmos, of space and time, as the creative act of a divine being, the results of the natural sciences do not prevent us. On the contrary, research in physics would probably describe this as the cosmological standard model of the Big Bang. I do not believe that the grandiose cosmic development takes its course simply as a meaningless play before empty seats. Like the American physicist Freeman Dyson I think that there is a purpose behind it — perhaps the plan to produce an ever more complex universe of diverse forms and filled with a spiritual principle. But that brings us into the realm of values and faith, in which we must modestly concede our ignorance.[28]

27. Gierer, *Biologie*, 43.
28. G. Börner, "Vom Urknall zum Weltall," *National Geographic Deutschland,* Dec. 2003, 112-15, here 115.

However, in today's religious view human beings no longer appear as the "crown of creation" directly created by God. Certainly they appear as unique products of evolution that on the basis of their conscious-ness, language, and freedom have developed a unique relationship to their environment, to the earth, the solar system, the Milky Way, the universe, metaphorically to "heaven and earth," as is poetically de-picted in the biblical creation story.

My conclusion is that science and religion both have their justifica-tion, independence, and autonomy (chap. I.5-6). But they can expand in the framework of a holistic overall view of all things:

- Religion can interpret evolution as creation.
- Scientific knowledge can make creation concrete as evolutionary process.
- Religion can thus attribute to the whole of evolution a meaning that science cannot read off evolution, but at best can conjecture.[29]

In the Jewish, Christian, and Muslim tradition people speak more pre-cisely of "faith" than of religion. However, this is not faith understood as "holding true all the doctrines which the church presents for belief," according to a traditionalist Roman Catholic formula. Rather, this is faith understood in a good biblical way as trust: "Faith is the assurance of things hoped for, the conviction of things not seen" (Heb. 11:1). Or philologically even more precisely in the translation that follows Lu-ther: "But faith is the foundation (Greek *hypostasis*) of what one hopes for and the certainty of things that one does not see." The reality of God is described here unambiguously: "By faith we understand that the world was created by the word of God, so that what is seen was made out of things which do not appear" (Heb. 11:3).

In this sense I believe what is the common faith of Jews, Christians, and Muslims, in God as "creator of heaven and earth." But if I make this faith my own, mustn't I then accept the miracles of the creator God that

29. Cf. S. M. Daecke, "Religion — Schöpfung Gottes in der Evolution. Zum Verhältnis von Evolution, Religion und Schöpfung," in *Gottesglaube — ein Selektionsvorteil?* ed. S. M. Daecke and J. Schnakenberg (Gütersloh, 2000), 179-203.

are narrated in the Bible? What about God's direct intervention in human history? Some scientists categorically declare that there are no miracles. This objection must be taken seriously.

5. Miracle

What about the miracle stories that already occur in the Hebrew Bible around the liberation of Israel from Egypt: the ten plagues of Egypt; the thornbush that burns but is not consumed; the smoke, earthquake, and thunder on Mount Sinai; the rain of manna and quail. And also the collapse of the walls of Jericho to the sound of the trumpets, the sun and moon standing still, all the healings of the sick and raisings of the dead, and the ascension of Elijah in a fiery chariot? These are miracles that are continued in the New Testament.[30] What are we to think of them?

Breaking the Laws of Nature?

God seems to have intervened, if not in the process of evolution, at least in the history of Israel, in such a way that here miracles take place not in a vague but in a strict modern sense, as the breaking of the laws of nature.

Without going into details, I want briefly to indicate some points of agreement with the view of leading biblical exegetes. But I do not want to violate the religious feelings of anyone for whose belief in God the miracles understood literally are important. I want to give a helpful answer to those modern men and women for whom the miracles are an obstacle to their faith.

If we want to do justice to the accounts of miracles in the Bible historically and hermeneutically, first of all we must be clear about the fundamental difference between the biblical understanding of reality and the modern understanding of reality. People in the time of the Bible were not interested in what is so important to us, today's children of the rational, technological age: the laws of nature. People did not think

30. Cf. H. Küng, *On Being a Christian* (London and New York, 1976), C.II.2: "Miracle?"

151

scientifically, and so they did not understand the miracles as breaking the laws of nature; they did not understand them as a violation of seamless causal connections. So nowhere in the Hebrew Bible and the New Testament is a distinction made between miracles that correspond to the laws of nature and others that break them. For every event through which God revealed his power was regarded at that time as a miracle, as a "sign," as a mighty act of God. God was at work everywhere, the creator and primal ground. Everywhere human beings could "wonder," they could experience wonders: in things great and small, in the history of the people and in the deliverance of the individual from deep distress, from the creation and sustaining of the world to its consummation.

Results of Biblical Criticism

The results of both historical and literary biblical criticism need to be taken seriously.

Historical biblical criticism has shown that many wonderful events that caused no problems for the faith of the people of the time (for example, the plagues of frogs, flies, or locusts in connection with the exodus from Egypt; Exod. 8:1-31) can be derived from natural events in Palestine or neighboring countries; with them the causality of nature was not broken in any way.

But *literary* criticism has shown that in the accounts of miracles we do not have records of historical events. Different traditions of the same event (for example, the journey through the sea; Exod. 13:17-22; 14:1-31) have often come together, and here the later ones further heighten the miraculous. There are also considerable differences between the various literary genres, for example, between a hymn, a popular narrative, and a court chronicle. Finally, narratives such as the miracle of the sun (Josh. 10:12f.), the miraculous feeding and raisings of the dead by the prophets Elijah and Elisha (1 Kings 17:7-24; 2 Kings 4:18-37, 42-44), or the prophet Jonah in the fish's mouth (Jon. 2) evidently have a legendary character.

All this makes it clear that miracles as the breaking of laws of nature cannot be demonstrated historically in the Bible, and those who think they can be demonstrated bear the burden of proof. The Bible with its miracle stories is in any case not primarily concerned with the narrated event itself but with the interpretation of what is narrated, not so much concerned with the form of the statement as with its content. So the miracle stories do not serve to communicate knowledge but to bring about wonder. They are untroubled popular narratives meant to evoke faith and amazement. And they have a deeper sense.

Pointers for Faith

Miracles are meant to be signs of the power of God: the Lord has done great things to us! These narratives set out to interpret God's word and strengthen faith, so they are at the service of the proclamation of the power and goodness of God. Nowhere is a belief required that miracles happened, or even that this or that event is really a miracle. Rather, simply faith in God is expected, which is at work in people who do such things, and for whose activity the miracles are sign-ificant, i.e., "signs."

To be specific, what is important is not the shaking of Mount Sinai but the message that Moses receives on this occasion. What is essential is not the plagues of Egypt but the testimony of God who demonstrates his saving power. What is significant is not the miraculous journey through the sea but the message of God whom the people experience as the God of liberation. Accordingly the miracles stand in the Bible as metaphors, just as in poetry metaphors too do not set out to overturn the laws of nature.

From this it is clear that such an experience of miracle is not in competition with a rational, scientific, and technological understanding of the world. The miracle stories are not meant to be proofs of God but pointers to his action in the world: pointers, but pointers that receive their clarity only through faith in him (and not in a second, evil principle). The message of these narratives is aimed at human beings in all their dimensions: body and spirit, space and time, individual and society. What do they proclaim? They proclaim not an unchanging unworldly and unhistorical God who unfeelingly leaves the world and human beings to their fate, but a God who gets involved with the destinies of the world, and commits himself for the people and for individuals. They proclaim a God who does not leave the world and human beings alone, who does not make history a dark, ominous fate for people but a connection of events that can be recognized in faith.

Thus the various biblical images and miracles can also be interpreted rightly in an evolutionary understanding of the world. However, this leads to a fundamental theological question that I now want to investigate further.

6. How Are We to Think of God's Activity?

Particularly in a rational trust in God we should avoid confusing scientific insights and religious confessions: driven by ethical and religious impulses (praiseworthy though they are), we may not use an anthropic principle to attribute to the process of evolution the direction toward a definite final state Omega and thus give it meaning that only religious faith, and not science, can give. I have argued for a Yes to an "Alpha" as "ground" of all things and will also plead for an "Omega" as a goal. But it must remain clear that here we are dealing with a Yes "beyond science,"[31] a Yes of rational trust.

Even those who accept an anthropic principle need in no way advocate a "supernatural" intervention of God in the world process. On the contrary:

- In the view of biologists a direct supernatural intervention of God in the rise and ongoing development of life seems more than ever unnecessary.
- But at the same time, leading biologists hold the view that from a scientific perspective the process of evolution as such does not exclude either an author (an Alpha) or an ultimate meaning-goal (an Omega).
- The existential question of the origin and meaning-goal of the whole process also arises for scientists as human beings. They may not evade this question, even if they cannot answer it as scientists. However, this includes an enlightened attitude to God.

31. Thus C. Bresch, *Zwischenstufe Leben. Evolution ohne Ziel?* (Münster, 1977), epilogue, 296-99.

A Spiritualized Understanding of God

It would be an all-too-external anthropomorphic notion to think that God as Lord and King "controlled" or "guided" events, even those that are apparently chance, even the indeterminate subatomic processes. In that case, how would we explain all the waste and dead ends in evolution, the species that died out and the animals and human beings who perished miserably? And how would we explain the infinite suffering and all the evil in this world and world history? Such a conception of a Lord God has no answer to this.

The biblical understanding of God as spirit has rightly been seen to be particularly helpful for an evolutionary worldview. The biblical evidence is very illuminating: tangible yet intangible, invisible and yet powerful, as important to life as the air we breathe, as laden with energy as the wind or storm — that is the spirit. All languages have a word for it, and the different genders given indicate that the spirit cannot be defined too simply: *spiritus* in Latin is masculine (as is *der Geist* in German), *ruach* in Hebrew is feminine, and Greek has the neuter, *pneuma*. So spirit is at any rate something quite different from a human being. According to the beginning of the account of creation in the book of Genesis, the *ruach* is that breath of air, breeze, or storm of God that moves over the waters, and according to the New Testament the *pneuma* stands in opposition to "flesh," i.e., to created transitory reality, and is the living power and force that goes forth from God.

So spirit is not the divine reason, as in Greek philosophy, but that invisible force and power of God that has both a creative and a destructive effect, for life or for judgment, which is as active in the creation as in history, in Israel as later in the Christian communities. The Spirit is "holy" insofar as it is distinguished from the unholy spirit, human beings, and their world, and has to be regarded as the spirit of the only Holy One, God himself. So the Holy Spirit is God's Spirit.

In the New Testament too the Holy Spirit is not — as often in the history of religions — a magical, substantial, mysterious, and supernatural fluid of a dynamic nature (a spiritual "something"), nor is it a magical being of an animistic kind (a spiritual being or ghost). In the New

Testament, too, the Holy Spirit is none other than God himself. God himself, insofar as he is near to the world and human beings, indeed becomes inward as the power that grasps but cannot be grasped, as the life-giving but also judging spirit, as the grace that gives but is at no one's disposal.

The Infinite Has an Influence on the Finite

For a modern evolutionary understanding of reality in which God as spirit is in the world and the world is in God, transcendence in immanence, it is fundamental that:

- God's spirit works in the regular structures of the world but is not identical with them. For God is pure spirit and constantly works in world history, not in the way of the finite and relative but as the infinite in the finite and as the absolute in the relative. I have already indicated two points of view in the section "How Are We to Think of God?" (chap. III.4).
- God's spirit does not work on the world from above or outside as unmoved mover. Rather, it works as the dynamic, most real, reality from within, in the ambivalent process of the development of the world, which it makes possible, permeates, and completes. It does not work high above the process of the world but in the passionate process of the world: in, with, and among human beings and things. It itself is the origin, center, and goal of the world process.

Nor does God's spirit work at especially important points or gaps in the world process. Rather it constantly works as a creative and completing support in the system of law and chance and thus as a governor of the world both immanent in the world and superior to the world — omnipresent also in chance and disaster — fully respecting the laws of nature whose origin it is. It is also the ground of the meaning of the world process that permeates everything and also embraces everything negative, and can of course be accepted and understood only in trusting faith. To avoid any misunderstanding, I shall make this yet more precise.

Life in the Cosmos?

No Competition between God and the World

It must by now have become clear that world *or* God is not an alternative: neither the world without God (atheism) nor God identical with the world (pantheism), but God *in* the world and the world *in* God. God and world, God and human beings are thus not two competing finite causalities side by side, where one wins what the other loses; they are in each other. If God really is the all-embracing infinite spiritual primal ground, primal support, and primal meaning of the world and human beings, it becomes clear that God does not lose anything if human beings in their finitude win, but that God wins when human beings win.

Keith Ward of Oxford, who, as we heard, has argued in a knowledgeable and detailed way with some English-speaking "new materialists" (chap. II.2), thinks it quite improbable that natural selection alone would have produced rational beings: a simpler explanation of the whole process is to accept the hypothesis of an invisible influence of God that actively or passively is determinative in each moment.[32] The Oxford biochemist and theologian Arthur Peacocke, who has likewise done sterling work in dialogue between scientists and theologians, has taken great pains to make the influence of God on the world and thus God's special providence understandable with the categories of physics.[33] Others too have attempted to connect God's activity with the quantum world or to locate it in chaos theory. But some objections to such attempts have been made from both physics and theology. The physicist and theologian John Polkinghorne, who has done no less service in dialogue, may be right when he says: "It is not possible to disentangle the causal web, asserting that God did this, a human being did that, and nature the other things. Faith may be able to discern, but inspection cannot demonstrate divine action of this kind."[34] So the all-embracing creative plan of the universe must be understood correctly, and not as a detailed scheme already existing in the idea of God. For Polkinghorne, the actual equilibrium between chance and necessity,

32. Cf. K. Ward, *God, Chance, and Necessity* (London, 1996), 76-95.
33. Cf. A. Peacocke, *A Theology for a Scientific Age* (Oxford, 1990), especially chaps. 3 and 9.
34. J. Polkinghorne, *Science and Theology* (London, 1998), 90.

contingency and possibility that we perceive seems to correspond to the will of a patient and subtle creator who is content to pursue his aims by initiating the process and by accepting that degree of vulnerability and uncertainty that always characterizes the gift of freedom through love.[35]

So theology may not take on too much nor extend its curiosity too far. I keep coming back to the famous "dispute over grace," the most important controversy over grace and freedom in the sixteenth/seventeenth centuries. At that time people wanted to solve the riddle of how the providence and omnipotence of God and human freedom could be combined. After endless disputes between Dominicans and Jesuits and more than 120 sessions in Rome, in 1611 Pope Paul V forbade either party to vilify its opponents. To the present day we are waiting for the papal declaration that was then held in prospect, and was to be published *opportune,* in due time. It is needed more than ever today. Most theologians have recognized that here we have no insoluble riddle but an unfathomable mystery of the activity of God himself. And this must also apply to the question of how an omniscient God can foresee not only determined processes but also the countless chance processes that evolution produces.

For me what is theologically relevant is not the *that (id quod)* of the activity of God and the cosmos, God and human beings, but the *how (modus quo)* of the collaboration that is ultimately hidden from us and we do not need to decipher. Here another aspect is more important for me, as suggested by the message of the Bible: most miracles take place for believers not in the cosmos but in the human heart, where God's spirit is at work. According to the apostle Paul, this is not an unholy human spirit, spirit of the time, spirit of the church, spirit of ministry, nor is it an enthusiastic spirit; it is the Holy Spirit, the spirit of freedom and love, which blows where and when it wills. It is God's gift, for which we may ask even in difficult times — and who does not have these? — again and again to be made free for a life and activity in peace, justice, joy, love, hope, and gratitude. And for me there is no finer hymn to God's

---

35. Cf. Polkinghorne, *One World: The Interaction of Science and Theology* (Princeton, 1987), 69.

spirit than *Veni Sancte Spiritus* ("Come, Holy Spirit"), written by Stephen Langton, archbishop of Canterbury, around 1200. It describes the effect of the spirit of God as light (I am quoting only a few verses here):

O lux beatissima,	O blessed light of life thou art,
reple cordis intima	fill with Thy light the inmost heart
tuorum fidelium.	of those who hope in Thee.
Sine tuo nomine	Without Thy name nothing can
nihil est in homine,	have any price or worth in man,
nihil est inoxium.	nothing can harmless be.
Lava quod est sordidum,	Lord, wash our sinful stains away,
riga quod est aridum.	refresh from heaven our barren clay,
sana quod est saucium.	our wounds and bruises heal.
Flecte quod est rigidum.	To Thy sweet yoke our stiff necks bow,
fove quod est frigidum,	warm with Thy fire our hearts of snow,
rege quod est devium.	our wandering feet recall.
Da tuis fidelibus,	Grant to Thy faithful, dearest Lord,
in te confidentibus,	whose only hope is Thy sure word,
sacrum septenarium.	the sevenfold gifts of grace.

But here we are going beyond the limits of this chapter on science and religion. Of course, I know that physiologists locate such stirrings not in the heart but in the brain, all of them determined by physical and chemical processes. We must face this problem. And we shall do so in the next chapter, in which I shall discuss the origin of human beings, the problem of brain and mind, brain research, the experience of freedom, and some other matters.

CHAPTER V

The Beginning of Humankind

Around 8,000 kilometers of sea lie between Australia and Africa today. But 2 billion years ago both formed one large southern continent (Gondwanaland) — together with India, New Zealand, South America, and Antarctica. In the late Cretaceous age, around 130 million years ago or even later, this gigantic landmass broke up and drifted farther and farther apart. Geologically speaking, Africa is a very old continent, on which we can study the geological history of our earth as nowhere else. At the same time, historically speaking Africa is also an age-old habitat of human beings — extremely significant for the beginnings of human culture that for the researcher into primal history begins in the Old Stone (Paleolithic) Age with the "tool-making being."

1. The Physical Development of Human Beings

Hominization required not just a change in physical characteristics. It required above all the development of intellectual capabilities — the presupposition for the development of techniques, culture, and social life. But first of all, there is agreement among specialists that rising to a permanently two-footed attitude and locomotion were fundamental to the development of the human being. According to most scholars, this change took place when the great forests retreated as a consequence of climatic change, the savannas extended, and the eating habits and ways

of life of early human beings changed. Only later did a considerable en-
largement of the brain take place, especially the associational area of
the cerebral cortex, which was to be decisive for the further development of human beings.

Phylogenesis

So far there is little agreement on the question of when the cognitive capacities characteristic of human beings and their interest in knowing
objects in the environment developed. We may assume that the development of speech played an important role here.

Phylogenetic research today largely agrees on two contrary insights.

First, human beings developed over the course of several million
years from their animal ancestors. A whole series of anatomical and
physiological peculiarities appears at least in embryo even among the
closest relatives of the human being, the higher primates, the anthropoids: from the number of chromosomes through the position of teeth
to the development of the brain. There are also analogies to human feelings such as anxiety, indifference, and joy. There are analogies in social
behavior: a long childhood, late sexual maturing, and the formation of
complicated social structures and social modes of behavior, often regarded as specifically human, already characterize the anthropoids.
Even the formation of (nonverbal) concepts, simple conclusions, and
judgments and the beginning of planned action based on them can be
established among chimpanzees, indeed, even the stages prior to a notion of the self. And yet:

Secondly, human beings occupy a special position over against all
animals. Not only are they the only living beings walking upright with a
rump kept vertical, they are also the living beings with the most highly developed brains. Above all, human beings possess consciousness, which is
the necessary condition for speech. Thus they are characterized by a capacity to think and speak purposefully. The possession of a complex syn-
tactical language is unique. It also distinguishes human beings from
their nearest relatives, the chimpanzees. Certainly chimpanzees can
learn words and their meaning and solve certain tasks by reflection, but
they have neither a speech center in the cerebral cortex (called Broca's

area after Paul Broca, who discovered it) nor a structure of larynx and vocal chords suitable for speech. It is undisputed that the possession of speech with complex sentence structures tremendously heightened the intellectual capacity of human beings. Only they have the capacity for strategic thought that weighs up alternative actions. Only they have the capacity for reflection. Consciousness and language are the presupposition for abstract thought and directed, intentional states of mind such as love and hate, hopes and fears, convictions and wishes. All this is the basis for cultural development, for religion, philosophy, and science.

There is no other being who like the human being also keeps reflecting on its origin and researching into it — not only in religion and philosophy but also in paleontology and science. But where did the adventure of the human being, so decisive for our earth, begin? According to most recent research, where is the cradle of humankind?[1]

Human Beings Come from Africa

The adventure began around 6 million years ago: the species of hominids, early human beings, which led to the modern type of human being, began to split away from that species from which its closest relatives, the anthropoids, developed. Granted, the genes of human beings differ from those of chimpanzees in only around 1 percent of the DNA chain. But this is around 30 million of the 3 billion blocks of the genome. The oldest genre of hominids known with certainty is the African Australopithecines ("southern apelike") from around 5 million years ago, which moved on two legs and clambered but did not develop any culture of tools. Members of the hominid society, 2.5 million years before any writing cultures, then began to make stone tools: *Homo habilis* ("capable man") cut sharp-sided splinters from small river pebbles, something no present-day anthropoid has proved capable of, even after intensive training. L. S. B. Leakey[2] has excavated the oldest known tool

1. F. Schrenk, *Die Frühzeit des Menschen. Der Weg zum Homo sapiens* (Munich, 1997), gives a brief and precise survey of the history of prehumans and primal humans. He is a paleontologist working with a group of researchers in Africa.
2. Cf. L. S. B. Leakey et al., eds., *Adam or Ape? A Sourcebook of Discoveries about Early Man* (Cambridge, Mass., 1971).

from the volcanic deposits in the floor of the Olduvai Gorge in East Africa, and on the basis of the strata has been able to date it to an age of 2.16 to 2.12 million years. Meanwhile numerous further discoveries have been made.

Africa and the other continents developed in a very similar way in the Early and Middle Stone Age. Discoveries of tools and burial places allow us to follow the development of *Homo habilis* to our immediate ancestors, *Homo sapiens,* very clearly. Between 2 and 1.5 million years ago there emerged *Homo habilis,* the "man walking upright," largely similar to present-day human beings in bodily form. Around 500,000 years ago human beings in groups and hordes mastered the use of fire. An intermediate stage then developed between about 200,000 and 35,000 years ago in cold Ice Age Europe, Neanderthal man. Partially divergent genetic material (confirmed by the most recent DNA analysis) indicates that Neanderthal man, with his compact, powerful bodily form, his receding forehead, and his great volume of brain, was probably not a direct descendant of *Homo sapiens,* but at any rate a relative. Scholars still dispute his psychological and intellectual capacities. He was certainly not still almost a wild beast, as was earlier assumed, but he was not close to a modern human being either, as was later claimed in exaggeration. It is indisputable that he had a developed technique of making tools and hunting; for the first time in the development of human beings he buried his dead with offerings in the tomb; and he engaged in linguistic communication and the communication of information, above all from parents to children.

Some scholars think that *Homo sapiens,* the anatomically modern human being, the human being of today, developed almost at the same time in several places in the world. But on the basis of overwhelming discoveries, which are also the most recent, most scholars are convinced that *Homo sapiens* comes from what was presumably not a very large group of early human beings in tropical/subtropical warm Africa, rich in wildlife, who in all probability lived around 200,000 years ago east of the great African-Syrian Rift Valley.

In the late Stone Age, probably far more than 100,000 years ago, this *Homo sapiens,* presumably in small hordes, made his long way over the globe: between around 40,000 and 30,000 years ago he suppressed the

Neanderthals in Europe and elsewhere. First skeletons were found at Cro-Magnon (Les Eyzies) in the Dordogne. But whereas his closest evolutionary relative in Africa, the chimpanzee, formed three different subspecies on his way to development, *Homo sapiens* has a quite unitary development. He is the creator of the famous cave paintings; he begins to play the flute, engages in tailoring and ceramic technology, and bakes clay figurines in the oven. He has an articulated language and probably also symbolic concepts. The population of the earth in the hunter-gatherer period presumably amounted to only a few million. It was the spread of agriculture around 10,000 years ago that brought a marked population growth, a differentiation of culture, and finally about 5,000 years ago, with the invention of writing in Mesopotamia and also at the same time in Egypt, the first high cultures — the beginning of the historical age.[3]

We should never forget that Aborigines, "bushmen," Asians, Europeans, and Americans are not different species of human being but form a single human species, the same human race. And even if we are very different in our external characteristics, as molecular genetic analysis shows, we all have a common biological origin. Under our skin we are all Africans. But what is the place of the development of religion in this phylogenesis of human beings?

Earliest Traces of Religion

"Natural peoples" and "civilized peoples" are not opposites. For although the original inhabitants of Africa or Australia developed no writing, no science and technology in the modern sense, they did have a "civilization." Their thought is logical, plausible, shaped by a "passion for order," for classifying things and relationships. Particularly in the Australian tribal cultures great importance is attached to civilization; it is a central characteristic that distinguishes human beings from the animal world and the savage. Civilization, understood comprehensively and including religion, is the totality of knowledge and modes of proce-

---

3. Cf. I. J. Gelb, *A Study of Writing: The Foundation of Grammatology* (Chicago, 1952); H. Haarmann, *Universalgeschichte der Schrift* (Frankfurt am Main, 1990).

dure that characterize a particular human society, whether they are of a technical, economic, scientific, social, or religious kind.

Today's hunters and gatherers in Australia and on other continents are by no means "Stone Age people" who have got stuck in time. Even these original inhabitants have changed. A long cultural history of several tens of thousands of years separates them from the Old Stone Age. They are not prerational, prelogical, as the first cultural anthropologists thought. Our "Western perspective" wrongly sees only our Western cultures in a historical context and the other cultures merely in a geographical context. Certainly the original inhabitants used very simple techniques, but this does not mean they had a simple, even unchanging and static, culture. In no way did they live in a timeless state. Rather, as anthropologists of our day have established, from time to time they adopted rituals and songs, but also artistic styles and techniques from other tribal groups; they discovered new holy objects and adapted their myths to changed circumstances.[4]

The Aborigines of Australia were for a long time a test case for the study of the development of religion. Cultural anthropology developed above all in a scholarly controversy over the Aboriginal tribes, and fronts formed here at an early stage.

Scholars of the late nineteenth century, whose scientific thought had been shaped by the notion of evolution and progress, such as Sir James G. Frazer (1854-1941),[5] saw the whole history of humankind in a scheme of stages: first magic, then religion, and today science. Fascinated by Darwin, they assumed without question that the early human beings were all human beings without religion, without God or gods. Only slowly, they thought, did religious customs and truths, sacrifice and prayers, develop from magical practices.

In opposition to this, other scholars, who believed in the Bible rather

4. Cf. M. Charlesworth, *Philosophy of Religion: The Historic Approaches* (London, 1972). Cf. also Charlesworth's collection of texts: *The Problem of Religious Language* (Englewood Cliffs, N.J., 1974); Charlesworth, *Religious Inventions: Four Essays* (Cambridge, 1997), especially essay 2: "The Invention of Australian Aboriginal Religion."

5. Cf. J. G. Frazer, *The Golden Bough: A Study in Comparative Religion*, vols. 1-2 (London, 1890); vols. 1-12 (3rd ed. 1907-15); Frazer, *Totemism and Exogamy: A Treatise on Certain Early Forms of Superstition and Society*, 4 vols. (London, 1910).

than in Darwin — one was P. Wilhelm Schmidt (1868-1954) in his multi-volume work and his Viennese Cultural Historical School[6] — attempted to provide a basis for an opposite scheme of development. They said the original Australians started from an original monotheism. Only with time did this develop into polytheism and finally degenerate into mere magic. At any rate, Australian tribes would still know a "Great Father."

Both extreme theories have now been shelved. They simply do not have an empirical basis because the cultures of the different tribal groups in reality developed quite unsystematically. It accorded with a Western hierarchical understanding of values to assume that religion developed from magic quite generally, as it were, step by step, from belief in souls to belief in spirits, from belief in spirits to belief in gods, and from belief in gods finally to belief in God. Today there is agreement among scholars that phenomena and phases overlap. Rather than speaking of phases and epochs (a "succession"), scholars therefore speak of strata and structures (a "superposition") that can be found in quite different stages of development phases or eras. And what about the "primal religion" of human beings, indeed a "primal monotheism"? Scholars today are also agreed about that: empirically a primal religion is nowhere to be found.

However, the first traces of the beginning of a religious sense already appear in the Old Stone Age and the Middle Stone Age, as in the most recent description of prehistoric religions by Ina Wunn.[7] The Mesolithic Age is less poor in a religious respect than was assumed earlier: "Evidently the notion of an all-powerful being was widespread — otherwise the discovery of masks makes no sense. Rituals were customary in the sphere of religious action connected either with hunting or with transitions in the life cycle. The cult of the dead had great significance. Burials according to more or less fixed rules were to safeguard the transition into the next world and/or make it possible for those left behind to have unbroken communion with the dead."[8] It was then the Neanderthals "who

6. Cf. Wilhelm Schmidt, S.V.D., *Der Ursprung der Gottesidee,* 12 vols. (Münster, 1926-55).

7. Cf. I. Wunn, *Die Religionen in vorgeschichtlicher Zeit,* Die Religionen der Menschheit, vol. 2 (Stuttgart, 2005), especially chap. 2.

8. Wunn, *Die Religionen in vorgeschichtlicher Zeit,* 199.

with their care for the fate of their dead embarked on a way in matters of religion and belief in the beyond which determined the religious notions of the following millennia"; from this "there developed the diversity of prehistoric religions on which the religions of the historical period then could build and enter on their triumphant course."[9]

But let's now turn to the question of psychological development and especially the problem of freedom in human history.

2. The Psychological Development of Human Beings

For classical European philosophy that begins with the Greeks, the essence of the human being consists in an intellectual capacity and a capacity for forming communities. Aristotle, the brilliant Greek thinker, who on the basis of his tremendous empirical knowledge was down to the Middle Ages *the* philosopher and scientific authority, framed a definition of human beings that has been influential to the present day. He saw the difference between human beings and animals as lying in the capacity for reason and defined the human being as a *zoon logon echon,* a being possessing reason (Latin: *animal rationale*), which is at the same time a *zoon politikon,* a companionable being capable of a regulated social life: in the Stoics and Christianity the element of freedom was then especially stressed. Aristotle already emphasized that it is not that the soul is angry or oppressed or thinks, just as it does not weave or build a house; rather, human beings do this by virtue of their souls.

The Body-Soul Problem

However, already in Plato, Aristotle's teacher, and following him also in Augustine and above all Descartes, we find a heightened dualism: the human being is understood as an antagonistic unity of mind *(res cogitans)* and body *(res extensa),* of freedom and regularity, which makes it difficult to bring together physis (nature) and psyche. On the other hand, the pantheistic monism of Spinoza, who wanted to assume

9. Wunn, *Die Religionen in vorgeschichtlicher Zeit,* 465.

only a single, divine substance with two attributes, extension and thought, does not represent a solution: Are we to integrate the world and all its misery completely into the Godhead and understand the individual self only as a modification of the one divine substance? Albert Einstein was to adopt this Spinozan determinism and precisely for that reason had difficulties in accepting nondeterministic quantum mechanics (cf. chap. I.3). Mediating between dualism and monism, Gottfried Wilhelm Leibniz (1646-1716) advocated a psychophysical parallelism, according to which the creator synchronizes soul and body without them influencing each other. But this proved to be a sheer postulate without an empirical basis.

Anthropogenesis, the coming into being of human beings, beyond doubt needs to be regarded from two different perspectives: it means a bodily change, a bio-evolution, and also a spiritual development, a psycho-evolution. First of all, the former was researched on the basis of numerous fossil finds, which could be investigated more and more closely with constantly improved methods of determining their age (amino-acid dating). Then the analysis of the modes of behavior of all animal organisms up to the human being attempted to explain the evolution of psychological processes: the origin of consciousness, intentionality, subjectivity.

However, models of totality and body-soul unity were increasingly developed. Comparative behavioral research has also worked out well-founded evolutionary models, so that the traditional Platonic-Augustinian-Cartesian body-soul dualism is out of date but by no means completely superseded. In any case, this was in need of explanation if it was to explain its reciprocal effect; the pineal gland deep in the brain, which Descartes assumed to be the seat of the soul, could not be demonstrated empirically to have this character. And how was a purely spiritual being to generate physical energy?

Psyche instead of Soul

Psychological development can be explained today on the basis of the integration of genetic, physiological, and ethnological theories. On this basis the expression "soul" — understood as the vehicle (substrate) of psychological processes and phenomena or also as the Aristotelian "form" (entelechy) of the body — is hardly used any more as a scientific term. The term used instead is "psyche"; this does not denote a principle of life distinct from the body, but in general the totality of conscious and unconscious emotional processes and intellectual functions.

A contemporary theology, too, has long given up the dualistic worldview: body and spirit are not two worlds, and the human being is not made up of two completely different "stuffs." So today people talk of animal "behavior" and human "behavior," thus using a terminology that deliberately leaves behind the difference between the bodily and the spiritual. Any mode of behavior embraces features that formerly were divided into body and soul. At an early stage the Protestant theologian Wolfhart Pannenberg adopted the insights of behavioral research and explained the well-known distinctive experience of a special world within the soul like this:

> For the anthropological study of behaviour, this experience is explained from the uniqueness of our corporeal behaviour. The inner world of soundless thought and conception only distinguishes the man who can already speak from the outer world. . . . Language, which is the condition for the emergence of a special spiritual inner world, itself arises through man's physical involvement with his surroundings. Thus, the distinction between the inner and outer worlds is not a primordial fact, but a derived one that grows out of man's corporeal behaviour. It follows from this that in man there is no independent reality of a "soul" in contrast to the body, just as there is not a body that is merely mechanically or unconsciously moved. Both are abstractions. The only reality is the unity of the living creature called man, which moves itself and relates itself to the world.[10]

Of course, those with a scientific training can still speak metaphorically of the "soul": negatively (a "soulless" house), in an antiquated way

10. W. Pannenberg, *What Is Man? Contemporary Anthropology in Theological Perspective* (Philadelphia, 1974), 48.

(a village of five hundred "souls"), poetically (the "soul" of Europe), liturgically ("My soul delights in the Lord"), or in a modern abbreviation (SOS = "Save our souls"). As long as one means this metaphorically and not in an objectifying way, misunderstanding can be avoided. But people today will speak of an honest, true, good "man" rather than of an honest, true, good "soul"; and the contemporary care of souls is about the whole physical person and not just his or her immortal dimension:

To sum up:

- It is neither the soul nor the brain, but the whole person who breathes, experiences, feels, thinks, wills, suffers, and acts: the "I," a "person."
- Body and psyche, brain and spirit, are thus given simultaneously and form a psychosomatic unity — psychologists and doctors attach great importance to this in theory and practice.
- Accordingly the bodily and the psychological are never to be had in isolation — not even in a dream.
- Many bodily and psychological characteristics (or at least dispositions) are already given to each individual in the cradle, bound up with the parental chromosomes.
- So a psychophysical process underlies every state of consciousness: there is no intellectual activity without a neuronal substratum.

But now another question becomes urgent: Does it follow from all this that the mind is a mere secondary effect of brain activity?

Conditioned Freedom

In the eighteenth-century French Enlightenment a mechanistic determinism began to extend causal physical determination to the whole human being: the human being became a "machine man," to use a phrase of J. O. Lamettrie's,[11] not essentially different from the animal and whose freedom of will was an illusion. Under the influence of Friedrich Engels and Ernst Haeckel, theoreticians of Marxism also thought along

---

11. Cf. J. O. de Lamettrie, *L'homme machine* (Leiden, 1748).

these lines. And beyond doubt such determinism is a presupposition of some neuroscientists today, who have remained philosophically in the nineteenth century and often do not reflect on it much.

In deliberate opposition to materialism and mechanistic science, the French existentialism of the twentieth century understood human beings in terms of their freedom, through which they determine what they are: "There is no determinism, man is free, indeed man is freedom," we read in the radical programmatic work *Existentialism Is a Humanism* by the young Jean-Paul Sartre. The philosopher and writer sees the risky freedom of the individual as an opportunity and at the same time as a compulsion to shape his life. What are called for here are not arbitrariness and randomness but commitment and responsibility. Human beings are either completely and always free or they are not: even those in prison and under torture are and remain free. This is a philosophy of resistance, born in the shadow of the Second World War and the Nazi German occupation. But coming closer and closer to Marxism under the influence of the Algerian and Vietnam wars by his support for the Stalinist Soviet Union, China, Cuba, and the Red Army Faction, the "committed philosopher" largely abandoned his original intentions.[12]

Sartre, too, emphasizes that the freedom of the individual is always realized only in a particular "situation" and therefore always comes up against limits. These limits have now become very much clearer from the results of behavioral research: human beings are preformed in two ways — by influences from the environment and by hereditary dispositions — and yet within limits they are free.

Environmentally Conditioned and Preprogrammed

On the one hand human beings are environmentally conditioned, shaped by external influences, dependent on conditions, conditioned in many ways and thus largely predictable in their behavior. American behavioral scientists such as the radical behaviorist B. F. Skinner ex-

---

12. On the centenary of Sartre's birth an excellent introduction to his life appeared, by the German philosopher H.-M. Schönherr-Mann, *Sartre. Philosophie als Lebenform* (Munich, 2005).

ploit this in demanding a human being programmed for the good, who must be guided by a "behavioral technology."[13]

But even Skinner does not deny human freedom. He knows that human beings are not just environmentally conditioned, are not totally conditioned, are not completely predictable. Beyond doubt the environment shapes human beings and their wills. But at the same time, human beings and their wills also shape the environment, insofar as the environment appears as an autonomous system.

On the other hand, as a construct that has come into being phylogenetically, the human being is preprogrammed genetically: as the German-speaking behavioral scientists (ethologists) in the school of the Nobel Prize winner Konrad Lorenz emphasize, human beings are driven on and guided in their forms of behavior, modes of actions and reactions by inherited programs. Hereditary dispositions are of fundamental importance for individual and social behavior.[14]

Here too there is a "but," emphasized by ethologists themselves. The innate does not work as a completely determining factor, as an inexorable fate that one merely has to tolerate and accept. As Lorenz's pupil Irenäus Eibl-Eibesfeldt says: the one-sided "view that human beings are programmed only through learning is wrong, as wrong as if one were to assert that human beings were completely pre-programmed."[15]

Happily the debate over determinism in education in the 1970s seems to be a thing of the past. At that time, depending on the ideological attitude, the view was put forward that human beings were 10 or 15 or 50 or 90 percent determined by the environment or conversely by their genes. In the meantime general agreement has been reached that human beings are determined as a "whole" by their genes and as a "whole" by their environment. But human freedom of will is now being put in question in a new and radical way by a science that focuses the problem of "mind and body" on the question "mind and brain": neurophysiological brain research.

13. Cf. B. F. Skinner, *Beyond Freedom and Dignity* (New York, 1971).
14. Cf. K. Lorenz, *On Aggression* (London, 1976); Lorenz, *Studies in Animal and Human Behaviour,* 2 vols. (London, 1971).
15. I. Eibl-Eibesfeldt, *Grundriss der vergleichenden Verhaltensforschung. Ethologie,* 3rd ed. (Munich, 1972).

3. Brain and Mind

Phylogenetic research already showed that the human spirit did not fall from heaven but was a product of evolution. We noted that the human brain is not unique; some intellectual capacities of human beings have prior stages among the anthropoids. So let's presuppose that without brain there is no mind and without the activity of certain brain centers there can be no intellectual achievement. But in that case a decisive question arises that must not be theologically covered up.

Determined by Physical-Chemical Brain Processes?

The fascination of brain physiologists by the object of their research is understandable: with the brain, evolution has beyond question produced its natural top product. The brain is by far the most complex structure in the whole universe, by comparison with which even a complicated computer works in a very simple way. This "grey mass" (large only by comparison with the smaller brain of the anthropoids) with its hollows and ridges displays structural levels and spheres of functions in which more than 10 billion brain cells are at work with the help of thousands of billions of links and guiding connections, extending over more than 100,000 kilometers. The processes of the brain are the result of both genetic disposition and social learning. The brain is not a mass fixed from early childhood, as was long believed. Rather it shows an amazing plasticity, power of regeneration, and capacity for change, and at the same time proves to be amazingly stable for our perception of ourselves and the world. As a result of new demands during our lifetimes, new neutron links can be built up in the brain and others dissolved.

Neurophysiological brain research has given us great insights in recent years. With the help of functional magnetic image resonance through new procedures that produce images — positron-emission tomography (PET) and functional magnetic resonance tomography (fMRT) — it has made impressive new discoveries: since the nerve cells (neurons with their continuations) use more protein and sugar with heightened intellectual activity, a heightened protein charge in different parts of the active areas of the brain can be measured. So states of consciousness can be correlated with activities in different parts of the brain. However, we are aware only of what is connected to the cerebral cortex, and this only to a small degree; processes outside that are unknown.

After all this research, it has become clear beyond dispute that all mental processes are closely connected with the electrochemical processes between the nerve cells in the brain, and these function in accordance with the natural laws of physics. Whatever conclusions one draws from this, no philosopher or theologian should enter into discussion with a neurobiologist without taking these physical and biological presuppositions seriously and recognizing the human potential of brain physiology. Those who prematurely and dogmatically introduce God into the debate over the freedom of the will or even introduce the incarnation of God, which is said to bring redemption from unfreedom and anxiety,[16] will a priori have lost the scientist. Having fully recognized the neurobiologist's scientific achievement, they will forfeit the chance of asking him bluntly whether he might not himself have his own dogmatic prejudice. For no science has a monopoly claim: just as philosophers and theologians should consider biological brain research, so brain researchers should consider questions of philosophy and theology. Be this as it may, instead of getting bogged down in trench warfare, here too I would like to build bridges. To that end I shall now make the question more pointed.

Is Free Will an Illusion?

Brain researchers have established more and more correspondence between the appearance of a particular process or state of consciousness and the activity of a particular region of the brain (identifiable macroscopically) or the (microscopic) circuits of neutrons from which the region of the brain is constructed. These insights are indubitable and welcome. However, neurophysiologists have now begun to draw momentous conclusions about the self or the self-consciousness of

16. Thus the Catholic moral theologian E. Schockenhoff in a discussion with the neurologist G. Roth in *Der Spiegel* 52 (2004).

the human being from this evidence: they argue that while we certainly experience that we are free in our will, decision, and action, science shows us that we are deceiving ourselves. The brain with its unconscious neuronal processes constantly precedes our will.

The Bremen researcher Gerhard Roth attributes to the limbic system with the basal ganglia (switches for muscle coordination) hidden deep in our brain the "ultimate decisions of human beings": the conscious I, he says, is "not the real master of our actions" and "freedom of will in the strict sense is a delusion." "In our thinking, feeling, willing, planning for action and the execution of our actions we human beings feel that we are free. Here our self feels that it is the cause of these states and actions. But this is evidently an illusion. Rather, psychological and neuro-scientific experiments and observations show that thoughts and intentions which come to our mind are largely caused and guided by the limbic system, which has a particularly strong effect on the frontal brain."[17]

So the feeling of being the author of our actions is as stubborn a delusion as the early notion that human beings are at the center of the universe. In fact, all our purposes and decisions, ideas and wishes, are determined by physiological processes. Everything is guided by the unconscious, by the limbic system, where for example even in childhood the decision is made as to whether or not one will become a sexual offender. Roth's view raises the question of what consequences such an application of neurophysiological insights would have for law and ethics.

Are all our everyday experiences of freedom deceptive? Or, to put it the other way around, are such conclusions from neurological experiments perhaps colored by conscious or unconscious philosophical assumptions? Wolf Singer of the Max Planck Institute in Frankfurt also claims that our intuition errs "dramatically"[18] in thinking that an "I authority" is responsible for decisions. Singer does not see any essential

17. G. Roth, "Das Ich auf dem Prufstand — Die Hirnforschung und ihre Sicht vom Menschen," radio broadcast on SWR 2, 10 June 2004; Roth, *Aus Sicht des Gehirns* (Frankfurt am Main, 2003).

18. W. Singer, "Selbsterfahrung und neurobiologische Fremdbeschreibung. Zwei konfliktträchtige Erkenntnisquellen," *Deutsche Zeitschrift für Philosophie* 2 (2004).

differences between conscious processes of the brain guided by us and unconscious, automatic processes. Singer's view wants to take account of the "trivial insight that a person did what he or she did because he or she could not do anything else at the moment in question, else he or she would have acted otherwise."[19] In logic this is called a *petitio principii*, a circular argument, begging the question, which presupposes what it wants to prove: "He could not do otherwise because he could not do otherwise." A circular argument easily arises when a brain researcher empirically establishes only what is structured by his consciousness and is attested with its help. The physicist or chemist as such will in any case hardly regard human beings as individual human beings in their uniqueness.

The Trivialization of Responsibility and Guilt by the Neurosciences

In such arguments it is amazing with what nonchalance, on the basis of short-term experiments, a neurophysiologist such as Roth foists his neurological hypothesis of the illusion of the freedom of the will, as a "deep-rooted foundational problem," on criminal law. This, he says, wrongly maintains a "principle of guilt and responsibility" that presupposes "all capacities of human beings to decide freely and rightly between right and wrong."

Of course, criminal law recognizes a limited capacity for guilt. But is the mental in principle merely an epiphenomenon of the neuronal? We should consider what pseudorelief such a neurological hypothesis brings the criminal: no guilt feelings — everything is illusion. I don't want to discuss the horrific Nazi crimes against humanity. But at the same time as Roth's report there was a terrible account in the German press of a clique of adult men and women in the Saarland who gang-raped a five-year-old boy and finally killed him. So are such monsters and all the adults who in Germany abuse at least 15,000 children every year unfree because of the mechanisms of the limbic system and therefore relieved from guilt and responsibility by a perfect scientific excuse?

19. Singer, "Selbsterfahrung und neurobiologische Fremdbeschreibung."

The victims and their parents will have little time for such a neurological trivialization of the guilt of child abusers. Instead of reflecting in a differentiated way on personal responsibility and guilt (and of course, also positively on merits), to appeal only to a "violation of social norms," as Roth does, seems empty in the face of almost total indifference to such social norms.

Authorities on forensic psychiatry such as Hans-Ludwig Kröber of Berlin find "suspicious the tendency of some brain researchers also to come forward as interpreters of the brain and to proclaim to an audience of lay people and amazed journalists with the aid of many colourful pictures that the freedom of the will is refuted and that criminal responsibility is a fiction. . . . In reality it is a very long way from the images from the PET, the functional positron emissions tomograph, to the question of criminal responsibility."[20] So when are we criminally responsible? "When we are in a position to make our decisions dependent on rational considerations, in other words when we are in a position to evaluate our wishes critically."[21]

In the Tübingen University Clinic, since January 2005 there has rightly been delight at the installation of one of the most modern pieces of diagnostic equipment in Europe (at the cost of 3.4 million euros), a combination of a computer tomograph (CT) and a positron-emissions tomograph (PET), which allows the smallest clusters of cancer cells to be recognized at an early stage. But unfortunately neurological hypotheses that declare that our understanding that we are free human beings is a delusion are partly to blame for the fact that the brain research that is making fantastic progress with the help of such instruments is today not just evoking hopes in the fight against serious diseases such as Alzheimer's, Parkinson's, schizophrenia, depression, and the regaining of

20. H.-L. Kröber, "Die Hirnforschung bleibt hinter dem Begriff strafrechtlicher Verantwörtlichkeit zurück," in *Hirnforschung und Willensfreiheit. Zur Deutung des neuesten Experimente,* ed. G. Geyer (Frankfurt am Main, 2004), 103-10, here 107f.

21. Kröber, "Die Hirnforschung bleibt hinter dem Begriff strafrechtlicher Verantwörtlichkeit zurück," 107f. Cf. also the warning by the Frankfurt criminal lawyer K. Lüderssen, "Ändert die Hirnforschung das Strafrecht?" in *Hirnforschung und Willensfreiheit,* 98-102, about brain research "which (probably innocently) has succumbed to the danger of a self-suggestive metaphysic" (102).

autonomy and freedom of decision. It is also encouraging anxieties that we human beings will become cold bio-automatons; guided by neurons, we could be exposed to every possible intervention to manipulate the consciousness and thus lose our identity and autonomy.

Happily, however, brain researchers too are becoming increasingly aware of the problems of such reductionist procedures, which are interested above all in what the human brain and the anthropoid brain have in common (and less in the differences). That human beings can think better but apes can climb better is one of these ridiculous levelings down. So now, after assessing the progress of brain research, it is time to show its equally clear limits.

4. The Limits of Brain Research

Functional magnetic resonance imagery gives us information — often very crude — about "where" things are in the brain, but not "how" cognitive achievements by neuronal mechanisms are to be described. It is never possible to read the feelings and thoughts of a person simply from the colorful patterns the tomographs produce from his or her brain activity. As for the "very indirect" measuring methods of the brain area, it is "rather as if one were attempting to discover the way in which a computer functioned by measuring its use of current while it was performing different tasks."[22] Of course, there are countless reflections on the biological foundations of an I-consciousness, but can these interesting speculations really overcome the gap in explanation between physical processes and consciousness? No, the more precisely the neuroscientists can describe the ways in which our brain functions, the clearer it becomes that none of their measurements and models embraces the central aspect of consciousness: subjectively by becoming aware of qualities such as color or smell, a reflection or an emotion. David Chalmers of Tucson, Arizona, explains that it is necessary to recognize that "conscious experience is an irreducible feature

22. Kröber, "Die Hirnforschung bleibt hinter dem Begriff strafrechtlicher Verantwörtlichkeit zurück," 107f.

of being."[23] We cannot expect that the relationship between brain and consciousness will be clarified in a flash, as the mystery of heredity was explained by Francis Crick and James Watson. Even Christof Loch, Crick's colleague, doesn't expect that.[24] So in 2004 brain research came to correct itself constructively in a surprising way.

Ignorance about the Decisive Levels of the Brain

A few months after Gerhard Roth's striking publications, in 2004 eleven leading German neuroscientists — remarkably also including Roth and Singer, who have already been cited — published a "Manifesto on the Present and Future of Brain Research."[25] In their introduction they said that the impression had been given that brain research was "on the threshold of wresting its last secrets from the brain." To reassure an alarmed public, they drew up a sober and balanced assessment of their young science, which was storming boldly ahead.

They said significant progress was being aimed at with the help of new methods:

- on the one hand on the *uppermost* level: research was being made into the functions and interplay of larger areas of the brain; the special tasks of the cerebral cortex and the basal ganglia, and thus a thematic division of the brain according to complexes of functions: understanding language, recognizing images, perceiving sounds,

23. Cf. D. J. Chalmers, "Das Rätsel des bewussten Erleben," *Spektrum der Wissenschaft,* Digest-ND, 4 (2004): 12-19. The same issue contains further illuminating articles on the riddle of the brain. Cf. Chalmers, *The Conscious Mind* (Oxford, 1996).

24. Cf. C. Loch, "Die Zukunft der Hirnforschung. Das Bewusstsein steht vor ihrer Enthüllung," in *Hirnforschung und Willensfreiheit,* 229-34.

25. Cf. "Das Manifest. Über Gegenwart und Zukunft der Hirnforschung," *Gehirn und Geist. Das Magazin für Psychologie und Hirnforschung* 6 (2004): 30-37. The manifesto is signed by Professors Christian Elger (Bonn), Angela Friederici (Leipzig), Christof Koch (Pasadena), Heiko Luhmann (Mainz), Christoph von der Malsburg (Bochum/Los Angeles), Randolf Menzel (Berlin), Hannah Monyer (Heidelberg), Frank Rösler (Marburg), Gerhard Roth (Bremen), Henning Scheich (Magdeburg), and Wolf Singer (Frankfurt am Main).

assimilating music, planning action, processes of memory, and experiencing emotions;

- on the other hand at the *lowest* level: today we largely understand the processes at the level of individual cells and molecules: the equipment of the nerve cell membranes with receptors, the function of neurotransmitters, the course of intracellular signal processes, the origin and further communication of neuronal stimulation;
- but not on the *middle* level: we know "terrifyingly little" of what goes on within hundreds or thousands of groups of cells: "We are completely ignorant about what takes place when hundreds of millions or even a billion nerve cells 'talk' to one another."[26]

All this amounts to an ignorance precisely at the decisive level of brain activity. For this is where thoughts and feelings, purposes and effects, consciousness and self-consciousness are made possible: "We still do not understand even the beginning of what rules the brain works by; how it depicts the world in such a way that direct perception and earlier experience fuse; how the inner action is experienced as 'its' activity and how it plans future actions. Furthermore, it is not at all clear how we can investigate it with present possibilities. In this respect to some degree we are still at the stage of hunters and gatherers."[27] Praiseworthy academic modesty (theologians too sometimes act as sheer "hunters and gatherers")!

The Big Questions of the Neurosciences

Fortunately, the neuroscientists who subscribed to the "Manifesto on the Present and Future of Brain Research" show themselves restrained about the "big questions": "How do consciousness and the experience of being a self arise, how are rational and emotional action linked, what about the notion of 'free will'? Today it is already permissible to ask the big questions of the neurosciences — however, it is unrealistic to think

---

26. "Das Manifest," 30-33.
27. "Das Manifest," 33.

that they will be answered in the next ten years. It even remains questionable whether we can approach them meaningfully by then. For that
we would need to know essentially more about the way in which the
brain functions."[28]

One can only agree. Even such a refined picturing procedure as a
"cyber-phrenology" cannot in fact fulfill the dream of an embodiment
of the mind. Some hope that a theoretical neurobiology will one distant
day supplement classical brain research, as quantum physics supple-
mented classical mechanics, then making it possible "so to speak to
understand the small uniqueness of the brain." That may be, but it
means that at present brain research has no empirically demonstrated
theory to offer about the connection between mind and brain, between
consciousness and the nervous system. To this degree one may hope
that in future all brain researchers will refrain from reductionist statements and keep to the closing sentences of their manifesto:

> But all the progress will not end in a triumph for neuronal
> reductionism. Even if at some point we have explained all the
> processes of the neuron which underlie human sympathy, being
> in love or moral responsibility, the distinctive feature of this "in-
> ternal perspective" nevertheless remains. For even a Bach fugue
> does not lose its fascination when one has understood precisely
> how it is constructed. Brain research will have to distinguish
> clearly between what it can say and what lies outside its sphere of
> competence, just as musicology — to keep to this example — has
> something to say about Bach's fugue, but can have no explana-
> tion of its unique beauty.[29]

There is a wealth of confirmation of this antireductionist view: for
example, the Tübingen behavioral neurologist Niels Birbaumer, who
plans to investigate even the electrical brain activity of the unborn, their
capacity to perceive and learn, with a novel magnetic encephalograph,
recommends to his colleagues "modest restraint in the generalization

28. "Das Manifest," 34.
29. "Das Manifest," 37.

and interpretation of neurobiological data." He remarks that he cannot say whether or not the will is free, as this cannot be measured. "Neither free nor unfree will can be observed, as we have no neuronal correlate of freedom. Freedom is certainly also a construct of the brain like all other behaviour and thought that human beings produce, but it is also and primarily a phenomenon which has grown up historically, politically and socially, and cannot just be derived from processes of the brain."[30]

The change of position of the American brain physiologist Benjamin Libet is interesting in this connection. In 1985 he was the first to carry out the much-cited behavioral physiological experiments that showed that the brain builds up a neuronal "readiness potential": for example, on raising the right or left finger or arm (a very small unit of the will), which is said to precede the subjectively experienced will to act by 350 to 400 milliseconds.[31] But does this "readiness potential" bind the will? In 1999 Libet then explained that the consciousness that lags behind in time is in a position to stop what the brain suggests as an action. So in all the pressure to act, "free will" at least has the power of veto. Libet's conclusion is now that the existence of a free will is at least as good a scientific option as denying it by the deterministic theory, if not a better one.[32]

Over against such short-term experiments on the "tug of the will" that is preceded by a potential for readiness, the Tübingen philosopher Otfried Höffe refers to a convincing intellectual experiment by Kant. Someone is required under threat of immediate death to give false evidence against an honest man. "Would he consider it possible in that case to overcome his love of life, however great it may be? He would perhaps not venture to affirm whether he would do so or not, but he must unhesitatingly admit that it is possible to do so."[33] So according to

30. N. Birbaumer, "Hirnforscher als Psychoanalytiker," in *Hirnforschung und Willensfreiheit,* 28.

31. Cf. B. Libet, "Do We Have a Free Will?" *Journal of Consciousness* 6 (1999): 47-57; Libet, *Mind Time: The Temporal Factor in Consciousness* (Cambridge, Mass., 2004).

32. Cf. Libet, "Do We Have?" 55.

33. I. Kant, *Critique of Practical Reason,* trans. T. K. Abbott (London, 1923), sec. 6, remark.

Kant, it is possible for him either to lie or to refuse to lie: "He judges, therefore, that he can do a certain thing because he is conscious that he ought, and he recognizes that he is free — a fact which but for the moral law he would never have known."[34] Höffe remarks: "Wherever someone acquires the attitude of honesty through education and self-education by appropriating the whole reality of morality, and thus remains honest even in a difficult situation, being ready to help or encourage, morality and freewill prove to be real."[35]

Besides, scientists have only recently begun to analyze these short-term experiments. It is pointed out that the experimenter communicates impulses to the brain simply through the attempted experiment and this immediately prompts unconscious neuronal activity. An analysis of the prehistory of an individual that made it possible for the decision processes of our own brain not to succumb to the limbic reflex in a particular situation would certainly be more illuminating than the analysis of milliseconds before a programmed movement of the finger. It is precisely here that we have freedom of the will: in the capacity of human beings to set themselves values and goals and pursue them in action, independently of the external and internal control of others, but rather in self-control, in "autonomy," in the "self-legislation" of the self. But in reality, is there a self at all?

Chemistry and Physics Do Not Explain the Self

Unlike the authors of the brain researchers' manifesto, Wolfgang Prinz of the Max Planck Institute for Cognition and Neurosciences in Munich thinks it is far from being demonstrated that on the basis of brain research "'our' picture of the human being has been considerably shaken." Like the beauty of a Bach fugue, he argues, so too the picture of the human being can remain untouched by any reduction and deconstruction; however, what certainly has to be revised is the naturalism that shapes this image of the human being and also that of

34. Kant, *Critique of Practical Reason*, 6.
35. O. Höffe, "Der entlarvte Ruck. Was sagt Kant den Gehirnforschern," in *Hirnforschung und Willensfreiheit*, 177-82, here 182.

some brain researchers but is hardly reflected on. Human beings are what they are not just through their nature but above all through their *culture,* and are so through and through, to the deepest roots of their cognitive achievements and the innermost corners and convolutions of their brains. "Therefore brain research can certainly do a lot here, but not everything. At all events it is of no use as the new leading discipline of the humanities, which it would very much like to be."[36] In a conversation Prinz is even clearer: "Biologists can explain how the chemistry and physics of the brain function. But so far no one knows how the experience of these comes about and how the brain produces meanings."[37]

The Berlin philosopher Peter Bieri regards the alleged empirical refutation of the freedom of the will as "a bit of adventurous metaphysics": "People look in vain in the material composition of a painting for the depiction or the beauty, and in the same sense one looks in vain in the neurobiological mechanics of the brain for freedom or a lack of freedom. There is neither freedom nor unfreedom there. The brain is logically the wrong place for this idea. . . . Our will is free if it controls our judgment as to what is rightly to be wanted. It is unfree if judgment and will fall apart."[38]

In connection with Aristotle,[39] the philosopher Thomas Buchheim of Munich observes that human beings do most of what they do by virtue of their brains: "Just as little as my hand boxes someone's ear, but I do, so just as little does my brain decide, but I myself. . . . When I am thinking with the brain, the brain does not think instead of me."[40] And whereas activities such as coughing, sweating, and dreaming are unfree and often even unconscious, the demonstration of a mathematical proof is not just conscious (as Singer thinks) but "in the consciousness also affirmed (judged affirmatively), and thus deliberately or

---

36. W. Prinz, "Neue Ideen tun Not," *Gehirn und Geist* 6 (2004): 35.

37. Prinz, "Der Mensch is nicht frei. Ein Gespräch," in *Hirnforschung und Willensfreiheit,* 26.

38. P. Bieri, "Unser Wille ist frei," *Der Spiegel* 2 (2005).

39. Cf. Aristotle, *De anima* 1.4.408b.7-15.

40. T. Buchheim, "Wer kann, der kann auch anders," in *Hirnforschung und Willensfreiheit,* 158-65, here 161.

willed,"[41] and this is not decided by a brain (erroneous objectifying talk) or even a "network of nerves"; I, the person, decide. "So if as whole human beings we repent of our deeds, then we should also be said to have committed them as whole human beings."[42]

Against the notion of the primacy of matter or the brain, the legal philosopher Reinhard Brandt of Marburg formulates the thesis: "In no brain cell and in no synapse does one have and will one discover the equivalent of a judgment, especially a negation. . . . As long as the formation of a judgment or insight and especially a negation have not been discovered, the spirit cannot be derived from any processes of the brain, however dynamic and democratically networked."[43] The neurologist and philosopher Detlev B. Linke of Bonn has worked out under the title "Freedom and the Brain"[44] how in particular creativity plays a decisive role in human thought and action and how the freedom of human thought and action manifests itself here.

Taking up Peter Bieri, the philosopher Jürgen Habermas makes a sharp distinction between causes and grounds: "Anyone who is subject to the causal compulsion of an imposed limitation," i.e., to a compelling cause, is in fact unfree. But anyone who "is subject to the uncompelling compulsion of the better argument" and decides on an action for particular reasons is free. The bending of an arm or finger induced by an experimenter is not a free action in terms of moral responsibility. Moral responsibility is always the result of a complex interweaving of considerations about means and ends, resources and obstacles, which have to be weighed up. Interpersonal communication, which is at the center of interest for Habermas and his ethics of discourse, is not a "blind event of nature" that runs its course as it were behind the subject's back. Already in the newborn child the human spirit develops only in social interaction, through cooperation and instruction. And to this degree the spirit by no means resides only in the brain, but is "em-

41. Cf. Buchheim, "Wer kann, der kann auch anders," 162.
42. Buchheim, "Wer kann, der kann auch anders," 164.
43. R. Brandt, "Ick bün all da. Ein neuronales Erregungsmuster," in *Hirnforschung und Willensfreiheit,* 171-76, here 175.
44. Cf. D. B. Linke, *Die Freiheit und das Gehirn. Eine neurophilosophische Ethik* (Munich, 2005).

bodied" in the whole human person. The self may be a social construc-
tion, but that does not mean it is an illusion.[45]
Here another aspect is important.

Experience of Freedom

In their everyday self-understanding even brain researchers constantly
presuppose responsible authorship in themselves, their colleagues,
and the patients. Simply to explain this self-understanding as an
epiphenomenon betrays a deterministic dogmatism that needs to be
investigated. Here the laboratory perspective needs to be expanded by
the perspective of the world in which we live, and external and internal
views need to be dovetailed. Alongside the neurological method, introspection is by no means to be despised. After all, in practice it must also
be used constantly by neurophysiologists if they want to interpret their
images and the processes they have established. They must then also
"look into themselves" instead of into the magnetic resonance imager:
the self-observation that is possible for anyone, supported by the observation of the conduct of others, cannot only look back. It can even grasp
psychological processes as they are happening.

Of course, everyone has his or her own perspective on things, as the
psychiatrist Manfred Spitzer of the University of Ulm observes: "So for
me things are again quite different from what they are for someone who
so to speak looks at me from outside. For me the sky is blue. But anyone
who roots around in my head, by whatever means, will not find anything
blue. And just as I can always decide for myself here and now, so it can be
that someone who roots around in my head will never find this freedom.
Nevertheless: for myself I am always free, just as for me the sky is always
blue."[46] Spitzer, who is very concerned that this insight should be used
in education, even thinks: "The better we get to know the machinery of
our actions and decisions in a neurological way, the freer we become."[47]

45. Cf. J. Habermas, "Um uns als Selbsttäuscher zu entlarven, bedarf es mehr,"
Frankfurter Allgemeine Zeitung, 15 Nov. 2004.

46. M. Spitzer, "Es gibt nicht Gutes, ausser man tut es — Die Hirnforschung und
die Frage, was uns zum Handeln antreibt," radio broadcast on SWR 2, 13 June 2004.

47. Spitzer, "Es gibt nicht Gutes, ausser man tut es."

Individuals experience others and themselves time and again as un-predictable, because they are free. So often someone says no when one expects yes and yes when one fears a no. Election and stock exchange pre-dictions — though people all too often succumb to the herd instinct — are often refuted. I experience in myself as an indisputable fact that how-ever much I am dependent and determined externally and internally in my whole being, this or that is ultimately up to me: whether I speak or keep silent, get up or remain sitting, prefer this or that drink or garment, this or that journey. However much my brain decides spontaneously that my eye will look at someone or my foot will evade an obstacle, as soon as this is not just a short physical movement (such as raising an arm or fin-ger) as in those experiments but lengthy processes that require my reflec-tion — for example, the choice of a profession, the acceptance of a job, the choice of a partner for life — I must grapple with different thoughts and alternative courses of action; I must decide, and in some circum-stances correct my decision. Here the whole of my life comes into view.[48]

The Tübingen developmental biologist Alfred Gierer is therefore right when alongside neurophysiology and introspection he emphasizes that our deliberate actions are a third access to our consciousness and our freedom: "In terms of information theory, the objective analysis of processes in the brain can produce only part of the information about states and processes of consciousness; the intersubjective communi-cation of conscious experience through language discloses more, and deliberate action even more. To some degree all three accesses are com-plementary, but even together they still do not provide a complete pic-ture."[49] If instead of the "somewhat dusty mechanics of the nineteenth century which preceded quantum physics" one goes by the insights of

48. To anyone interested in a comprehensible but highly differentiated account of the problems of the freedom of the will, I recommend P. Bieri, *Das Handwerk der Freiheit. Über die Entdeckung des eigenen Willens* (Munich, 2001). In my own experi-ence, in the first four decades I had more than enough opportunity to explore the different dimensions of freedom; cf. H. Küng, *My Struggle for Freedom: Memoirs* (London, 2002).

49. A. Gierer, *Biologie, Menschenbild und die knappe Ressource Gemeinsinn* (Würzburg, 2005), 73. Cf. Gierer, *Die Physik, das Leben und die Seele* (Munich, 1985); Gierer, *Die gedachte Natur. Ursprung, Geschichte, Sinn und Grenzen der Naturwissen-schaft* (Munich, 1991).

the mathematical theory of decision, then it is necessary to "reckon with limits in principle to the deciphering of the relationship between brain and mind."[50] This would also meet the age-old basic problem of the freedom of the will: "Presumably the will of others cannot be disclosed completely with objective means. We do not even know ourselves sufficiently — our look inwards is incomplete — and in many respects we experience ourselves first in our own actions."[51] Here we should broaden the horizon yet further over the problem of brain and mind.

The Spiritual Cosmos

Modern research into the brain is as far from explaining the riddle of the origin of the mind in human beings as microbiology is from explaining the origin of life. It hardly looks at the spiritual cosmos with all the wonders of science, art, music, culture, philosophy, and religion, although these are the powers that shape the neuronal processes. Brain research is far removed from the concrete world in which we live, and even further removed from the world of history. For historiography a cerebral explanation by means of a "neuronal turn," of the kind proposed by the Frankfurt medievalist Johannes Fried,[52] would be a rather barren "extreme task in intellectual sport," as the modern historian Marcus Völkel asks: "What would move us to describe Chartres Cathedral, the Civil Code or the machete scars of the victims of Rwanda as pure epiphenomena of neuronal processes?"[53]

The fascinating images of the brain thus initially give information only about *where* thinking, willing, and feeling take place, and not, as we noted, *how* thinking, willing, and feeling come about, far less *what* the content of this thinking, willing, and feeling is. Anyone who looks at the pattern of neuronal stimulation by no means sees the human being with feelings, thought, and will. A map is not yet a landscape, a cartog-

50. Gierer, *Biologie*, 73.

51. Gierer, *Biologie*, 45.

52. Cf. J. Fried, "Geschichte und Gehirn. Irritationen der Geschichtswissenschaft durch Gedächtniskritik," in *Hirnforschung und Willensfreiheit*, 111-33.

53. M. Völkel, "Wohin führt der 'neuronal turn' die Geschichtswissenschaft?" in *Hirnforschung und Willensfreiheit*, 140-42, here 141.

rapher is not yet a geographer, far less a traveler. The different colored markings of the zone of the brain affected in hearing music or looking at a picture cannot produce the sound of music or paint a real picture before our eyes.

The neurobiologist grasps only what can be measured and experimentally verified in the brain. But the world of human feelings, freedom, will, love, consciousness, the I, the self, cannot adequately be described in this physiological perspective on the brain. And how is the neurobiologist to be able to discover in the brain that it is not only the possibility of self-reference that distinguishes the human being from the animal but the reference to transcendence (no matter what one may personally think of this)? However fruitful a psychological investigation of religious feelings, acts, and experiences and a comparison with pathological phenomena (hallucination, etc.) can be, as William James demonstrated at a very early stage,[54] we get little help from a "neurotheology" of evangelical apologists who even want to produce a neurobiological proof of God, because human beings need faith and religion as much as they need to eat and drink.[55]

In his excellent "Operating Instructions for a Human Brain," the Göttingen neurobiologist Gerald Hüther again points to the plasticity of the human brain: it changes depending on use and becomes as we use it. Indeed, at any point in our life we can decide to use our brain in the future in a rather different way. Unlike geese or moles, we human beings have "a brain which to some degree first programmes itself by the way in which it is used. So we must decide how and for what we use it."[56] The most primitive stage of knowledge is the "if-then-knowledge" that is also innate in apes. But anyone who remains at the stage of this simple cause-and-effect connection remains primitive. Moreover, many people soon discover that several causes work together in most phenomena. The highest stage of knowledge is self-knowledge. Only

54. Cf. W. James, *The Varieties of Religious Experience: A Study in Human Nature* (New York, 1902).

55. For criticism see F. W. Graf, "Brain me up! Gibt es einen neurobiologischen Gottesbeweis?" in *Hirnforschung und Willensfreiheit*, 143-47.

56. Cf. G. Hüther, *Bedienungsanleituung für ein menschliches Gehirn* (Göttingen, 2001), 99.

the human brain has succeeded in "developing an overarching notion of the nature of human beings and their place in the world . . . , that of the transcendental (or transpersonal or cosmic) consciousness."[57] There is a whole series of basic attitudes (often forgotten today) for using one's brain in a more comprehensive, complex, and networked way than before: "Meaningfulness, honesty, modesty, caution, truthfulness, reliability, obligation. . . ."[58]

So freedom is an experience not just of thought and feeling but of action. But it is also an experience of doing nothing, failing and incurring guilt. For in my actions I can also directly experience this negative aspect: I have not done it but I should have; I have given a promise but not kept it; I am guilty, I acknowledge my guilt and ask for forgiveness; but I also require from others an acknowledgment of their guilt where I was not guilty.

Indeed, what would morality be without responsibility, what would responsibility be without freedom, what would freedom be without a tie? Particularly at a time when there is a threat of lack of orientation, support, and meaning, this question must be taken very seriously — for the sake of the threatened humanity of human beings that needs to be strengthened. Human morality, the human ethic, also developed only slowly. Yet in all the changeability since human beings became human, a certain constancy is evident.

5. The Beginnings of the Human Ethic

The question of the beginning of all things also includes questions such as, Where do specific ethical values, criteria, and norms come from? I shall go into them briefly and succinctly. "Only human beings can have an ethic. To recognize biological facts does not mean to be free of the responsibility of working out such an ethic," writes the molecular physician Gerd Kempermann of Berlin.[59]

57. Hüther, *Bedienungsanleitung für ein menschliches Gehirn,* 118.
58. Hüther, *Bedienungsanleitung für ein menschliches Gehirn,* 123.
59. G. Kempermann, "Infektion der Geistes. Über philosophische Kategorienfehler," in *Hirnforschung und Willensfreiheit,* 235-39, here 239.

Evolutionary Biological and Sociocultural Factors

Theologians, too, should not dispute that the ethical behavior of human beings is rooted in their biological nature.[60] Sociobiologists such as Alfred Gieler rightly note the evolutionary biological factors in the development in human behavior: the human being, coming from the animal realm, initially had a primarily selfish orientation and necessarily so. Particularly in the early phases of the process of humanization, the human being was strongly tied to the basic biological conditions of his life for the sake of his survival. But already in higher animals there is a cooperative behavior among all those who are related or socially intimate that is produced genetically. Perhaps here we can already note a kind of "reciprocal" altruism understood as a disposition to help others at one's own expense without a deliberate orientation: "As you act to me, so I act to you." An action is performed with the expectation of receiving something in return.

So social researchers with equal justification also point to the sociocultural factors that play a role in ethical behavior in the various societies. A biological and mechanistic interpretation is not in fact enough to explain the origin of ethical values and criteria. There is no doubt that with the capacity to speak there also developed among human beings a unique capacity for cooperation that despite the genetically innate capacity for learning had to be learned socially. With the evolution of strategic thought there also developed a capacity for empathy, a feeling for the fears, expectations, and hopes of others, a fellow feeling that became basic to human social behavior.

After the period of hordes of hunter-gatherers, the higher cultural development could build on the basic biological conditions. Concrete ethical norms, values, and insights gradually emerged — in a highly complicated sociodynamic process; in this sense an "autonomous morality" is also being advocated by theologically open ethicists.[61] Depending on where the needs of life make themselves felt, where urgent and pressing matters emerge in interpersonal relationships, from the

---

60. Cf. Gierer, *Biologie,* 75-93.
61. See the numerous publications by A. Auer, F. Böckle, C. Curran, G. Gründel, G. Hunold, W. Korff, D. Mieth, etc.

beginning orientations for actions and regulations for human behavior have imposed themselves: particular conventions, instructions, customs, in short, particular ethical criteria, rules, norms. Over the course of the centuries, indeed the millennia, they have been tested everywhere among humankind. They had, so to speak, to become established.

The Primal Ethic as the Basis for a Global Ethic

There is no people without a religion, much less without an ethic, i.e., without quite specific values and criteria. Already in the tribal cultures there are unwritten norms, not given propositional form, a family, group, tribal ethic, handed down in stories, parables, and comparisons, which — if they are recognized as "good" — are universalized:

- a sense of mutuality, justice, generosity (perhaps in reciprocal giving);
- a deep reverence for all life (for example, in settling conflicts, in punishing violence, in dealing with nature);
- particular rules for the sexes living together (for example, the prohibition of incest and a rejection of libertinism);
- great respect for parents (and at the same time care of children).

It is striking that certain elementary moral standards seem to be the same all over the world. In the view of cultural anthropologists, unwritten ethical norms form the rock on which human society is built. One can call this a "primal ethic" that forms the core of a common ethic of humankind, a global ethic. This is not meant in the sense of a single "primal religion," to be found in some tribe or people (but which in fact cannot be discovered). On the contrary, such a primal ethic occurs in every possible tribe and people. So a "global ethic" does not have its foundation only in the basic norms that different religions and cultures have in common today (synchronically). It is also based (diachronically) on the basic norms of tribal cultures that already became established in prehistoric times (before the beginning of written sources). Even if of course not every norm is an element of an ethic that was given originally, to emphasize the continuity given through all the transformations, it can be said that the global ethic lived out today in space is ultimately based on a biological evolutionary primal ethic that has been tried out in time. But what does this mean for the ethic of the high religions, above all for that of the Bible, which indeed is also relevant for the ethical orientation of many scientists?

Even the Biblical Ethic Has a History

Only after periods of acclimatization and testing can there be a general recognition of such experienced norms as will later also be formulated in propositions. Indeed, in individual cultures they were put under the will of the one God, in exemplary form in the Ten Commandments of the Hebrew Bible as these were received by Israel according to the Sinai tradition by a revelation of God: not only "Do not murder, steal, bear false witness, commit adultery," but also "I am the Lord, your God. . . . You shall not . . ." (Exod. 20:1-17; Deut. 5:6-21).

However, the Ten Commandments, too, have a history. The ethical instructions of the Hebrew Bible did not fall from heaven any more than the narratives about the beginning and end of the world. Research into the Old Testament[62] has broadly demonstrated this: not just for the later ethic of the prophets and the even later ethic of the wisdom literature (which already sounds very "secular"), but also and in particular for the early ethic of the law of Moses. The instructions on the "second" tablet for interpersonal relations reach back into the pre-Israelite, seminomadic moral and legal traditions; they have countless analogies in the Near East. That does not exclude the possibility that a series of impressive basic instructions for the people of Yahweh was brought from the wilderness by the group around Moses and bequeathed to all Israel.

But whatever may be the origin of the Ten Commandments, these fundamental minimal demands for a human life in society precede the origin of belief in Yahweh, and if we compare them with the ethic of the peoples between Egypt and Mesopotamia, they are not specifically Isra-

---

62. The publications of A. Alt, W. Eichrodt, J. L. McKenzie, G. von Rad, W. Zimmerli, etc., are important for the ethic of the Hebrew Bible.

elite. In that case, what is specifically Israelite? That these demands are set under the authority of Yahweh, the God of the covenant, to whom the obligations of the "first table" and above all the basic command-ment of being committed to Yahweh alone, excluding all other deities, refer.

So the characteristic feature of biblical morality does not consist in the discovery of new ethical norms but in the fact that the instructions handed down were put under the legitimating and protective authority of the one true God and his covenant. The norms that came into being on the basis of human experiences are thus not a voluntary human law or a merely general divine law for Israel, but the categorical demands of the one true God of the fathers known from history. By being accepted into the new relationship with God, morality received a new motivation (gratitude, love, the gaining of life, the gift of freedom became decisive motives) and was given a dynamic (existing norms were taken further, newly developed, or adopted).

But what new element does the specifically Christian ethic bring by comparison with the ethic of the Hebrew Bible? For a majority of West-ern scientists Christianity is still the ideological background, but in the global scientific community, influences from other religions are in-creasingly playing a role.

The One Light and the Many Lights

Is there a distinctively Christian feature in ethics? People look for it in vain if they seek it abstractly in some idea or principle, some disposi-tion, a horizon of meaning or a new disposition or motivation. "Forgive-ness"? "Love"? "Freedom"? Though these are indispensable for Chris-tians, they are not specifically Christian. Many others live and act by them. Act against the background of a "creation" or "consummation"? Others also do that: Jews, Muslims, humanists of very different kinds. But what then is the criterion of the Christian, the distinctively Chris-tian? It is not an abstract something, a Christ idea, a Christology, or a christocentric system of thought, but the concrete crucified Jesus as the living Christ, as the one who is the norm.

There is a vividness about Jesus as a concrete historical person: he can be perceived and realized in a way that an eternal idea, an abstract principle, a universal norm, an intellectual system cannot. For believers, too, he can represent a basic model of a view of life and conduct that can be realized in many ways. He makes possible in a specific way what people are calling for on all sides in the face of a lack of orientation, loss of norms, meaninglessness, drug addiction, and violence: a new basic orientation and basic attitude, but also new motivations, dispositions, actions, and finally a new horizon of meaning and the determination of a new goal.

So already in the New Testament Jesus is called the light: "the light of men" (John 1:4), "the light of the world" (8:12). One can learn from him what a selfish society of egotists so lacks: to be able to take heed and to share, to forgive and to repent, to practice restraint and renunciation, and to offer help. After all, it depends on believers whether Christianity, by really taking its bearings from its Christ and letting him give light, illumination, to the spirit, can provide a spiritual home, a house of faith, hope, and love.

According to the New Testament, non-Christians, too, can know the real God; God is also near to them. And if for Christians Jesus Christ as the light is also the decisive criterion for Christian action, Christians cannot avoid seeing that there are also other lights:

- For millions of people, the majority of them scattered all over the world, Moses is the leading figure and the great liberation, and they find their pointer to life in the Torah of the Hebrew Bible.
- For hundreds of millions of Muslims in the past and present the Qur'an is the "light" that illuminates their way; the prophet Muhammad sent by God personally embodies this message of the Qur'an in a convincing way.
- For hundreds of millions of people on this earth in the past and the present, Gautama is the "Buddha," the "Awakened," the "Illuminated" and thus the great light.
- For millions of Chinese Confucius in his teaching and his basic attitude of humanity is still the guiding light.
- For hundreds of millions of Indians Hinduism with its various current and different manifestations, with its faith in an all-

embracing cosmic order *(dharma),* is the framework of life that provides orientation.

If more than 6 billion people populate this planet, no religion can dispute with others their way to salvation. Rather it is important in recognition of human freedom, especially the real freedom of faith, for each to respect its own path of faith and to encounter the other in dialogue, so as to better understand itself. In the one world society all human beings are concerned with the fate of the earth, no matter what their religion, philosophy, or worldview. The directives of the global ethic can be a basic orientation for this responsibility for the world, and this by no means excludes a special orientation on one's own religion. On the contrary, each can contribute to a global ethic in its own way.

But what is the future of humankind? What is the future of the earth, the cosmos? Since at least in physics the theories of the beginning and the end of the cosmos hang together and there are also various parallels between beginning and end in the biblical visions, in an epilogue I want to talk about the "end of things," though of course it is as hidden as the beginning.

The End of All Things

—◁᷅◦◦᷄▷—

Like the prophet Joel (2:10), the New Testament too speaks of the sun being darkened and the moon losing its light, the stars falling from heaven and the powers of heaven being shaken in the last tribulation (Matt. 24:29). Aren't these spooky enough visions in the light of theories of the end time in physics? But it is necessary to warn against theological fallacies about the end of the world as much as against fallacies about the beginning of the world. Here too theology has to make up for the understandable prejudices it has produced among scientists.

Hypotheses of the End in Physics

Of course, astrophysicists also speculate about the end: in around 5 billion years the Andromeda Galaxy will collide with our Milky Way and billions of stars will be hurled around the universe. At the same time, the sun will swell up into a "red giant." Then all life still existing on our earth will die out. Is all that so certain? Much that is taught in physics about the "last three minutes" of the universe is speculative. Moreover, the American physicist Paul Davies gave his book, which is a good summary of futurological research, the appropriate subtitle "Conjectures about the Ultimate Fate of the Universe."[1]

---

1. Cf. P. Davies, *The Last Three Minutes: Conjectures about the Ultimate Fate of the Universe* (New York, 1994).

The majority of cosmologists today begin by assuming that our world is anything but stable, unchanging, indeed eternal; Harald Fritzsch calls it a "world between beginning and end."[2] However, there is a dispute over the question raised again after the discovery in April 1992 of what are so far the oldest structures (fluctuations) of the universe, namely, whether the expansion of the universe that began with the Big Bang will one day come to a stop and then turn into a contraction or whether it will continue permanently.

The first hypothesis starts from a "pulsating" or "swinging" universe, but as we have heard, so far it has not been possible to verify this in any way. According to this hypothesis, one day the expansion will slow down and turn into a contraction, so that the universe will again draw itself together in a process lasting many billions of years and the galaxies with their stars will finally condense faster and faster until possibly — scientists talk of at least 80 billion years after the Big Bang — with the dissolution of the atoms and atomic nuclei into their elements there will be another Big Bang, the Big Crunch. Then perhaps a new world could arise in a renewed explosion. Perhaps, such a universe "oscillating" between phases of contraction and expansion is no more than pure speculation. Indeed, strong "faith" is needed to accept without any empirical evidence that any Big Crunch would be followed by a Big Bang that would produce a new world with totally different laws of nature.

The second hypothesis, which today has the majority of astrophysicists behind it, is that the expansion of the universe, which is measured as being very flat (most recently by the French CNRS [National Committee for Scientific Research]), is constantly progressing without being braked and turned into contraction. Indeed, the universe, possibly accelerated by a "dark energy" distributed all over the universe (vacuum fluctuations?), is extending faster and faster. Here too the stars undergo development: when their store of energy is used up, in heavy stars there is a supernova explosion (with possibly a billion times more light than the sun); the inner part of the mass collapses into the center and a neu-

---

2. Cf. H. Fritzsch, *Vom Urknall zur Zerfall. Die Welt zwischen Anfang und Ende* (Munich, 1983). Cf. his most recent work, *Das absolute Unveränderliche. Die letzten Rätsel der Physik* (Munich, 2005).

tron star forms. With smaller stars, for example, the sun, finally a "white dwarf" forms, perhaps as large as our earth; this is stabilized by the pressure of the electrons from collapsing through the force of gravity. So from the matter transformed within the stars and ejected, new stars and generations of stars form. In these, once again nuclear processes will take place in which the matter within the star finally burns into "star ashes" (iron and nickel). Cold will slowly enter the cosmos, death, silence, absolute night. But long before that our sun will first inflate itself into a "red giant" and swallow up the earth, until it too goes out because its hydrogen is used up.

Is all this also pure speculation? By no means, for the constant expansion of the universe is observable, and the different stages of the development of stars have been verified by astronomers with astonishing precision. But should we be afraid of something that, if it happens at all, will happen only in 5 billion years, when the stock of hydrogen within the sun is exhausted?

Apocalyptic Visions of the End

The pressing threatening problem for our average contemporaries is not so much the end of our universe, of whose tremendous temporal and spatial extent in any case the biblical generations had no inkling. The problem is rather the destruction of the world for us, the end of our earth, or more precisely of humankind: the destruction of the world as the end of humankind, brought about by human beings.

In the face of all the global catastrophes, wars and famines, earthquakes, the tsunamis and other natural catastrophes, many "born-again" Christians quote the oppressive, terrifying vision in the New Testament and thus foment anxieties: "And you will hear of wars and rumors of wars; see that you are not alarmed; for this must take place, but the end is not yet. For nation will rise against nation, and kingdom against kingdom, and there will be famines and earthquakes in various places; all this is but the beginning of the sufferings. . . . Immediately after the tribulation of those days the sun will be darkened, and the moon will not give its light, and the stars will fall from heaven, and the powers of the heaven will be shaken" (Matt. 24:6-8, 29).

Now we do not need to read any stories about the end of the world from Poe to Dürrenmatt or to watch disaster films to know that we are the first generation in human memory capable of putting an end to humankind by unleashing nuclear forces. The "small" atom bombs on Hiroshima and Nagasaki and the reactor accident in Chernobyl have shown people everywhere what a large-scale nuclear war would mean: the earth would become uninhabitable. But today, now that the danger of a large nuclear war has declined as a result of the end of the Cold War, more and more people are fearing "small" nuclear wars between fanatical nationalistic peoples or sparked off by terrorist groups. And they fear above all the collapse of the environment, which could likewise destroy our earth: climate change, overpopulation, catastrophic pollution, a hole in the ozone layer, polluted air, poisoned ground, chemically polluted water, a shortage of water. Even the British astronomer and cosmologist Martin Rees, who has been cited on various occasions for the somewhat hypothetical many-universes theory (cf. chap. II), in his most recent book under the title *Our Final Century?* goes into gloomy prognoses, catastrophic scenarios, and criticisms of science in view of the extremely real "man-made problems."[3]

These are apocalyptic visions that could become reality unless humankind stirs itself energetically to produce more defensive and reform measures in all areas — from climate protection to birth control. But particularly in the leading Western power, the USA, so far ecological and social change is yet to come.[4] Rather, there the criminal atrocities of Muslim fanatics on 11 September 2001 have led to an unprecedented boom in Christian "end-time" literature. The modern belief in progress that was disseminated from the time of the first technical romances of the future by Jules Verne in the 1860s has turned into postmodern skepticism and pessimism. History and fantasy, apocalyptic and esotericism, Christian and pseudo-Christian are mixed up here. The Left Be-

3. Cf. M. Rees, *Our Final Century? Will the Human Race Survive the Twenty-First Century?* (London, 2004).

4. For the problems of a new paradigm of a global politics and a global economic, cf. H. Küng, *A Global Ethic for Global Politics and Economics* (London and New York, 1996). Cf. H. Küng and D. Senghaas, eds., *Friedenspolitik. Ethische Grundlagen internationaler Beziehungen* (Munich, 2003).

hind series, which has grown to eleven novels, has sold millions of copies; it shows how on the return of Christ "the evil" will be rejected and "left behind." Even better known is the film *Armageddon,* in which Christians defeat the power of evil in the final battle; here Americans as a matter of course identify themselves with "the good." In this way they also often legitimate their military policy and preventive wars in the present over oil and hegemony. President Ronald Reagan, who did not always distinguish clearly between virtual and real reality and foresaw a "star" war, already believed, like Jehovah's Witnesses, in "Armageddon," according to the book of Revelation (16:16), the mythical place at which the demonic spirits gather "the kings of all the earth" for the great final battle, from which the annihilation of this system of things will proceed.

It is bad that some people regard exciting novels such as Dan Brown's *The Da Vinci Code* about the "Last Supper" and the "Holy Grail" as historical works, indeed, that even an intelligent American president such as Bill Clinton took a novel about the threat to the USA from a biological attack (richly documented with the support of neoconservative circles in the Pentagon) as genuine and gave relevant instructions to the military.[5] All these apocalyptists with their vast following of conservative Christians urgently need an explanation of what the apocalyptic passages of the Bible really mean.

The Significance of the Biblical Visions

To think that we have exact predictions about the end of the world or at least of our earth in the New Testament reports of the last tribulation, the darkening of the earth and the moon, the falling of the stars and the shaking of the powers of heaven, and to regard them as a kind of chronological "un-veiling" (Greek *apo-kalypsis*) or as information about the "last things" at the end of world history, is to misunderstand the texts.

Just as the biblical narratives of God's work of creation were taken from the environment of the time, so too the reports of God's final

---

5. Cf. R. Preston, *The Cobra Event* (New York, 1977). Cf. the illuminating criticism by the Basel historian P. Sarasin, *Anthrax. Bioterror als Phantasma* (Frankfurt am Main, 2004).

work were taken from contemporary apocalyptic, a contemporary current stamped by expectations of the end around the beginning of the common era. The spooky visions of the book of Revelation are an impressive warning to humankind and to individuals to recognize the seriousness of the situation. But just as the biblical protology cannot be a report of events at the beginning, so biblical eschatology cannot be a forecast of end events. So here the Bible is not speaking any scientific language of facts, but a metaphorical language. Here, too, it is again true of biblical language that:

- Images are not to be taken literally; otherwise faith becomes superstition.
- But images are not to be rejected simply because they are images; otherwise reason degenerates into rationalism.
- Images may not be eliminated or reduced to abstract concepts, but have to be understood correctly: they have their own reason, depict reality with their own logic, and seek to disclose the deep dimension, the overall meaning of reality. So it is important to translate what they mean once more from the framework of the understanding and imagining of that time into the thought world of today.[6]

None of these biblical announcements can be the film script for the last act of the human tragedy. For they do not contain any special divine "revelations" that could satisfy our curiosity about the end. In them we are not given any details about what will happen to us and how things will turn out. Like the "first things," so too the "last things" are not accessible to direct experiences. There are no human witnesses to either the "primal time" or the "end time." And just as we have no clear scientific extrapolation, so too we have no precise prophetic prognosis of the definitive future of humankind, the earth, and the cosmos. The biblical picture of the great public judgment of all humankind, the billions and trillions of human beings, is likewise an image.

6. K. P. Fischer, *Kosmos und Weltende. Theologische Überlegungen vor dem Horizont moderner Kosmologie* (Mainz, 2001), gives a survey of the understanding of the end of the world among Catholic and Protestant theologians.

What then is the meaning of these poetic images and narratives of the beginning and the end? They stand for what cannot be fathomed by pure reason, for what is hoped for and feared. The biblical statements about the end of the world are a testimony of faith to the completion of God's work on his creation: at the end of the history of the world and human beings we also find — God! Therefore theology has no occasion to favor one or another scientific model of the world, but it does have an interest in making God understandable as the origin and consummator of the world and human beings. Here too everyone is faced with an option, a decision of faith. According to the message of the Bible, the history of the world and human life move toward that last goal of goals that we call God, God the consummator. And if human beings cannot prove him to be the creator God either, they have good reason for affirming him: in that rational, tried, enlightened trust in which they have already affirmed God's existence. For if the God who exists is truly God, then he is not just God for me here and now and today, but he is also God at the end. If he is Alpha, then he is also Omega: God, as the liturgy says, forever and ever.

Dying into the Light

I personally have accepted Blaise Pascal's "wager" and have put my stake on God and the infinite against the void and nothingness — not on the basis of a calculation of probability or mathematical logic but on the basis of a rational trust. I do not believe in the later legendary elaborations of the New Testament message of the resurrection but in its original core: that this Jesus of Nazareth did not die into nothingness,[7] but into God. So trusting in this message, I hope as a Christian, like many people in other religions, not to die into nothingness, which seems to me to be extremely irrational and senseless. Rather, I hope to die into the ultimate reality, into God, which — beyond space and time in the hidden real dimension of the infinite — transcends all human

7. For the original understanding of the biblical message of the resurrection, cf. H. Küng, *On Being a Christian* (London and New York, 1976), chap. V, "The New Life"; Küng, *Credo: The Apostles' Creed Explained for Today* (London and New York, 1993), chap. IV: "The Descent into Hell — Resurrection — Ascension."

reason and conceiving. What child without any special knowledge would believe that the cocoon of a caterpillar would achieve the shining existence of a butterfly, no longer tied to the earth? Of course, I am aware of the abiding risk of this wager in unconditional trust, but I am convinced that even if I lose the wager in death, I will have lost nothing for my life; at all events, I will have lived a better, happier, more meaningful life than if I had not had hope.

This is my enlightened, well-founded hope: dying is a farewell inward, an entry and homecoming into the ground and origin of the world, our true home, a farewell perhaps not without pain and anxiety, but hopefully in composure and surrender, at any rate without weeping and wailing, and without bitterness and despair, but rather in hopeful expectation, quiet certainty, and (after everything that has to be settled is settled) ashamed gratitude for all the good things and less good things that now finally and definitively lie behind us — thank God.[8]

So I can understand the unfathomable totality of reality:

God as Alpha and Omega, the beginning and end of all things.
And therefore a dying into the light.

I began this book with the saying about light on the first page of the Bible in the book of Genesis.

I would like to end it with the saying about light on the last page, the Revelation of John:

And there will be no more light, and they will need neither the light of a lamp nor the light of the sun. For the Lord their God will shine upon them, and they will rule from eternity to eternity. (Rev. 22:5)

8. Cf. H. Küng and W. Jens, *A Dignified Dying* (London, 1995).

A Word of Thanks

As early as the 1970s I turned to the question *Does God Exist? An Answer for Today* (1978), following my book *On Being a Christian* (1974), and in doing so studied the most recent state of research into cosmology in astrophysics and microbiology. In 1994, in a semester colloquium with my Tübingen colleagues at the Institute of Physics, Professors Amand Fässler, Friedrich Gönnenwein, Herbert Müther, Herbert Pfister, Friedemann Rex, Günther Staudt, and Karl Wildermuth, entitled "Our Cosmos: Scientific and Philosophical-Theological Aspects," I was able to test my views and finally to sum them up in twenty-two theses.

After I had completed my trilogy, the Religious Situation of Our Time series — *Judaism* (1991), *Christianity* (1994), and *Islam* (2004) — an invitation from the German Society of Natural Scientists and Physicists to give the ceremonial lecture at their annual gathering in Passau on 19 September 2004 was a challenging occasion to concern myself afresh with the basic questions of cosmology, and after that of biology and anthropology.

I was reassured that I could show the difficult passages of my manuscript to knowledgeable professional colleagues from the natural sciences. I am extremely grateful to Professors Amand Fässler (theoretical physics), who has already been mentioned in the text, Ulrich Felgner (logic, foundations and history of mathematics), Alfred Gierer (developmental biology), and Regina Ammicht-Quinn (theological ethics).

I received an encouraging response from a wide public when in the summer semester of 2005, for the twenty-fifth anniversary of the Studium Generale at the University of Tübingen that Walter Jens and I refounded, I offered my reflections in five lectures. The Centre for Information Technology of the Tübingen University Clinic was kind enough to record all the lectures on DVD; I am most grateful to the head of the Audiovisual Media Division, Rudi Luik.

I have certainly written this book, too, by myself, by hand, from first line to last. But it has been an inestimable help to me to be supported by the well-tried team of the Global Ethic Foundation. I am grateful to Professor Dr. Karl-Josef Kuschel, Dr. Günther Gebhardt, and Dr. Stephan Schlensog for many improvements in style and content. Stephan Schlensog also looked after typesetting and layout in his customary way. The reliable Anette Stuber-Rousselle produced the several revisions of the manuscript, supported by Inge Baumann and Eleonore Henn. Marianne Saur kept reading the manuscript for readability, and Katharina Elliger did valuable work on the proofs. Ulf Günnewig and Carina Geldhauser were responsible for liaison with the libraries, and Carina Geldhauser also helped me in revising the section on mathematics.

Tübingen, July 2005   *Hans Küng*

Index

Aborigines, 165-67
Abraham, 115
acoustics, 19
Adam and Eve, 129-30
adaptation, 86
adenine, 137
Africa, 161, 163-65
African Australopithecines, 163
African-Syrian Rift Valley, 164
Albert, H., 29n.39
Alpha and Omega, 154, 205-6
America (Jesuit journal), 100
amino-acid dating, 169
Anaxagoras, 44
Anaximander, 44
Anaximenes, 44
Andromeda Nebula, 10, 135, 199
animals, 131, 139, 192
Anselm of Canterbury, 67, 121
anthropic principle, 147-49, 154
anthropogenesis, 97, 169, 179
anthropoids, 162-63
antiprotons, 59
apes, 190
Archimedes, 82
Aristarchus of Samos, 3

Aristotle, 9, 44, 106, 108, 124, 130,
  168, 185
Armageddon, 203
astronauts, 119-20
Astronomia nova (Kepler), 4
atheism, 48, 52-53, 58, 68, 70, 73,
  103, 141, 157
Atkins, Peter, 48
atoms, 13, 26
Audhumla, 112
Augustine, 106, 109, 120-21, 131,
  168
Australia, 165-67

Babylon, 115
Bach, J. S., 182, 184
Bachmann, Ingeborg, 126
Barbour, Ian G., 8n.10, 39
Barth, Karl, 38
basal ganglia, 176, 180
beliefs, stages of, 167
Benk, A., 39n.52
Bergson, Henri, 97, 140
Bible, 53, 108-9, 117, 121-22, 124,
  155, 157; and ethics, 194-95; infal-
  libility of, 30, 38, 41; metaphorical

209

language of, 116-18, 197, 203-5;
and science, 90-91, 93-94, 110-20,
129
biblical criticism, 93, 117, 129,
152-53
Bieri, Peter, 185-86, 188n.48
Big Bang, 3, 12, 16, 44-45, 63, 66,
118, 124; Christians' use of, 54-55,
68; confirmation of, 10-11, 76,
105; and expansion, 9-12, 54-55,
59-63, 74, 76, 78, 200-201; origin
of, 13, 56, 59-61, 67-68, 71, 78
Big Crunch, 200
Binnig, Gert, 56
biogenesis, 129, 137-38
biogeography, 88
biology, 86, 89, 95, 131; molecular,
87-88, 136
Birbaumer, Niels, 182
black holes, 22-23, 32, 57, 63, 66, 70
Bohr, Niels, 13, 22, 72, 113, 126
Boltzmann, Ludwig, 59, 146
Boltzmann's constant k, 59, 146
Borman, Frank, 119
Born, Max, 13
Börner, Gerhard, 149
Boyle, Robert, 34
brain, 139, 162, 174-82, 189-90;
body-soul problem, 168-71; brain
research, 173-91; and judgment
formation, 186; readiness poten-
tial of, 183
Brandt, Reinhard, 186
Brecht, Bertolt, 6
Brief History of Time, A (Hawking),
16
Broca, Paul, 163
Broca's area, 162-63
Brod, Max, 6
Brouwer, L. E. J., 20
Brown, Dan, 203
Brownlee, Donald, 134

Bruno, Giordano, 55
Buber, Martin, 103
Buchheim, Thomas, 185
Buddha, 111, 196
Buddhism, 107-8, 110-11
Bultmann, Rudolf, 38
Burali-Forti, C., 19
burials, 167

Cantor, Georg, 19, 41
carbon, 11-12, 60, 132, 135, 137
Carnap, Rudolf, 25n.34, 26-27
Carter, Brandon, 147
Castelli, B., 4
causality, 40, 87, 129, 142, 186, 190
celestial mechanics, 19
cells, differentiation of, 139
cerebral cortex, 162, 175, 180
Chalmers, David, 179
chance, 14, 67, 139-47, 155-58
Chance and Necessity (Monod), 140
chaos theory, 115, 142, 157
Chernobyl, 202
chimpanzees, 162-64
Christianity, 113-14, 125, 168,
195-96; and the end times, 201-3;
and God as creator, 110, 123, 150
Christogenesis, 97-98
church, and opposition to science,
5-6, 52-53, 89-100, 130
Civil Code, 189
Clinton, Bill, 203
CNRS (National Committee for Scientific Research, Geneva), 200
Cobb, John, 102
Cold War, 202
communist, 141
communities, 168
complementarity, 41, 126
computers, 23-24, 31
computer tomograph (CT), 178
Comte, Auguste, 25, 95-97

Index

Confessions (Augustine), 120
Confucianism, 110
Confucius, 196
Congregation for the Doctrine of Faith, 7, 55, 99-100
Congress on General Relativity and Gravity, 23
consciousness, 162-63, 169, 181-82, 188
constancy of species, 86-87
constants, cosmic, 59-60, 66, 76, 80, 146-47
contraction of the universe, 54, 62, 200
contradictions, in mathematics, 19-21, 117
"Copernican shift," 3-4, 46
Copernicus, Nicolaus, 3, 5, 34
Cornwell, John, 22
corpuscular theory, 13
cosmic order, 1-2, 58-60, 123, 125
cosmogony, 110-11
cosmology, 9-12, 29, 38-39
cosmos, 9-12, 32, 58-60, 74-77, 189-91
Cours de philosophie positive (Comte), 95
creation, 67-68, 71, 115-16, 120-25, 149; and the Bible, 110-20, 155; dating of, 90, 94; instinctive opposition to, 61-62, 67-68, 72; myths of, 110-12, 115
creationism, 93-95, 98, 131
creativity, 186
"Creator God." *See under* God
Crick, Francis H. C., 48, 136, 180
Critique of Pure Reason (Kant), 46-47
Cro-Magnon skeletons, 165
Cuénot, C., 99
cult of the dead, 167
cultural anthropology, 166, 193
cytosine, 137

Daoism, 110
dark energy, 76-77, 200
dark mass problem, 59
dark matter, 76-77
Darwin, Charles, 6, 86-94, 98, 136, 138, 166
David, 114
Davies, Paul, 148, 199
Da Vinci Code, The (Brown), 203
Dawkins, Richard, 48
Democritus, 140
Denzler, Georg, 5
De revolutionibus orbium coelestium libri VI (Six Books on the Revolution of Heavenly Spheres) (Copernicus), 3
Descartes, René, 19, 34-35, 46, 53, 67, 121, 168-69
Descent of Man, The (Darwin), 89, 91
determinism, 169, 171-73, 183, 187
Deuteronomy, book of, 114
Deutsch, D., 65n.24
dharma, 197
dialectical materialism, 54, 141
Dicke, Robert H., 147
Dictionnaire de la Bible, 98
Dirac, Paul, 13, 22
Ditfurth, H. von, 45n.3, 57n.15
DNA, 88, 136-39, 163-64
dogmas, papal, 92, 96
Dominicans, 158
Drake, Frank, 132-33
dualism, 34-35, 168-70
Du Bois-Reymond, Emil, 73
Dürrenmatt, F., 202
Dyson, Freeman, 149

Easterbrook, Greg, 45
Edda, 57, 112
Eddington, Sir Arthur Stanley, 9
Eibl-Eibesfeldt, Irenäus, 173
Eigen, Manfred, 141, 143-45

Einstein, Albert, 7-10, 13-15, 22, 54, 72, 74, 76, 105, 107-8, 121, 169

élan vital, 97, 140

electricity, 7, 9

electrodynamics, 13, 74

electromagnetic energy, 13, 126

electron charge *e,* 59, 146

electrons, 11, 13-14, 59, 201

Elijah, 152

Elisha, 152

embryo, 88, 111, 162

embryology, 88

empiricism, 25, 72

end times, 201-3

energy, 13, 55, 60, 146

Engels, Friedrich, 171

Enlightenment, 35, 171

entropy, principle of, 55

Enumerability — Decidability — Computability (Hermes), 20

environment, 32, 96, 125, 172-73, 202

Essay on the Principles of Population (Malthus), 88

ET (film), 133

eternity, 106-7, 121

ethics, 176-77, 186, 192-94, 197

ethologists, 173

evil, problem of, 98

evolution; Bergson's view of, 97, 140; and biblical account of creation, 118, 129; and chance, 136, 140, 142; dead ends in, 140, 155; of human beings, 89, 174; Teilhard de Chardin's view of, 97-100; theory of, 73, 86, 94, 136, 139-40

excluded third, principle of, 18

existentialism, 172

Existentialism Is a Humanism (Sartre), 172

expansion, and the Big Bang, 9-12, 54-55, 59-63, 74, 76, 78, 200-201

extraterrestrial life, 58, 105, 131-36

faith, 105, 117, 150, 157, 190, 205; Kant's view of, 46-47; and miracles, 151, 153-54; and questions of ultimate origin, 120-27, 145, 149-50

Fascism, 26

Fässler, Amand, 59, 74n.44

Feigel, Herbert, 25n.34

Feuerbach, Ludwig, 49-50

Feynman, Richard P., 14

fireball, primal, 10, 58, 71, 74

First Three Minutes, The (Weinberg), 56

Fischer, Ernst Peter, 71

Fischer, K. P., 204n.6

Flew, Anthony, 95

fMRT. *See* functional magnetic resonance tomography

formalism, 20

fossils, 87-88

fourth dimension, 9, 74

Frank, Philipp, 25n.34

Frazer, Sir James G., 166

freedom, 186-97; and brain processes, 176-78, 183; experience of, 187-88, 191; philosophical views of, 158, 168, 171-73; of the will, 73, 173, 175-78, 183-85, 188n.48, 189

"Freedom and the Brain" (Linke), 186

Frege, F. L. G., 20, 24n.33

Freud, Sigmund, 49-50

Fried, Johannes, 189

Fries, Jacob Friedrich, 28

Fritzsch, Harald, 200

fugue, 182, 184

functional magnetic resonance tomography (fMRT), 174, 179
fundamentalism, 93-94

Gagarin, Yuri, 119
galaxies, 10-12, 23, 43, 76, 135
Galileo Galilei, 4-7, 34, 38, 41, 52-53, 89, 91, 94, 100, 143, 148
Game, The (Eigen), 141
Gamow, G., 57n.15
Gautama. *See* Buddha
Gell-Mann, Murray, 15n.14, 75
General Morphology of Organisms (Haeckel), 91
generationism, 131
genes, 87, 139, 163
Genesis, book of, 68-69, 71, 112-26 passim, 155
Genesis Flood, The (Morris and Whitcomb), 118
genetic code, 137
Gierer, Alfred, 138, 148, 188, 192
gluons, 74
Gocconi, Giuseppe, 132
God: activity of, 130, 151-59; belief in, 48-53, 150, 205; biblical understanding of, 117, 155; as creator, 45, 60, 102, 109-10, 114-16, 120-21, 124-25, 137, 143-44; death of, 27, 50-51, 89, 109; of the gaps, 60, 79-80, 143, 159; human beings as image of, 90, 93, 115-16; as hypothesis, 79-81, 95-96; knowing the mind of, 16-17, 21-22, 108-9, 148; as light, 125-27, 159, 195-97, 206; and the origin of life, 90, 130, 139, 141-44, 157; and Pascal's wager, 57-58, 205-6; proofs of, 46-48, 66-71, 81-82, 86, 144, 148-49, 153, 190; rejection of, 15-18, 25, 27, 68, 71, 73, 175; as spirit, 155, 158-59; as uncaused

reality, 81-83, 107, 121; views of, 65, 97-109, 196
Gödel, Kurt, 18, 20-24, 25n.34, 30, 146
Gödel's theorem. *See* incompleteness theorem
God Particle, The (Lederman), 105
Goenner, Hubert, 65
Goethe, Johan W. von, 12, 106
Gondwanaland, 161
Gott, Richard, 71
grand unifying theory (GUT) (Hawking), 15-18
gravity, 4-9, 11, 13-14, 23, 61, 74, 76, 146, 201
Gross, D. J., 41
guanine, 137
guilt, 177-79, 191
GUT. *See* grand unifying theory
Guth, Alan, 63

Habermas, Jürgen, 100, 186
Haeckel, Ernst, 73, 91, 171
Hahn, Hans, 25n.34
Haldane, J. B. S., 22
Harrison, Edward, 63
Hartshorne, Charles, 102
Hawking, Stephen, 15-18, 21-24, 48, 70-71, 146
Hebrew Bible, 110, 116, 151-52, 194, 196. *See also* Bible
Heckmann, Otto, 55
Hegel, Georg Wilhelm Friedrich, 85, 95-96, 100
Heidegger, Martin, 79
Heisenberg, Werner, 13, 15-16, 22, 30, 33, 40, 72, 80, 113, 118, 126
heliocentric theory, 3, 5
helium, 11, 59
Heraclitus, 44
heredity, 87, 136-37, 172-73
Hermes, Hans, 20

Hilbert, D., 20
Hinduism, 110-11, 196
Hiroshima, 202
Höffe, Otfried, 183-84
Holy Spirit, 155-56
Homer, 1
hominids, 163
hominization, 32, 129, 161
Homo erectus, 85, 89
homogeneity problem, 59
Homo habilis, 163
Homo sapiens, 85, 89, 164-65
horizon problem, 59
How I Believe (Teilhard de Chardin), 98
Hoyle, Fred, 55, 64, 67, 70n.37
Hubble, Edwin P., 9-10
Hubble Space Telescope, 9, 63, 135
Humanae vitae (Paul VI), 92
human beings, 12, 51, 89, 124-25, 191-97; development of, 146-48, 162-63; on earth for 200,000 years, 32, 43, 85, 130, 164; freedom of, 171-73; in God's image, 90, 93, 115-16; progress of, 95-96; psychological development of, 168-73; spirit of, 130-31, 174, 186-87
Humani generis (Pius XII), 92, 99
humanism, 50-51
humanization, 192
hunters-gatherers, 164-65, 192
Hüther, Gerald, 190
Huxley, Thomas, 90
Huygens probe, 129, 135
hydrogen, 11, 59, 201

Ice Age, 164
I-consciousness, 179-80, 185-86
illusion theory (Freud), 49-50
immanence, of God, 101, 106-7, 156
immutability, of God, 102
incarnation, 98, 175

incompleteness theorem (Gödel), 18, 20-24, 30, 146-47
indeterminacy, 13-14, 23, 30, 108; molecular, 143
Index of Prohibited Books, 5
infinity, 70, 156; of God, 106-7
inflation model, 59
information theory, 188
Inquisition, 5-7, 55; Roman, 94
intentionality, 169
International Congress of Palaeontology, 99
intuition, 176
intuitionism, 20
iron, 201
Islam, 110
Israel, 114

Jainism, 110
James, William, 190
Jehovah's Witnesses, 203
Jesuits, 158
Jesus, 98, 195-96, 205
Joel, 199
John Paul II, 6, 7n.8
Jonah, 152
Judaism, 110, 123, 125, 150, 195-96
Jupiter, 4
Jupiter Symphony (Mozart), 52

Kanitscheider, B., 38n.46, 71n.40
Kant, Immanuel, 34, 36, 40, 46-48, 52, 70, 81-82, 183-84
Kempermann, Gerd, 191
Kepler, Johannes, 3-4, 7, 34, 41, 148
kingdom of God, 102
Kline, Morris, 21
knowledge, and subjectivity, 40, 46
Kraft, Victor, 25n.34
Kröber, Hans-Ludwig, 178
Kuhn, Thomas S., 3, 52

Lamettrie, J. O., 171
Landau, Lev, 71
Langton, Stephen, 159
language, 162-65, 170, 188, 192; of the Bible, 118-19, 204-5; of poetry, 119, 204-5
Laplace, P., 79
Large Hadron Collider, 77
Last Supper, 203
law: criminal, 176-78; meta-natural, 147-49; natural, 28, 141-43, 147, 151-52; universal, 136, 140
LBT telescope, 54
Leakey, L. S. B., 163
Lederman, Leon, 105
Le Fort, Gertrud von, 6
Left Behind series, 203
Leibniz, Gottfried Wilhelm, 7, 19, 24n.33, 34, 79, 145, 169
Lemaître, Georges, 9, 57n.15
Lesch, Harald, 134
Lessing, Gotthold E., 34
Leuba, James H., 103
Li, Lin-Xin, 71
Libet, Benjamin, 183
life: chance in the origin of, 139-45; conditions for origin of, 129-30, 132, 134-39, 146, 148; definition of, 130-31
light, 7-9, 23, 54, 59, 125-27, 146
light-year, 132, 135
limbic system, 176, 184
Linde, Andrei, 63, 66
Linke, Detlev B., 186
Loch, Christof, 180
logical positivism, 24-29
logicism, 20
Logic of Scientific Discovery, The (Popper), 27
Lorenz, Konrad, 173
Lucas, George, 135
Luria, S. E., 140n.12

Luther, Martin, 5-6, 150

"machine man," 171
macrocosm, 74-75, 77
macromolecule, 143
magic, 166-67
magnetic encephalograph, 182
Maistre, Joseph de, 96
Malthus, Thomas R., 87-88
"Manifesto on the Present and Future of Brain Research," 180-81
many-universes theory, 23, 62-69, 146, 148, 216
Mariner space probe, 133
Mars, 135
Marx, Karl, 49-50
Marxism, 119, 171-72
Mary, 92
materialism, 48-49
mathematics, 15, 18-24, 29-31, 40, 148
matter: in Big Bang, 10-12, 15, 54-55, 59, 142; unitary theory of, 15, 17-18, 21-22
meaning: determination of, 26-27, 29; in evolutionary process, 144-45, 148-49; of reality, 79, 81-83
Melanchthon, Philipp, 5
Mendel, Gregor, 87
Mengel, Karl, 25n.34
Mesolithic Age, 167
methane, 136
Metz, J. B., 100
Michelangelo, 124
microcosm, 74-75, 77
Milky Way, 4, 10, 23, 75, 78, 85, 131-33, 135, 199
miracles, 50-54
missing links, 93
Moltmann, Jürgen, 36
monism, 33n.42, 73, 101, 168-69

Monod, Jacques, 48, 140-41, 143
monogenism, 92, 130
monotheism, 167
morality, 183-84, 191, 195
Morris, H., 118
Morrison, Philip, 132
Moses, 93, 115, 194, 196; books of, 94, 114; law of, 194
Mozart, Wolfgang Amadeus, 52
M theory, 70, 72
Muhammad, 196
music, and physics, 52
Muslims, 123, 125, 150, 195-96, 202
mutation, 87, 131, 137-38, 140

Nagasaki, 202
nanotechnology, 75-76
Napoleon, 79
NASA, 64, 133-34
National Radio Astronomy Observatory, 132
naturalism, 184
natural sciences, 26, 73-74
natural selection, 87-88, 138, 141, 157
Nature, 132
nature, 53-54, 97, 100-101, 108
Nazism, 26, 172, 177
Neanderthal man, 164-65, 167-68
necessity, and chance, 139-45, 157-58
neo-positivism, 25
Neurath, Otto, 25n.34
neurons, 174-75
neurosciences, 181-84
neurotransmitters, 181
neutralinos, 77
neutrons, 11, 59, 74-75
neutron star, 200-201
"new materialists," 157
New Testament, 110, 126, 155-56, 196, 199, 201, 203, 205. *See also* Bible

Newton, Sir Isaac, 7-8, 13-14, 34, 39, 53, 69
New York Times, 134
Nicholas of Cusa, 41, 109
nickel, 201
Nietzsche, Friedrich, 50, 58, 82, 109
nihilism, 50
nitrogen, 11-12, 60
Noah, 115
No End to the Galileo Case (Denzler), 5
noosphere, 97
Novalis, 12
nuclear forces, 13, 60-61, 146, 202
nucleic acids, 136-38

Ogden, Schubert, 102
Old Testament. *See* Hebrew Bible
Olduvai Gorge, 164
Omega Point, 97-98, 141
omnipotence, 158
omnipresence, 106, 108
omniscience, 158
On the Origin of Species by Natural Selection (Darwin), 86, 91-92
"Operating Instructions for a Human Brain" (Hüther), 190
opium theory (Marx), 49-50
optics, and mathematics, 19
origin, question of, 56-58, 78-79, 83
original sin, 93
Our Final Century? (Rees), 202
oxygen, 11-12, 60

Paganini, 56
Paleolithic Age, 161
paleontology, 88
Paley, William, 86
Pannenberg, Wolfhart, 170
pantheism, 157

Papal Academy of Sciences, 92
paradigm shift, 3-4, 46
paradoxes, in mathematics, 19, 21
particle accelerators, 74, 77
Particular Council of Cologne, 91
Pascal, Blaise, 57-58, 77, 120, 205
Paul, 158
Paul V, 158
Paul VI, 92
Peacocke, Arthur, 39, 157
pendulum, law of, 4
Penrose, Roger, 22, 70
Pentateuch, 114
Penzias, Arno A., 12
perpetuum mobile, 55-56, 61-62
pessimism, 202
petitio principii, 177
Pfister, Herbert, 72
*Philosophiae naturalis principia
    mathematica* (Newton), 7
photons, 11
photosynthesis, 138
phylogenesis, 162-63
physics, 7-8, 17, 30-31, 40, 68-69;
    and questions of ultimate reality,
    44-45, 51-52, 72, 78-79, 113
Physics of Immortality, A (Tipler), 68
Pius X, 91
Pius XII, 92, 99, 130
Planck, Max, 13, 24, 41, 59, 146
Planck's constant *h,* 59, 146
planets, 3-4, 12
Plato, 41, 44, 106, 108, 168
pleroma, 97
Plotinus, 107
Poe, Edgar A., 202
Politzer, H. D., 41
Polkinghorne, John, 39, 157
polytheism, 167
pope, 30, 38, 91
Popper, Karl, 24-29, 52
positivism, 24-29, 95-96

positron-emission tomography
    (PET), 174, 178
positrons, 11
Post, Emil L., 20
prayer, 117
Preskill, John, 23
Primal Mystery, 78-83, 107
Principia mathematica (Whitehead),
    100
Prinz, Wolfgang, 184-85
Process and Reality (Whitehead), 101
process philosophy, 100-102
process theology, 102
progress, belief in, 95-98, 141, 202
projection theory (Feuerbach), 49-50
proteins, 136-37, 174
protons, 11, 59, 74-75
"proto-universe," 71
Psalms, 118
psyche, 169-71
Ptolemy, 3
pulsars, 78
Purusha, 111
Pythagoras, 1, 69
Pythagoreans, 41

quantum mechanics, 13, 15-16, 72,
    136, 169
quantum theory, 7-8, 15, 17, 30, 40,
    157; Einstein's rejection of, 10,
    13-14, 105, 108
quarks, 41, 59, 65, 74-75
quasars, 74
Qur'an, 108, 110, 117, 123, 196

radiation, and the Big Bang, 11-12,
    59, 68, 105
Rare Earth (Ward and Brownlee),
    134
rationalism, 35-36
Ratzinger, Joseph, 100
Reagan, Ronald, 203

realism, 8
reality: as inscrutable, 46, 59, 74-75, 78-83, 107-8; meaning of, 2, 31-33, 40-41, 52, 72; questions of, 25-29, 52-53, 72; unity of, 33-35, 113
reason, 35-37, 53; and belief in God, 58, 81-82, 123-24; as human distinctive, 148, 168; Kant's critique of, 46-48, 70
red giant, 32, 199, 201
reductionism, 36, 182, 184
Rees, Martin, 43, 64, 66-67, 146, 202
Reese, Thomas, 100
Reichenbach, Hans, 25n.34
relativity, theory of, 7-9, 13, 22, 100
religion, 48-51, 110-12, 165-68, 197; and science, 30-31, 41, 73, 149-50, 159; and views of God, 96-97, 101
Rendell, Lisa, 64
responsibility, principle of, 177-79, 186, 191
Revelation, book of, 203-4, 206
"riddle of the world," 73-75, 77
Riedl, Rupert, 142, 145
Rig-Veda, 111
RNA, 88, 138
Robespierre, 95
Roth, Gerhard, 176-78, 180
Rousseau, Jean-Jacques, 46-47
Russell, Bertrand, 20, 24n.33, 100

Sagan, Carl, 48, 71, 133
Sakharov, Andrey, 100
Sandrum, Raman, 64
Sartre, Jean-Paul, 172
Saturn, 4, 129, 135
Schäfer, Lothar, 70n.36
Schlick, Moritz, 24, 25n.34, 26
Schmidt, P. Wilhelm, 167
Schmitz-Moorman, Karl, 99n.19
Schrenk, F., 163n.1
Schrödinger, Erwin, 13

Schulz, Walter, 40
Schwarzschild, Karl, 23
science: and the Bible, 120-29; and God, 48, 51-53, 102-5, 108-9, 154; limits of, 27-31, 51-52; and religion, 6-8, 19, 73, 112-14, 149-50, 159; and theology, 38-39, 53, 97-98, 118-20, 157, 175
science fiction, 131
scientific correctness, 67-68, 70
"Scientific View of the World" (Vienna Circle), 24-25
scientism, 96
Scopes, J. T., 93
Second World War, 172
self, 184-87
self-knowledge, 175-76, 187, 190-91
senses, 25, 27, 113
set theory, 18-19
Shiva, 111
Siddhartha Gautama. See Buddha
Sikhism, 110
silicates, 132
Singer, Wolf, 176-77, 180, 185
singularity, theory of, 44-46, 54, 69-72
Skinner, B. F., 172-73
Smolin, Lee, 63
Smoot, George, 105
socialism, 50-51
solar system, 131, 134
soul, 169-71
space, 40, 54, 120-22
space-time, 8-9, 13, 15, 22, 74, 106-7
speculation, cosmological, 62-68, 72
speed of light c, 59, 146
Spencer, Herbert, 87
Spinoza, Baruch, 34, 105, 108, 121, 168
Spitzer, Manfred, 187
Stardust project, 134
stars, 11, 23, 200-201

Index

Star Wars (film), 134-35
steady state theory, 55-56, 68, 70
Stoics, 168
Stone Age, 161, 164, 166-67
Strauss, Johann, 56
string theory, 15-16, 70
subjectivity, 169
sun, 9, 11, 64, 78, 146
"superlaw," 147
supernova, 200
superstring theory, 15n.14, 70, 72
Supreme Court, 93
survival of the fittest, 138

Taschner, Rudolf, 23-24
Teilhard de Chardin, Pierre, 38, 92, 97-100, 141
Templeton, Sir John, 127
Ten Commandments, 194-95
Terrestrial Planet Finder, 64
Thales of Miletus, 44
theogony, 110
theology, 30, 37-39, 48, 130, 170, 192; and science, 53, 105, 108-9, 118-20, 157, 175, 199, 205
"theory of everything," 34, 43
thermodynamics, second law of, 55
Thomas Aquinas, 124, 131
thought, and images of the brain, 163, 189
thymine, 137
Tillich, Paul, 108
Time, 60
time, 40, 45, 54, 100-101, 106, 120-22, 124
Tipler, Frank J., 68-70
Titan, 129, 135-36
TOE. *See* unified theory of every-thing
tomographs, 179
tool culture, 161, 163-64
Townes, Charles, 61-62

transcendence, of God, 101, 106-7, 115, 156, 190
trust, in God, 81-82, 205-6
Turing, Alan, 24

UFOs, 132
unified theory of everything (TOE), 16
universe, 1-3, 5, 14-18, 32, 131-32, 200; alternate, 23, 62-69, 146, 148; as expanding, 9-10, 54-55, 78; as finite, 54-56, 63, 80; and God, 15-16, 106, 124; origin of, 2, 17, 58-60, 72, 76
Ussher, James, 90

Vatican Council, First, 96
Vatican Council, Second, 99-100
Veni Sancte Spiritus (Langton), 159
Venus, 4
verification principle, 28-29
Verne, Jules, 202
Vienna Circle, 24, 25n.34, 26, 97
Viennese Cultural Historical School, 167
Viking space probe, 133
Vilenkin, Alexander, 63
Vishnu, 111
vitalism, 97, 139, 141-42, 147
Völkel, Marcus, 189
Voltaire, 34
Voyager space probe, 133

wager, Pascal's, 57-58, 205-6
Waismann, Friedrich, 24n.33, 25n.34
walking upright, 161-64
Walter, Ulrich, 120
Ward, Keith, 48, 157
Ward, Peter, 134
warp of space and time, 9, 74
Watson, James D., 136, 180

wave theory, 13
Weber, Carl Maria von, 56
Weil, André, 20
Weinberg, Steven, 56, 57n.15, 65, 68, 112
Weizsäcker, Carl Friedrich von, 113-14
Wenner Gren Foundation, 99
Wheeler, John Archibald, 72
Whitcomb, J., 118
white dwarfs, 32, 57, 201
Whitehead, Alfred North, 20, 97, 99n.19, 100-103
Wilberforce, Samuel, 90
Wilczek, F., 41
Wilkinson Microwave Anisotropy Probe (WMAP), 54, 76

Wilson, E. O., 33n.42
Wilson, Robert W., 12
WIMPs (weakly interacting massive particles), 76
Wittgenstein, L., 24n.33, 26, 52
WMAP. See Wilkinson Microwave Anisotropy Probe
world, 45, 85-86, 95, 200-201; and God, 57-59, 169; models of, 3-4, 6, 8, 14, 16-17
"world formula" (Heisenberg), 14-18, 146
Wunn, Ina, 167

Yahweh, 116, 194-95
Ymir, 112